MAKING IT

Music, Sex & Drugs in the Golden Age of Rock

TED MYERS

**CALUMET
EDITIONS**

Minneapolis

**CALUMET
EDITIONS**
Minneapolis

SECOND EDITION DECEMBER 2022
Making It Copyright © 2017 by Ted Myers.

10 9 8 7 6 5 4 3 2

ISBN: 978-1-960250-35-3
Book and cover design by Gary Lindberg

MAKING IT

Music, Sex & Drugs in the Golden Age of Rock

TED MYERS

Intro

STOP! DON'T READ THIS BOOK…if you're expecting the story of a likeable young guy who aspires to rock stardom, struggles, shows he has the stuff, and finally makes it, stop right now. This isn't that book. This is a true story, not a novel or a Hollywood movie. It's about me, a likeable young guy who aspires to rock stardom and, like thousands of others, doesn't make it. But on my way to the bottom, I meet some amazing people and have some wonderful adventures. So, if you think you can handle the ending, read on…

Age 5 – I attempt the Jimi Hendrix method on mandolin –
lefty, upside down and backward.

PART 1 – EAST COAST

Chapter One

Since I Don't Have You

Perhaps I was scarred at an early age by my inability to make Janie Schindelheim love me. She was the prettiest girl at P.S. 40, our elementary school, a building that was already a hundred years old when we went there in the 1950s. It stood across First Avenue from Stuyvesant Town, the red-brick labyrinth of a housing project on Manhattan's East Side, where Janie and I grew up. We were both ten years old. She was in my fifth grade class when I first noticed her.

Her brown hair was flecked with golden highlights that would catch the sun. Her pouty mouth made her look grown-up and sexy, even at ten. She had this amber, translucent skin, and when her hair was pulled back in a ponytail, as it usually was, you could see little blue veins in her temples.

Sometimes I would hang around outside her house on the off chance she would come out to play. One snowy day I got lucky. I was outside the back entrance of her building, freezing my ass off, and then there she was, melting my heart in her winter coat and knitted cap with the pom-pom on top. I acted casual, like, "What a coincidence, seeing you here—right outside your building."

"Let's make snow angels," she said.

Then we lay on our backs in a patch of virgin snow and flapped our arms and legs. Boy, I wouldn't have been caught dead making snow angels with anyone but Janie Schindelheim.

This experience gave me hope and a sense of delicious anticipation of things to come. At that age your capacity to hope, your boundless optimism, has yet to be crushed by the deluge of disappointments life has in store.

The high point of my relationship with Janie came in February of that year, 1956. She made me a valentine in class and gave it to me. I was walking on air for weeks. And that was as close as I ever got to making her mine.

Janie turned into Jane. We went through junior high together, then high school. But she never gave me a second glance. She always went out with the older, handsomer guys. One day, when we were in tenth or eleventh grade, she and her boyfriend of the moment (whose name and face I have conveniently forgotten) and me and my sort-of-girlfriend, Dora, a Polish immigrant with big blue eyes and a gap between her front teeth, cut school and went to my parents' apartment to make out. Both my parents worked, so we knew there would be no one home. Janie and her guy went into my sister's bedroom and closed the door. Dora and I were in my room.

What a strange feeling it was to be making out with one girl and to know that the girl of my dreams—and she had never ceased to be that—was right in the next room making out with—or maybe even fucking—some other guy.

Jane was two-timing Whatshisname with a guy who lived in our neighborhood, Harold Doolin. I was appalled because I knew him. He was older—big, tough, and good-looking—and a neighborhood bully. When I was eight he chased me with his cap gun and when he caught me, instead of pointing it at me and pretending to shoot me with it, he grabbed my arm, held it close against my skin and fired, burning me. Yes, even as a child, Harold Doolin was malevolent enough to figure out how to hurt someone with a cap gun.

One day, about a week after the make-out session, Harold and a buddy of his cornered me in an elevator and beat the shit out of me. As the blows landed on my face I heard a high-pitched ringing in my ears, like a sound effect in some B science fiction movie. Blood trickled from my nose and mouth. I kept asking "Why? Why?" But I never got an answer.

I don't know when it dawned on me—somebody had seen me, Janie, Dora, and Whatshisname go into my building together. It got back to Harold and he assumed that I had been with Jane. So, not only did I not get the girl I wanted, I got a beating for doing something I desperately wanted to do and never did.

In all those years I never proclaimed my love for Jane; never gave her the slightest inkling. She always treated me with cool indifference, and I acted the same. I was too afraid of rejection, especially *that* rejection. I knew she would turn me down, knew I wasn't handsome enough. That was a reality I couldn't face, so I just kept mum.

Jane grew up, moved to San Francisco, and married Jann Wenner. They started *Rolling Stone* magazine together on a loan from her father. In 1995 Jann left her for a guy.

Jane and Jann Wenner in the early days of Rolling Stone.
Photo: Baron Wolman, Iconic Images/Baron Wolman

* * *

In 1992, shortly after I had completed production on my first compilation project for Rhino Records, *Troubadours of the Folk Era*, I met Holly George-Warren, who at the time was a staff writer for *Rolling Stone*. I asked her if she knew Jane Wenner, and she did. I gave her a package for Jane: the three CDs, which chronicled the urban folk revival of the 1950s and '60s, and a short note. I wrote it by hand and made it sound as casual as I possibly could. I told her about my job at Rhino, my wife and my two kids, and told her to look me up if she was ever in LA. I congratulated her on her great success and added some quip, like "I think you are the only person I know who has a publishing empire." Holly delivered it, but I never got a reply.

* * *

There was another girl in elementary school and junior high, with none of the mystery or allure of Janie Schindelheim, but a sweet, good-natured girl named Carla Wise. I didn't think much of her at the time, didn't think she was very pretty but, in retrospect, she was quite pretty. She was petite, had very white skin and freckles, lovely red lips, and a turned-up nose. But she had this unruly mop of frizzy black hair (a "jewfro"!) and that just wasn't cool in 1958. Carla pursued me shamelessly. She used to show up outside my window and yell up to me at all hours of the day and night. One day at school she cornered me in the cafeteria where you return the trays.

"Hey, Teddy," she said, trying to sound casual, "I've got two tickets to the Dick Clark Saturday night show. It's this Saturday. Wanna go?"

The *Dick Clark Show* was a spin-off of *American Bandstand*. It was broadcast live from a New York theatre every Saturday night. It was more of a concert setting, as opposed to *Bandstand*'s "dance party" format. The artists all lip-synched to their records, but I didn't care. I jumped at the chance to see The Diamonds, Jimmy Clanton and the *pièce de résistance*, Ritchie Valens, doing his double-sided hit, "La Bamba" and "Donna," in person. Little did I suspect that he and one of my biggest all-time idols, Buddy Holly, would both be gone in just a few weeks. That concert had a profound effect on me.

Was it not scoring with Janie Schindelheim that had set me on this road, or my admiration for the pop stars of the 1950s? Truth is, when I convinced my parents to get me a guitar and lessons at age thirteen I was motivated as much by the desire for popularity as a love of music. Ask any rock musician why he got into it and, if he has a shred of honesty, he'll admit it was to 'get chicks.' I wasn't tall, athletic, or handsome, so learning how to play and sing was a natural shortcut for me to the attentions of the opposite sex. And it worked.

IT'S SO EASY TO
BE POPULAR

When You
**PLAY TODAY'S
MOST POPULAR INSTRUMENT
THE GUITAR**

* * *

I started out playing folk songs on my nylon-stringed classical guitar, but it wasn't long before I convinced my parents to get me an electric guitar and an amp. My first electric guitar was a gray sunburst, solid-body Supro. It was inexpensive, but to me incredibly cool. As luck would have it, I had a good ear and a natural gift for picking up and replicating songs I heard on records and the radio.

During eighth grade at Junior High School 104, by far the best guitar player in the school—the best musician, for that matter—in fact, the most talented person in the school—was a blind Puerto Rican kid named José Feliciano. José played the shit out of his nylon string guitar. He was trained in classical, flamenco, and various Latino folkloric styles. He also sang really well. He was a *monster*. José loved to perform and was often called upon to play at school assemblies—and he never failed to blow my mind.

After I got my electric guitar, José told me if I let him play it for the upcoming talent show, I could back him up on rhythm guitar. I immediately agreed, secretly hoping that Janie Schindelheim would be watching. The show was a success. José and I played—appropriately enough—"La Bamba." He wailed on the electric guitar parts, teaching my guitar some tricks I hoped it would remember, and I played acoustic rhythm guitar and sang harmony. Being up there in front of all those people was a heady experience. There was the worship and adoration I had always craved. I scanned the admiring faces in the crowd, hoping I would see Janie Schindelheim. Lots of people came up and congratulated me afterward, but not Janie.

* * *

1959 was a seminal year for me… literally. In February I was shaken by the deaths of Buddy Holly and Ritchie Valens. That same month The Skyliners hit the charts with "Since I Don't Have You." That song really struck a chord in me. There was something heart-rending and very different about it from the rest of the doo-wop and rockabilly that dominated the airwaves. Looking back, I think it was that unexpected and emotionally evocative third chord change, and the melody that went with it, that made the song stand out. When I saw The Skyliners on TV, there were things about them that were different too: they had a girl in the group, and one of them was playing an electric guitar—unusual for a doo-wop vocal group. "Since I Don't Have

You" seemed to go with the sense of loss I felt with the sad news about Buddy and Ritchie, and it became embedded in my consciousness.

* * *

That summer I went to a co-ed camp in upstate New York for July. The previous summer I had gone to Boy Scout camp and hated it. I quit the Scouts to pursue my newest interest—girls. I brought my acoustic guitar, which made me in-demand at weenie roasts and the like, where we would all sit around the fire singing stuff like "Cumbaya." I could accompany any of those three-chord folk ditties in a range of keys, plus I had developed a fairly decent repertoire of current pop and rock 'n' roll hits, and, yes, this made me... popular.

Sometimes the camp would charter buses and take us on field trips. One, I remember, was to the Tanglewood Music Festival in Massachusetts. This involved quite a long bus ride and an overnight stay. We camped out in tents. On the bus, boys and girls paired off and, when riding at night, it turned into a make-out fest. I was sitting next to a girl named Lorraine, frizzy off-blond hair and a face that could not launch even a single rowboat, but she had a reputation for being 'fast.' Lorraine showed me how to "French kiss" and even let me feel her up under her blouse—but over her bra. That night in the tent, I discovered what the guys meant by 'blue balls.'

The only other item of note about that month at camp was that one of our counselors, a guy named Mel Schwartz who couldn't have been more than twenty-one at the time, had written the #10 song in the country, "Baby Talk" by Jan & Dean. This made a profound impression on me. I asked him, "How did you get the song to Jan & Dean?"

"I played it for a publisher, he liked it, paid for a demo and he got it to Jan & Dean."

"Did you make a lot of money from it?"

"Not much so far. When the money comes in, the publisher takes fifty percent and gives me the other fifty percent—if he's honest."

As an interesting footnote, when United Artists Records released the album of my band Glider in 1977, the graphic designer was none other than Dean Torrence of Jan & Dean, who had—very prudently—developed another skill besides music with which he could make a living. When I told someone I was going to write a book about my life, they quipped, "You should call it *Six Degrees of Ted.*" Yeah, now I see what they meant.

When camp ended, I joined my parents and kid sister in a bungalow colony called Schreyer's, where they rented a three-bedroom apartment for the summer. The owner was a smart farmer named Rudy Schreyer, whose ancestors probably had farmed that land since the days of the Dutch settlers. He had the foresight and business acumen to build a cluster of bungalows and apartment structures on his land near a small lake and rent them out to city dwellers looking to escape the summer heat of New York City. I was only at Schreyer's for a month and, looking back, it's mind-boggling that so much in my sexual awakening could have transpired in so short a time. At camp I had learned about making out, but at Schreyer's it kicked up a notch. That's where I met Laura Hunt. She was quite a beautiful girl—about my age—with dirty blond hair and an odd birthmark on her right eyelid that somehow added to her glamour and mystery. I thought she was out of my league.

There was a recreation hall where they would have social events—mostly folk dancing—every weekend. One night, as the dance was winding down, Laura asked me to walk her home. I was surprised and elated. I couldn't believe my luck. Her parents owned a private summer home on a small ridge that overlooked our swimming lake. This was not on Schreyer's land, but an adjoining lot owned by the Hunts. Laura invited me in. Her parents were not home—probably still at the dance. We sat on the couch and put on the radio. She let me put my arm around her. The lights were low and at some point I got up the nerve to kiss her—and she kissed me back. My head swam. I was ecstatic. She made me leave soon after, sure that her parents would be getting home any minute, but there was a promise in her eyes of more to come.

The next day I was in the stratosphere. I couldn't contain my excitement. Laura Hunt was going to be my girlfriend. I just had to tell someone. So, when the guys all met on the baseball diamond for our daily baseball game, I whispered to Ronnie Elkind, "Laura Hunt let me kiss her. Don't tell anyone!"

Well, I'm sure it won't come as a surprise that Ronnie told Stevie, and Stevie told his little sister, and she told EVERYONE. And when I went to see Laura later that day, she told me she never wanted to speak to me again. And that was the end of my very brief love affair with Laura Hunt. "Since I Don't Have You" was still playing on the radio that summer, and it became my "loss theme" once again. I was inconsolable.

I started hanging around with a kid named Mark Blumenthal, who was a year older than me. His parents owned a large private home up the road maybe half a mile from Schreyer's. Mark had a .22 rifle, which he let me shoot. We would go out into the woods and have target practice on bottles and tin cans and—God help me—frogs. He also had an electric guitar, a Fender Jazzmaster, just like Buddy Holly's.

One night, Mark invited me to a party at someone's house. It was another private home on the same road as the Blumenthals' house. No adults were present. There were Mark, a girl he was going with, his teenage sister Nicky and her boyfriend, another couple maybe a year older than me, and a red-haired girl with freckles whom I had never met. Her name was Ellie. She was thirteen, the same age as me, a little taller and nicely developed. There was a phonograph and a stack of 45s. Everybody slow-danced real close, arms tightly around each other. I could tell this kind of party was a pretty new experience for Ellie as well. I was sitting right next to her on the couch and she suddenly blurted out, "Isn't there supposed to be necking and petting?"

I took this as my cue. She let me put my arm around her and my hand casually landed on her right breast. She did not object. It was very dark. I guess everybody else was doing the same thing. She let me kiss her, and even opened her mouth. I was making remarkably fast progress. Before we said goodnight, Ellie and I resolved to meet the next day by a small deserted lake in the woods across the road.

The next day was warm, muggy and gray. Gnats and mosquitoes buzzed in the air and cicadas raised a racket in the high grass. I walked out to the lake. It was really just a pond, surrounded by marshy reeds and some nice, soft grassy spots. She had gotten there before me and had staked out a good spot. There was not a soul in sight. She had brought a large beach towel and we laid down on it and began to kiss. Before long I was on top of her. She let me put my hand up under her sweater. After some fumbling I undid her bra (a first), and she allowed me to fondle her bare breasts. She was not as beautiful or mysterious as Laura Hunt, but this was, by far, the most exciting thing that had ever happened to me. Until the next day.

We decided to meet again the following day, same place, same time. I had to walk down a wooded path that snaked through a grove of maple trees, and when I rounded a curve she came into view. Standing there in the hazy afternoon light, red hair flying in the breeze, stark naked. What a sight! She looked like Botticelli's "Venus." Her skin was ivory white and dotted all over with little freckles. And she was a real redhead, there was no doubt about that.

I wasted no time in taking my clothes off, but she insisted that I keep my underpants on. We lay on the beach towel and I explored her all over with my hands and mouth. Then I was on top of her and we were kissing. The only thing between us was my white cotton jockeys, and they were stretched pretty thin.

We continued our secret rendezvous daily for what little remained of the summer. She never let me go 'all the way,' and I suppose at some level I was relieved. And I never breathed a word about it to anyone. I might have been dumb and naive, but I was a fast learner, and the Laura Hunt episode had taught me that no good can come of kissing and telling.

Chapter Two

Confessions of a Teenage Beatnik

In September 1960 I started at the High School of Music & Art in upper Manhattan. If New York City was the cultural center of the universe at that time, Music & Art was the cultural incubator of New York City, turning out scores of notable alumni in both fields. We had a far higher academic standard than that other performing arts school, the one that came to be known as the *Fame* school. Our school day started at 8:30 and went until 4:00, so we could get a full academic load in addition to our major, either music or art.

By then I was playing folk music at the Four Winds on 3rd Street, one of the lesser coffee houses in Greenwich Village that let just about anyone get up and play, then pass the basket for small change. These were called 'basket houses.' José Feliciano was on a somewhat parallel, if more advanced, trajectory than me. He would appear at some of the better coffee houses. By 1961 he was headlining and getting paid real money. One night I went to The Gaslight on MacDougal Street—or maybe it was the Bottom Line on Bleecker—to hear him play.

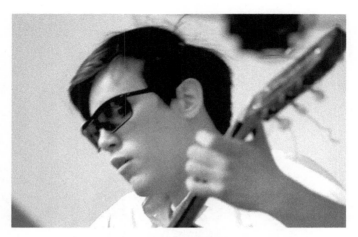

José. Photo: IPE Collection

I found myself a seat in the corner at the last empty table. Just as José started his set, this guy, a couple of years older, with a baby face and a funny, old-fashioned worker's cap—black corduroy, with a snap on it—came in and sat at my table. "Okay?" he says.

"Sure."

"Man, this guy can play, huh?"

"You're tellin' me. We went to junior high together. We used to jam," I told him.

"Oh yeah? You a musician too?"

"Yeah, I play a little guitar—not like him, though."

"You ever hear of Woody Guthrie?"

"The folk singer? Yeah. Used to play with Pete Seeger in the Almanac Singers, right?"

"Yeah, he's sick now. Dyin' in a hospital in New Jersey. I came to New York to see him."

"Really? Where you from?"

"All over. I ride the rails."

"You play music?"

"Little bit."

"Oh yeah? What's yer name, man?"

"Bobby."

That was a few months before Bobby Dylan became a household name in the folk world, but then he was just another kid in a funny hat.

13

Bobby. Photo: IPE Collection

* * *

As a member of the Columbia Record Club, I started buying LPs by jazz greats like Miles Davis and Dave Brubeck. I loved jazz. Of course, it was musically much different than folk music, so much more complex and so-phisticated. And the way a virtuoso jazz player could improvise around a set of chord changes was truly impressive. But what made me want to be a jazz musician was simply the fact that I thought they were the coolest of the cool, and that's what I wanted to be—the coolest of the cool. I sold my solid body Supro and got a used, big, fat hollow-body Gibson jazz guitar. I began taking lessons from jazz guitarist Billy Bauer, best known as a member of Lennie Tristano's sextet in the 1940s. I started jamming with the black jazz musi-cians from M&A, often schlepping my electric guitar and amp on the subway from Manhattan to the all-black Brooklyn neighborhood of Bedford Stuyve-sant, where I miraculously walked with impunity to and from the home of my pal, pianist Jimmy Hunter, never encountering so much as a bad word.

Jimmy was a gifted jazz piano player. At seventeen, he could hold his own with any professional jazz group. Many of the other black jazz musicians at M&A were also incredibly good, but I'm surprised that Jimmy Hunter never broke through in the jazz world. I often wonder what became of him.

At Music & Art I was an art major. You had to take an entrance exam to get in, and I didn't have enough formal music training to get in as a music major. M&A was a hotbed of culture, coolness and precociousness. At fifteen I adjusted my image daily to an ever-vacillating concept of what I thought was hip. One day I would show up in ripped tennis sneakers, no socks, jeans and a black turtleneck (The Beatnik), the next I was in sunglasses, a continental suit, skinny tie, tight pants and pointy black shoes (The Jazz Hippie).

Rock 'n' roll was at an all-time low. Elvis was in the army, Chuck Berry was in jail, Buddy Holly was dead, and Little Richard was preaching the Gospel. I liked some of the girl group records, like the ones Phil Spector was making, but for us teen-hipsters the rock of the early '60s was a non-starter. My musical heroes were Miles Davis, John Coltrane, Thelonious Monk, Pete Seeger, Theodore Bikel, Joan Baez, and—errm—The Kingston Trio.

My first girlfriend, Sophia, was as ga-ga over classical pianists like Glenn Gould, Vladimir Horowitz and Sviatoslav Richter as a bobbysoxer over Sinatra. I liked some of that stuff too, especially baroque, but most classical did not ignite my blood and touch my soul—not like jazz, folk and old rock 'n' roll.

Sophi was a beautiful and brilliant Italian-born artist with sandy brown hair that she would usually wear pulled back in a long single braid down her back. She was pretty in an exotic way: almond-shaped brown eyes and a sweet, heart-shaped mouth. Her long neck made her look like a painting by Modigliani. And she had amazing breasts, even at fourteen. She had been accelerated in elementary school because she was so damned smart. She knew about everything: classical music, art, literature—even science. I turned her on to jazz. Her parents were terrific too—bona fide European intellectuals. We were pretty much inseparable for our sophomore and junior years. I was definitely in love with her.

* * *

In my early years of high school I often ran with the uptown preppy set—guys from Trinity prep school. I met them through Carl Engstrom, a guy

I'd become friendly with in junior high, whose parents lived on Gramercy Park, a tony neighborhood that was within our school's district. These were the sons of wealthy Manhattan families, often celebrities. There was Aram Saroyan, son of William Saroyan, Alan Montoya, son of the flamenco guitarist Carlos Montoya, Art Vanderhoven and Carl, whose parents were merely rich. At one of their parties I got friendly with a young jazz drummer named Fred Mason who also went to Trinity. His mother was a Park Avenue socialite from North Carolina. Fred had a Southern accent and a cool, deadpan delivery that made his charm irresistible—to girls as well as fellow jazz hippies like me (the term "hippie" originated from "jazz hippie," and this was how we referred to ourselves in the early 1960s).

My art skills finally came in handy when I learned to forge the New York State seal on the New York driver's license application. In those days your driver's license was simply an application form filled out on a typewriter and stamped with the New York state seal. No photo, no embossing, just a little piece of green paper. I was able to make up fake I.D.s for all my friends by simply drawing the state seal in the appropriate box. You could get as many blank application forms as you wanted at the local DMV. It was a painstaking process. It took a lot of practice to make my ink drawing of the seal look authentic. If only I had applied that kind of concentration and dedication to my schoolwork.

The drinking age in New York was eighteen, so at sixteen we were able to pass in a dimly lit nightclub. And somehow having this little green piece of paper made me feel more like an adult. I hated being a kid; hated being under the control of parents, teachers or any authority figure. I was determined to grow up fast, leaving them all behind, and I was prepared to do anything I could to hotwire the process.

With our forged I.D.s we made the rounds of the legendary jazz clubs of New York: the Five Spot, the Village Gate, the Village Vanguard, the Half Note, the Jazz Gallery and Birdland. We got to see just about every giant of modern jazz alive at that time: Miles, 'Trane, Monk, Mingus, Roland Kirk, Eric Dolphy, Herbie Mann, Nina Simone and many others. Fred and I also started a jazz combo with Jimmy Hunter on piano, various sax players and several different bass players. One of these was Eddie Gomez, who was a year ahead of me at Music & Art, but who would soon become the legendary bass player for the Bill Evans Trio.

Around this time Fred's mother began dating Miles Davis (shocking for a Southern belle of her generation), and, through this connection, Fred arranged to take lessons from Coltrane's drummer, the great Elvin Jones. Our alto sax player, David Kalish, was studying with John Handy III. I was still taking lessons from Billy Bauer, but I was very resistant to learning how to read music. Billy always made the mistake of writing something out for me to practice and then playing the melody down for me. My excellent ear proved to be my undoing. As soon as he played the tune, I would echo it back to him, pretending to read it off his sheet music. Once I played it, I knew it. It soon became evident—at least to me—that I lacked both the chops and the discipline to become a jazz musician. We took a few casual gigs at high school dances where we were expected to play rock 'n' roll, and that seemed to me more suited to my limited technical abilities. Besides, with rock 'n' roll I got to use a lot more of the cool effects on my amp, like reverb and tremolo.

Unbeknownst to my jazz cronies, I was also a secret folkie. I would tote my acoustic guitar down to Washington Square every Sunday for the Big Hootenanny, walking south on Avenue B from 14th Street, through the teeming tenement streets that smelled alternately of pizza ovens and dog shit. I then turned west through the East Village on St. Marks Place, across Astor Place, in the center of which was a big black cube of a sculpture on which someone had scrawled "Give me Librium or give me meth," then across West 8th Street, and finally south again on Fifth Avenue.

The Big Hootenanny in Washington Square Park happened every Sunday around the circular fountain once the weather got warm enough. It had been going on since the '50s and attracted hundreds of folk musicians from all over the city. Most of the big names in the urban folk revival had jammed there at one time or another: Ramblin' Jack Elliott, Dave Van Ronk, Mary Travers. There were traditional balladeers and several blue grass groups, playing a vast assortment of mostly stringed instruments. Often, casual passersby would join in, singing along with an age-old refrain, like:

> *Come all ye fair and tender maidens*
> *Take warning how you court your men*
> *They're like a star on a summer's evening*
> *They first appear and then they're gone*

One of my favorite Village haunts was the Café Wha? where I could sit on a Saturday or Sunday afternoon nursing a cup of coffee for hours and hear great folk and comedy acts like Len Chandler, Richie Havens, Hugh Romney (who in a later incarnation became *Woodstock*'s Wavy Gravy) and a goateed gent named Noel Stookey, who later changed his name to Paul and joined Peter Yarrow and Mary Travers to become Peter, Paul & Mary. But at that time everyone referred to him as "the toilet man" because the high point of his act was his imitation of a flushing toilet.

Every Sunday, folk musicians would flock to Washington Square for the Big Hootenanny.

The arty, bohemian atmosphere of the Village fascinated me. The ancient, narrow streets, alleys and lanes were populated as much by the ghosts of James, Poe, Faulkner, Eugene O'Neill and Dylan Thomas as by the odd assortment of characters—artists, musicians and poseurs—that now sauntered by. I spent as much time in the Village as possible. Occasionally I would get up at three o'clock in the morning, and while my parents slept soundly, get dressed (in my black turtleneck beatnik garb), put on my dark glasses and walk down to the Café Figaro at Bleecker and MacDougal and sit there, looking deep, reading something like *Illuminations* by the tragic teenage poet Arthur Rimbaud, hoping to meet some cool beatnik chick dressed all in black. I'd sit there until the place closed at 6 a.m., then go to school.

* * *

One of my closest friends was Alan Schwartz, an unusually mature, four-teen-year-old classical violinist who studied with an urban legend named Bobby Nutkoff. Bobby claimed to be taking lessons from the ghost of Paganini, and the way he played, we had no reason to doubt it.

Alan occupied a vacant apartment one flight up from his mother's apartment in a seedy building on First Avenue, about half a mile uptown from Stuyvesant Town. It's unclear how he was able to squat in this place undetected, but apparently the landlord either never came around or didn't care. There were a couple of ratty mattresses on the floor, some orange crate furniture, a phonograph and a small collection of jazz albums. I remember spending many a blissful night with Alan, getting wasted on rotgut vodka and listening to Miles Davis' album *Jazz Track*. This was an album that had the soundtrack to the French film *Ascenseur pour l'èchafaud* on one side, and a monumental sextet session on the other that featured Coltrane *and* Cannonball Adderley on saxes, as well as Bill Evans, Paul Chambers and Jimmy Cobb. We had a couple of parties at chez Alan, and at one of them I lost my virginity.

Needless to say, we were all very drunk. There was Alan, me, a couple of single girls whose names and faces I don't remember, my friend Alfred Perkins, a black guy who was quite a bit older than us—probably nineteen at least—and Alfred's girlfriend, whose name I also can't recall. She was a foul-mouthed, grossly unappealing white chick with bad skin, who, as they say, had been around the block many times. There was a little laundry room at the back end of the apartment, and I recall trying to seduce one of these young single girls in there, but I was rebuffed. Eventually she and her girlfriend went home. Alan decided to crash downstairs at his mother's, and Alfred and his girlfriend were getting it on—right in front of me—on Alan's mattress on the floor. I was pretending to be passed out on another mattress nearby. Eventually Alfred passed out next to her. And there it was: wide open opportunity, staring me right in the face. She beckoned to me and I slid onto her, sinking into flaccid layers of flesh like it was quicksand. There was some furtive fumbling with my pants. I produced a condom (my Boy Scout training had taught me to always be prepared) and offered to use it. She said, "Don't bother. I'm pregnant anyway, so I let all my men come in me." One can't always choose how these moments will unfold, especially when you're trying to hotwire reality.

Of course, I would have greatly preferred to lose my virginity with Sophi, but she was nowhere near ready for sex. The first summer we knew each other, she got a nanny job, working for a wealthy family with a summer home on Fire Island. I went out there to visit her one blazing hot, blue-sky-white-sand day. It was her day off, so we lazed around on the beach and went for a swim. The water was clear and warm, the beach beautifully uncrowded. Afterward, we went back to her room. It was a small guest room, with wood-paneled walls that was like a little knotty pine cabin. We started making out on the bed, and she took off her bathing suit top and let me kiss and fondle her wonderful breasts. It was one of the most exciting experiences of my life—way better than fucking Alfred's girlfriend.

* * *

My second consummated sexual experience came some time in my junior year. We used to congregate in big clumps of humanity outside the school in the mornings and after school as well. One day this girl known as Renny, whom I hardly knew, came up to me and announced: "I've decided to lose my virginity, and I've decided to do it with you." A rush of warm affirmation coursed through me like heroin. For a guy obsessed with acceptance by the opposite sex, who was incredibly insecure about his attractiveness, and who above all was determined to will himself into instant adulthood, this was like a shot of adrenalin to my feeble ego.

I took her to a crash pad downtown at 48 Grand Street that belonged to a couple of college guys. It was well known in the hipster community simply as "Grand Street." This was a place you could go to do anything you wouldn't want your parents to know about, mainly sex and drugs. In the back was a tiny bedroom with a single bed in it called The Ballroom, and that's where I took Renny.

She took off all her clothes and lay on the bed like a patient on an operating table. She was not beautiful, but not hard to look at. Her compact body was trim and beautifully shaped. I undressed as quickly as I could, fearing she might change her mind at any second. Then I remembered the condom. This was not optional; there was no 'pill' in those days, so I started rifling through my pockets, trying to find it. A shudder of panic passed through my body, causing me to lose my erection. What if I had forgotten it? I held my pants aloft and shook the contents of my pockets out onto the floor. Amidst the loose change and used Kleenex, there it was. I struggled to get enough of an erection back to put it on. I had never felt so unsexy in my life. Finally, I was able to unroll the condom onto my pathetic member.

"Is it in yet?" she kept asking.

"I... I think so..."

It was all over in seconds. On the subway ride back uptown we didn't speak, hardly looked at each other.

A few weeks later my parents got a call from the local police precinct, telling them to bring me in. Renny had accused me of rape. It felt like I'd been punched in the stomach. What could possibly motivate her to do such a thing? My father took me down to the 13th precinct. I told the truth about the incident, and the cops seemed to know that she was a nut job. To my relief they sent me home with no charges. But I never spoke to that lunatic again.

My parents looked at me differently after that. I had shed my childhood image forever and was now an interloper in their home.

* * *

Sophi went to Italy the second summer of our romance, and I went on a cross-country camping trip. It was a chaperoned group of about twenty kids in my grade, on a big tour bus that took us across most of America, as far west as Yellowstone National Park. We camped on all kinds of farms and ranches and in national parks. But the most interesting thing about that trip for me was meeting fellow musician Jody Stecher on the bus and learning about bluegrass music. Bluegrass was a very authentic branch of folk music that many urban kids had embraced in the early '60s, but it was truly a part of the culture of the Appalachian Mountains of West Virginia, Tennessee, North Carolina and Kentucky that had remained little changed in one hundred years.

At sixteen, Brooklyn-born Jody Stecher was a virtuoso bluegrass banjo player. He had freckles, short brown hair and a thin upper lip. His idol was Earl Scruggs, who is generally acknowledged as the progenitor of the rapid-fire, three-finger banjo picking style that has come to be known as "Scruggs picking." It entered the mainstream consciousness with "Dueling Banjos" in the 1973 movie *Deliverance*. Since I was the better of the two guitar players on the bus, I got to play Lester Flatt to Jody's Earl Scruggs. Lester Flatt was the flat-picking guitar player that accompanied Scruggs' lightning picking throughout most of his career. The guitar parts were pretty easy, especially compared to what Jody was playing, and he taught me a lot about the music of Appalachia.

When we got back to the city, we continued to meet up at the Sunday hoots in Washington Square. Jody went on to a long career as a professional folk musician, mastering a wide array of stringed instruments and eventually forming a duo with his wife, Kate Brislin, and recording for Rounder Records.

Jody Stecher (L) and me pretending to be Flatt & Scruggs, summer 1962

* * *

When Sophi and I saw each other again after the summer, she told me she had fallen in love with someone else. It was a guy named Robby: blond, handsome, sophisticated and rich—everything I was not. I was heartbroken. I wrote her pathetic letters, begging her to come back to me. I was too young to understand that there was nothing I could say or do. I couldn't undo her love by begging, nor wishing, nor willing it away.

Eventually my grief subsided sufficiently for me to fall madly in love with Edie Hasselman. She was, simply put, the best-looking girl in the entire school. She was not beautiful in the traditional, commonplace 'cheerleader' way; her beauty was completely natural and unselfconscious. It was as if she didn't know she was beautiful. She had long blond hair, big blue eyes and exquisitely shaped lips. But what made her so breathtaking was the sweetness and kindness that radiated from those eyes. She looked like what most Northern European Christians imagine when they think of an angel. She was from a blue collar Bronx family. Not dumb, but definitely not an intellectual. It didn't matter; I could just sit and stare at her—she didn't have to say a word.

There was only one problem: she had a boyfriend. She had been going with a guy named Peter Blankfield, who was an art major in our grade as well. He was a quiet sort. I really didn't know him well, but he was tall, handsome and, like me, had long hair before it was fashionable. I thought he was cool. Why Edie would give me the time of day was a mystery to me. But she did. One time, close to the end of the term, she came with me, my sister, and my parents on a trip to Jones Beach. I guess, at some level, I was showing off to my parents what a beautiful girl I could attract.

Another time we met at Fort Tryon Park on the upper end of Manhattan. It was a glorious spring day. We were walking along blissfully, holding hands, and then we spotted—*Peter*. He had been tailing her. What followed was this weird game of cat and mouse, where Edie and I tried to elude him, and he kept popping up, stalking us. The park had intricate pathways, rocks and trees, and Peter would suddenly emerge from behind a rock or tree, always some distance away, but close enough for us all to make eye contact. And then there were The Cloisters, a museum that was constructed from medieval European abbeys and was a labyrinth unto itself. He never approached us or said anything. Edie never approached him either. I wondered why she didn't just go to him and say something. I expected her to leave me there and go with him, but she stuck with me. It was awkward and surreal.

I liked Peter. He was not confrontational, and even though he was much bigger than I was, he never threatened me or even said anything to me. I got the feeling he was just hurt. After that, I kind of backed away from Edie. I think she really loved Peter deep down, and I had just confused her for a minute. Who knows why girls do stuff.

* * *

My new best friend, Jay Bernstein, and I decided to get our own apartment. I had decided to move out of my parents' house, and I convinced Jay to go in on the rent with me. Jay was a voice major at Music & Art who lived near me in Stuyvesant Town. We would take the long subway ride to and from school together every day. His curly brown hair and thick, black-framed glasses reminded me a little of Buddy Holly, but his face was ravaged by serious acne. He sang in the M&A chorus, probably the best high school chorus in the city. He had an amazing *basso profondo* voice. When he was preparing for the annual Christmas concert, he would regale me all the way to and from the subway with excerpts from Handel's *Messiah*...

> *King of kings and lord of lords*
> *And He shall reign forever and ever...*

We found a place for rent in a tenement building on Stanton Street on the Lower East Side. This was the *lowest* of the Lower East Side. It was $35 a month. I had inherited a fairly valuable coin collection from my grandfather, and I sold it, bit-by-bit, to pay the rent. Jay would always go home at night to his parents in Stuyvesant Town, but I decided to live there full-time. I left a note for my parents telling them I would be in touch, and moved out. In a subsequent phone call, I agreed to keep attending school if they would not try to get me to move back home. My poor parents were beside themselves.

The place had bare wooden floors, one bedroom, a W.C. and a bathtub in the living room that had a white metal cover, so it could double as a kitchen table. The first thing I did in the apartment was to knock all the plaster off one wall of the living room, exposing the bare brick. When one of my friends came over to admire the place he said, "Wow! This is like somethin' out of *The Subterraneans*!"

In the mornings when I went to school, I would often encounter neighborhood junkies or old drunks who had sought shelter from the cold in our hallway and passed out on the stairs. One time an old man insisted on showing me his swollen balls, as if I was some kind of medical authority. They were the size of grapefruits.

During our brief sojourn at 65 Stanton Street, Jay and I played host to a constant parade of colorful characters, from the uptown preppies to the downtown hipsters. There was the pretty young artist next door, Anne Frank (yes, that was actually her name), who wound up going with one of my new friends, a tall, handsome black guy named Chris. Her place was far better appointed than mine. She had lacquered the floor glossy black, had some decent furniture and knew how to keep the place clean. Many a night Anne, Chris, Alfred Perkins (in whose girlfriend I had lost my virginity) and I would sit around in her living room passing a bottle of cheap Chianti. I was at last living the life of an adult—a bona fide member of the Beat Generation.

One day I cut school with Cookie, a buxom black girl I had taken out a couple of times. She had radiant dark brown skin and a beehive hairdo that could hold up the Chrysler Building. Mixed race couples in those days were still head-turners, even in New York, especially when the girl was black and the guy was white. While I was genuinely attracted to Cookie, I confess I also enjoyed shocking the straights we passed on the street and in the subway. She wanted to see my pad, so I took her to Stanton Street. We made out on my seedy mattress on the floor. She was a great kisser and I loved her abundant lips. She smelled of hairspray and some kind of musky perfume I didn't care for much, but that didn't keep me from being turned on. I unbuttoned her blouse, and tried to undo her bra. I had little experience at bra-undoing, and this one was like a combination chastity belt and bullet proof vest. Her breasts were formidable, and I was dying to liberate them from this cruel bondage, but alas, it was not to be. In the end, Cookie demurred. She was not quite the swinger I hoped she might be.

And then there was Leo C.V. Jones, the Wild Man of Greenwich Village, a bushy-haired, bearded black man around forty with no fixed address who could often be seen playing chess with the old men in Washington Square Park. He wasn't hard to spot; he was the one yelling, "Check, mothafucka!" One night he showed up with the legendary Lydia Savage, Park Avenue debutante and nymphomaniac. I had met her through Fred Mason, who had been screwing her on a regular basis, but how had Leo met her? He took her into my bedroom and proceeded to noisily fuck her brains out. There was no door on the bedroom, and I had to sit there and listen. I tried going next door to Anne's, but she was not at home. I came back and turned up the Miles Davis record as loud as it would go, but it was no use.

One night I went to my parents' house for dinner. My dad flipped out and started beating me and crying. I was on the living room sofa, and he just started flailing away at me with open hands. I just covered my head and took it—my dad was no pugilist. "Do you know what you're doing to your mother? She's been crying her eyes out every night," he kept saying. It freaked me out. My parents had never raised a hand to me and had rarely shown much emotion of any kind—unless you count annoyance. I had never seen my cold, undemonstrative mother cry even one tear. In fact, even after my dad died more than fifty years later, I didn't see her cry. But I saw my dad cry that night, and that was enough.

I gave up the apartment and moved home.

* * *

By my senior year I was sick of high school. I decided to drop out and get a job after the fall semester. My parents, who were both educators, took it hard, but they now realized they had little-to-no control over me, and I was gonna do what I was gonna do.

I got myself a minimum wage job at Mark Cross Ltd. in the mail order department. I sat and processed forms all day, filling orders for address books bound in fine Morocco leather and silver-plated pen and pencil sets. It was the most unbearably tedious experience of my life. Even worse than school.

After about a month, I let my parents enroll me in an expensive Upper West Side private school for underachievers called Robert Louis Stevenson School. I found that, in my almost three years at Music & Art, I had completed all the math and science requirements needed to graduate, so all I had left to take were my easy subjects: English, art, history, drama. As I said, it was a school for underachievers; next to these bozos I was a genius. At the end of the term they told me I was going to be Valedictorian. I guess you could say I had mixed feelings, and in keeping with my anarchist leanings I decided to cut school for the graduation. I wasn't going to make any hypocritical speeches, that much was certain, so I just didn't show up.

At Robert Louis Stevenson I became friendly with a fellow guitar player named Johnny Meyers. His parents were Orthodox Jews, and he knew Hebrew. He taught me some Israeli folk songs and we used to perform these together, singing harmony. We also discovered smoking pot together. In those days you could score a 'nickel bag' in the Village for $5.

The pot high was very different from alcohol in that, while alcohol tended to dull the senses, pot amplified them. It also didn't mess with your motor skills so much, so it was fun to get out and explore. I'd be walking down the street and suddenly stop and get caught up in the ant action that was taking place in some crack in the sidewalk, or stare at the brazen redness of a potted geranium until Johnny interrupted my reverie and pulled me away. It was good to go out as a team, since either one of us could get so easily sidetracked; the other one could always get us back on course.

We often scored from a couple who lived in a seedy hotel on Waverly Place. They were heroin addicts. One day we were smoking a joint with them. The girl was white and the guy was black. There was a crib in the room containing a little brown baby girl. We were pretty high, and we asked her what it felt like to have a baby. I'll never forget her reply. She said, "Ever have to take a shit so hard you have to hold on to the sink?"

* * *

In the summer of 1963, as a graduation present, my parents gave me what was, up to that point, the greatest experience of my life. They sent me with a camp group—the same camp that sponsored the cross-country trip—on a camping trip around Europe.

We landed in Holland and spent a few days living with Dutch families. I stayed with a family in Noordwijk, which is on the coast. They were really nice, and I remember they had a boy a year or two older than me, who subsequently visited me in New York and stayed with my family. He

27

had a little motorbike on which he drove us around to show me the sights. In Noordwijk there were actual dykes to keep the sea from overrunning the low-lying fields. They ate buttered toast with chocolate sprinkles for breakfast. I thought this was a marvelous idea, especially since the chocolate was about the best I had ever tasted.

Bud Rose, an American who taught at the university in Amsterdam, led our group. He drove an old Citroen, a car the like of which I had never seen before. It looked like it was made out of cheap, corrugated aluminum, the kind of stuff we would bang on in metal shop in junior high. The seats in it looked exactly like beach chairs, with plastic or vinyl netting slung on hollow aluminum frames.

Amsterdam was riddled with canals, and everyone rode bicycles. We rented bikes and rode around the city, which was magnificent and old. All the people we met spoke excellent English. One kid in our group had studied German in school, and he tried speaking in German to some Dutch people. That did not go over well at all.

Then we all boarded a big bus and, with our Dutch bus driver, Job, and two college-age Dutch counselors, Gerard and Tini, we set out across the continent, camping out in seven countries in about six weeks.

The first place we went was Dachau. This was an all-Jewish group of kids and the camp that sponsored the trip was a Jewish camp, and so this was an important stop for us. We got the grim guided tour and viewed the notorious ovens where so many thousands of dead bodies were cremated, and we heard all the grim statistics. Instead of making the reality more palpable, being there somehow distanced me from it. The unimaginable horror humans are capable of perpetrating on their fellow humans numbed me. It was enough to make me want to drop out of the human race.

But the high point of the trip for me was Paris. I had been a below-average French student in high school, but upon my arrival on the continent, my musician's ear kicked in and I realized I had an amazing knack for picking up languages. I even picked up some Italian while in Italy. But in France, I was instantly immersed in the language and culture. I would translate American folk songs into French—and make them rhyme.

One of the guys I had played bluegrass with in Washington Square, Carl Nobler, told me to look up a friend of his in Paris, a certain Scott Miller. So, when I got to Paris, I hit the streets, feeling an indescribable sense of freedom I had never experienced before. I was in a strange city in a strange country, yet I knew the language well enough to speak and understand. I was thousands of miles away from the control of my parents and teachers.

I descended into the metro. I went to the address Carl Nobler gave me. It was in a cool neighborhood on the *rive gauche*. An attractive brunette in her thirties answered the door. In my flawless accent, I said "Bonjour, je cherche un monsieur Scott Miller."

"Mais, Scott Miller est une jeune fille," she said.

"Vraiment?" I was taken aback.

"Oui. Etes vous Francais?"

"Non, Americain."

"Well, so are we," she replied.

My French was so good, she couldn't tell I wasn't French. Cool!

Anyway, Scott Miller did indeed turn out to be a girl. She and her family were very welcoming, as most Europeans were in those days. They insisted I stay for dinner. Her dad was Warren Miller, a fairly well known author, who had written a popular novel of that time called *The Cool World*. I felt I was, at last, where I belonged—in my element. I was in Paris, hanging out with a celebrated author on the Left Bank. If only this could be my life from now on…

* * *

Upon my return to New York that summer, before going off to college, I worked in the mailroom at New York City Community College, a two-year vocational college in Brooklyn where my father was Dean of Students. One day a girl who also worked there said to me, "You look like a Beatle." I was highly offended, assuming she meant the insect. Then she showed me a picture in the newspaper of the four mop-tops, said to be the latest rage in England. I had been wearing my hair quite a bit longer than was socially acceptable in those days, and so I was intrigued when I saw these Brits copping my look.

It was a few months later that I actually heard The Beatles for the first time. I remember walking down MacDougal Street, and a car went by with the radio blasting "I Want to Hold Your Hand." Something about the chord changes was so unusual, so appealing that I ran after the car so I could hear the rest of the song. Until then I'd thought The Beatles were just music industry hype, cooked up to appeal to twelve-year-old girls. But the next day I went out and bought their first album (later I learned that *Meet The Beatles* was not their first album, but it was the first one released in the US). Because I still considered them fodder for little girls, I smuggled the album home under my coat, so no one would see, and I played it clandestinely—over and over. The melodic appeal of the songs was so powerful it changed my musical sensibility forever. The tug-of-war between folk and jazz was over; from now on I would be a pop songwriter. I would write heart-rending-yet-interesting melodies with unpredictable, emotionally evocative chord changes. And Lennon & McCartney were my new heroes.

Chapter Three

College, Sort of

I had applied to just one college: a tiny, ultra-progressive school in Vermont called Goddard. They had no tests, no grades, and you could make up your own courses. It sounded right up my alley. My high school friend Johnny was going there as well. When I got there, to my great surprise, there was my ex-girlfriend Sophi and her boyfriend Robby! She, being a wonderful artist, had been accepted at Cooper Union, but since Robby was going to Goddard, she had opted to follow him there. I had long since gotten over my grief at losing her, and we were now friends. I still admired her intellect and her great sense of humor, so I was overjoyed that she would be in college with me.

I had a great time at Goddard, so much so that I kind of forgot to go to class. Nobody there was supervising me, nobody breathing down my neck, telling me to do stuff. So I did whatever I wanted, never considering that there might be consequences.

The thing that interested me the most about college life, about being away from home for the first time, was that my odds of getting laid increased exponentially. My sex life really began with Ginny Sue Robbins, the 'Sex Goddess of Goddard.' She was a pretty brunette with a charming North Carolina drawl, about my height (5'7") and generously proportioned. She was a free spirit, whip-smart, funny, a brilliant painter and writer, played a good blues piano, and she rode a Honda motorcycle. One night she put me on the back of her bike and drove us up a steep, grassy hill to a little shack they called "The Hideout."

Inside, there was an old wood stove, a candle on a low table and some grimy blankets on the floor. It had a pleasant, earthy smell that reminded me of mushrooms. And there Ginny Sue showed me new aspects of sex that were a revelation to me. She was a couple of years older than I and assumed the role of tutor and mentor. We got down on the blankets and began to make out. She was an excellent kisser.

"Okay," she said, "just lay back and trust me." She unzipped my pants and peeled off all my clothes, gently kissing each new patch of exposed flesh. Once I was completely naked, lying on my back, splayed before her, she slowly and seductively shed her own clothes, piece by piece. The next thing I knew she had my cock in her mouth. This was a new and wondrous sensation to my inexperienced penis. She licked me like a popsicle and then took my whole member into her mouth. It was as if she could feel what I was feeling. I knew nothing about forestalling orgasms or "saving" it for coitus. I was hot as a firecracker and my fuse was burning fast. When she sensed I was about to come, she slowed down still more, 'milking' the moment to prolong what was, up to that point, the greatest orgasm of my life.

You'd think I would be done for the night, but no. "Your turn now," she said sweetly. We switched places and she instructed me, without being at all intimidating. I sucked her nipples until they were hard, then kissed my way down her torso, lingering on her belly button, and then I was face-to-face with a wet, pulsating vagina for the first time in my life. She told me how and where to use my tongue and how to find that magic little button called the clitoris. And she talked me through coaxing it to the brink of orgasm. At eighteen I was a walking semen factory, and by now I was hard as a rock again. Since she had gotten me off only minutes earlier, I was able to enter her and bring her to repeated orgasms before I finally had my second of the night.

After my two fumbling attempts at coitus in high school, this was the first really complete sexual experience of my life. I felt little romance with Ginny Sue, but it developed into a unique friendship. There was no pretense of faithfulness or commitment; her sexual exploits were legendary on campus; she was faithful only to her own freedom. But I have her to thank for my lifelong appreciation of guiltless, wanton sex.

We were on the forefront of the New Morality, which roughly coincided with JFK's New Frontier. We eschewed the stultified moral values of the

'50s with a vengeance. It was only later, when I got into relationships that were more emotional, that I found that certain laws of sexual nature were immutable, and if you fell in love with someone, you wanted that person to love you to the exclusion of all others.

A few weeks after my tryst with Ginny Sue, JFK was dead, and the New Frontier was over. But the New Morality went on.

There was no shortage of liberated coeds at Goddard who were also enthusiastic supporters of guiltless, wanton sex. After a month or two I hooked up with a petite, bespectacled blond named Dee. She was a little older than I and wore her straight blond hair parted slightly to one side and draped over one eye like Veronica Lake. She drove a cute little Renault Dauphine. Growing up in Manhattan, someone with a car was still a bit of a novelty to me. We would go on road trips to other towns, sometimes visiting other schools where she or I knew people. At Windham College I ran into my old heartthrob Edie. Her boyfriend Peter was elsewhere. She promised to come visit me at Goddard.

* * *

That first year at college was also when I started writing songs. The first one was a mournful, self-pitying folk ballad, but with a simple-yet-memorable melody and some chord changes that departed from the standard folk lexicon. I had also been writing short stories and poetry, but I now felt strongly that songwriting was my true calling.

Johnny, my guitar-playing friend from high school, and I wrote a bunch of songs that were parodies of '50s rock 'n' roll. Enlisting several other guys, we organized a show in which we performed these send-ups. It was sort of like a precursor to Sha Na Na, but with original material. There was a take-off on Little Richard called "20 Minutes Makes a Hardboiled Egg". There was a mock doo-wop ballad called "Soggy Pillow," and then there was my social comment on the current crackdown on marijuana at Goddard, "The Heat Is on Again." We performed this in the little theater adjacent to the Community Center building, drawing a surprisingly large and enthusiastic crowd—a testament to just how starved for entertainment everyone was.

* * *

At Goddard we had a mid-winter 'work term,' where we would vacate the campus for three months—December, January and February—and find jobs, preferably ones that would be meaningful to our future career aspirations. I wanted to do music, but had no idea how to apply this to the working world. I went home to New York and got a job as a volunteer counselor in a Harlem city-funded daycare center. I lived in my parents' home, so I was able to work for no money.

On February 7, 1964 I decided to go out to Idlewild (now Kennedy) Airport to witness the arrival of The Beatles for the first time in the US. Because of my inability to accurately estimate time, and the succession of subways and buses I had to take to get there, I arrived too late to see the Fab Four. There were still quite a few people milling around in the terminal, including fans and reporters, and I noticed, just a few feet away from me, there was Brian Epstein, wearing a black bowler hat and long topcoat, talking to reporters. The idea passed through my mind to go up and talk to him. I wanted to say, "Hey, Mr. Epstein, I can do what they do—sign ME!" But in the end sanity prevailed and I went home.

* * *

I went back to Goddard in March. Sophi and Robby had gotten thrown out of school for cohabitating in his dorm room, Johnny transferred to a 'real' college, and I became close friends with Steve, a short, bearded psych major with thinning brown hair and a perpetual mischievous grin.

My roommate was a tall, blond, mercurial filmmaker named Wendell Jones. He was incredibly creative, handsome, and exuded a romantic, dangerous air. He rode a Vincent Black Shadow, the King of Motorcycles and wore a black leather motorcycle jacket. He was older and more experienced than I, and I held him in awe. His girlfriend was Phoebe, a short, rather dumpy and plain brunette. This was a guy I figured could nail any girl he wanted, and he fell head over heels for someone to whom I wasn't in the least bit attracted. Of course, he didn't have anything to prove. He was not as caught up with looks as I was, and I was—precisely because I was so terribly insecure about my own looks. I was determined to attract the hottest, most prestigious girls on campus—the 'A-list' girls. Especially blonds. Blonds became my new obsession, because there were so few of them in my upbringing. A blue-eyed straight-haired blond represented to me everything my family—and especially my mother—was not. But more of that later.

Wendy—as we called him—was working on a claymation animated short film, and the set was our collective desks. Our desks were actually one long piece of wood, painted flat white, that was a built-in shelf running the full width of the room beneath two large windows. Wendy had constructed a backdrop of a forest that stood about a foot high and ran all across the desk. He had sculpted little figures, the characters in his film, which was a sort of twisted fairy tale that I gathered drew influences from "Hansel and Gretel," "Little Red Riding Hood" and "Rumpelstiltskin." There was a little boy, a little girl, a wolf, an ogre, a witch and a prince. He had his 16mm movie camera set to click off one frame at a time, and he would painstakingly move each character a fraction of an inch, then click the frame, then move it some more, then click. He had the focus and patience of a tabby cat stalking a mouse.

One night Wendy came into the room, clearly agitated. He had a small bottle of bourbon and kept pacing the room, taking pulls on the bottle, which was already half empty. It seems he and Phoebe had a big fight and had broken up. I had never seen him like this. "She doesn't want me anymore, she doesn't want me anymore," he kept saying. After a while he went storming out of the dorm and roared off on his bike. That was the last anyone ever saw of him. Word came late that night that he had been in a head-on collision on the Barre Road, and he was dead. I went into town to the hospital with Phoebe, Steve and Phoebe's roommate, Sue, but it was a futile journey. There was nothing any of us could do.

Wendy's funeral was held in his hometown of Annandale on Hudson in New York State. This was also the home of Bard College where a few people I knew were attending, Jane Schindelheim among them. I caught a ride with Phoebe, Sue and Steve. Steve drove, Sue sat in front with him and I sat in back with Phoebe. She was white and still as a gravestone. She didn't weep; she didn't speak. She just sat, frozen, the whole way. I didn't even want to guess what was going through her mind.

The funeral was not worthy of the charismatic Wendy. It was a dreary, predictable, WASPy affair. A clergyman muttered some platitudes at the gravesite, and then everyone retired to Wendy's parents' home for tea and cake.

No one this close to me had ever died before, at least no one this close in age. My Aunt Rose had died of cancer a few years earlier, after smoking heavily for years, but she was my parents' age, and that seemed old to me.

I knew I should be overcome with emotion at Wendy's death, but I was unable to muster a single tear. I just felt numb. Maybe I pushed the grief away subconsciously, but I couldn't get in touch with my feelings of loss, which I knew were lurking there somewhere.

At the reception I met a tall, good-looking guy who was a childhood friend of Wendy's and who was now attending Bard. He had an odd name: Chevy Chase (wasn't that a town in Maryland?). He told me he played drums and piano. He looked pretty cool, so I filed him away for future reference.

My friends from Goddard drove back that afternoon, but I opted to stay and hang around Bard for a day or two. I tried to find Jane, but was told she had gone to New York to visit her parents, so I hung out with some other people I knew from high school.

The next day the weather was pretty nice and, having no other options, I decided to hitchhike back to Vermont in my black funeral suit. I got stuck somewhere between northern Massachusetts and southern Vermont. I stood there with my thumb out for hours, but no one even slowed down. It began to get dark—and cold. Finally I came to a pay phone and called the local cops. They came over and picked me up and let me spend the night in their pokey under some old army blankets that stank of urine. In the morning I set out again. The minute I stuck out my thumb a car screeched to a halt. It was a beat up VW Microbus. Behind the wheel was a wild-eyed young man with a mustache, sandy curls and wire-rimmed specs. "Hey man, where ya headed?" he asked.

"Goddard College in Plainfield, Vermont."

"Oh yeah? Is that a cool spot?"

"The coolest," I said.

"Okay," he said, "I'll drive, you roll."

And he tossed me a bag of marijuana and some rolling papers.

Tom (that was his name) drove me straight back to Goddard, and a very pleasant drive it was. He hung out for a few days, during which we all stayed quite high. Then he split for parts unknown. My dorm room had been cleared of all Wendy's possessions—all, that is, except the film set and little clay figures. Gazing at them suddenly brought forth the suppressed grief. Tears finally flowed. I looked out the window at the beautiful spring weather, the birds chirping loudly in the trees that were shooting out new leaves and said, "You're missing a beautiful day, Wendy."

* * *

True to her word, the beautiful Edie actually came to visit me at Goddard. She stayed with me in my dorm room, which I occupied alone for the rest of the semester. At last I had her all to myself. There was no sign of Peter. I didn't even ask her about him, for fear he would pop out from behind a tree or something. She was so sweet, so lovely, and so—innocent. I just couldn't put the moves on her, and indeed, she was not sending out any signals that she wanted me to. I respectfully slept in the vacated bed, while she slept in mine. We never even snuggled. After that we lost touch for a while.

Edie

* * *

Toward the end of the semester I started going with Jen, an 'A-list chick.' She was tall (maybe 5'8"), graceful, and slinky. She had dirty blond hair, brown eyes, full lips and skin prone to occasional acne. Skin problems notwithstanding, she had charisma and a lot of campus cachet. Yes, she was a status symbol, but I was also genuinely crazy about her.

Steve and I hatched a scheme to go to Martha's Vineyard, an island off Cape Cod, for the summer and start a folk music coffee house—a 'basket house.' We recruited several classmates to join the venture. Each had a specific field of expertise, which would be his or her role in the running of the operation. We had Bob, who had been a short order cook, Henry, who had been an accountant, Steve, who was sort of a jack-of-all-trades and I was in charge of the entertainment. If I couldn't get any entertainment, I would *be* the entertainment. Jen and her friend Jane, another pretty blond, volunteered to come along and be the waitresses. I was thrilled that Jen liked me so much she wanted to spend the whole summer with me.

A few days before school let out I found a letter in my box from Goddard. Basically, it said that my academic performance that year had been "sub-standard" (an understatement—it had been nonexistent). I was welcome to return for the fall semester, but if I didn't demonstrate a greater interest in my studies, I would be asked to leave.

Chapter Four

Café Moska

We arrived on the island before the summer tourist season really got underway. Almost immediately, we scoped out an abandoned storefront that looked like it had been some kind of appliance store, or maybe even a coffee shop, because it had some kitchen appliances we could use. It was right on the street where the Vineyard Haven ferry landed, a great location for tourists. We found out the property was owned by one Henry Koenig, a wealthy German-Jewish immigrant, who apparently owned half the Island.

We excitedly told him of our plan to start the coffee house, and run it for just this one summer. He was highly amused by our youthful enthusiasm and naiveté. "Okay," he said. "You can hev the place. If you voud make some money, you can pay me rent." We were dumbfounded and beside ourselves with joy.

At the end of a deserted beach road we found an old hotel that had gone out of business where we obtained tables, chairs and dirt-cheap restaurant supplies. We had to go to Boston to buy the espresso machine, but no self-respecting coffee house could be without one. We found a beautiful used one—a real antique—in a classified ad in a Boston newspaper.

We named the place the Café Moska, which Bob insisted meant "brotherly love" in Arabic or something (many years later I learned that the word is actually *moksha*, which means "release from the cycle of death and rebirth" in ancient Sanskrit). We all slept in a large space in the back of the store, behind the kitchen, which we partitioned with blankets hung from ropes, like in *It Happened One Night*.

We made enough to keep the doors open. We even booked a couple of paid acts into the place: an old country & western singer named Dusty Rhodes, a hulking guy in his late forties with a booming baritone voice, who played guitar and sang old cowboy songs, and The Holy Modal Rounders, a whacky duo who sang weird, old-timey songs in warbled, surrealistic voices. We never paid Henry Koenig one penny of rent, and he never asked us for it.

One day, in perusing the local underground paper, we saw that my old friend José Feliciano was playing the Newport Folk Festival and would be coming to the Vineyard immediately after that to play the island's biggest—and only other—folk music venue, the Mooncusser in Oak Bluffs, which was just down the road a mile or two. We hatched a scheme for a preemptive strike: we would go to Newport, find José, and drive him back to the Vineyard.

It was crowded at the festival and quite chaotic outside the main gate, but I managed to get a message backstage to José. After a long wait, he emerged with his "handler," a mousey Puerto Rican woman named Alma, who was very shy and said little. Jen and I waylaid them, bundled them into her old Plymouth, and we were off to Martha's Vineyard. José and I hadn't seen each other in years, and he was jovial and talkative.

As per the plan, José's gig at the Mooncusser did not start until the next night, and I had gotten him to agree to play at the Moska the night we arrived back at the Vineyard. I noticed that Steve—ever the optimist—had already placed two big posters in the windows: "ONE NIGHT ONLY – JOSE FELICIANO." Good thing he'd agreed to do it—and lucky for us he couldn't see the signs in the windows. That night José and I alternated sets to a packed house. Mission accomplished.

* * *

Everyone who got off the Vineyard Haven ferry had to pass by our place. One day I was out front reviewing the passing parade, and along comes a tall, lanky kid with a guitar. Always on the lookout for free talent, I accosted him. "Hey, kid," I said. "You any good on that thing?"

"Not bad," he drawled in his North Carolina twang.

"Ever play a gig?"

"A what?"

"You know, a gig—playing live in front of people."

"Nope," he said.

"How'd you like to audition for us?"

I brought him inside and he played us "Don't Think Twice, It's All Right" by Bob Dylan. Nothing new there; this was part of the standard folk repertoire that just about everybody played back then. But he had something special, and his finger picking and singing were impeccable. He was just sixteen years old, but I hired young James Taylor (then called 'Jamie') on the spot. He played in our coffee house at least once a week for the entire summer, sometimes accompanied by his friend, Danny 'Kootch' Kortchmar.

Being two years our junior, Jamie treated us more like his mentors than friends. He was still a high school kid and we were college "adults," so we didn't socialize that much. But one Sunday he invited us out to his parents' house in Menemsha on the west end of the island. The house was a beautiful, rustic-but-modern structure; all weathered wood and beamed ceilings. It stood alone on a little rise overlooking a vast expanse of deserted white-sand beach. There was nothing and no one anywhere near it. If this wasn't paradise on Earth, I don't know what was.

Jamie's parents were not around—probably why he invited us that day. We hung out in the living room for a while listening to records by Lightnin' Hopkins and Ian and Sylvia. I lit up a joint and passed it around. When it came to Jamie, he looked at it dubiously.

"Never smoked pot?" I said.

"Nope," he said, "this will be a first." He took a big hit, held it in and let it out in a fit of coughing and laughter. Everyone laughed and applauded.

Later, Jen and I walked down to the beach, shed all our clothes, and walked and waded in the surf, pretending we were the first and only people on Earth.

Memory is a funny thing. I told that story of my first meeting with young Jamie Taylor so many times over the years, it became a vivid, deeply ingrained memory. But then, maybe a year after I had finished a draft of this book, someone gave me a link to a YouTube video of an interview someone did in the '70s with James and Carly Simon, who were married at the time. The interviewer asked him what was his first gig and, to my utter amazement, he said he had played (with Danny Kootch) at the Unicorn in Oak Bluffs on Martha's Vineyard at the age of fifteen, in the summer of 1963, a year before I met him. Carly expressed doubt. She had been an old Vineyarder since she was very young, and she said she didn't remember there being a Unicorn on the Vineyard, but James was certain there was. It wasn't there in the summer of '64, of that much I'm sure. A year or so later, I was to play at the original Unicorn, which was a long-established coffee house in Boston. So maybe my memory of that initial conversation was a result of my own desire to spin a good yarn and claim credit for discovering James Taylor. Or maybe not. I just don't know anymore.

Young J.T. Photo: IPE Collection

* * *

Another of our regulars was David Simons, aka Bruno Wolf who, until recently, had been the harmonica player for the Jim Kweskin Jug Band, a big name in the folk world and a local New England favorite. Dave lived in sort of a commune on the island that was started by the Kushi family, proponents of the macrobiotic diet and students of George Ohsawa, author of the book *Zen Macrobiotics*. In addition to being a staunch macrobiotic, Dave was a heroin user. Go figure.

Dave was also an extremely unique and entertaining solo performer, playing guitar, harmonica, and other stringed instruments and singing quirky, hip-yet-traditional folk songs. I'll never forget his version of Leadbelly's

"When I Was a Cowboy," with its "Come-a cow, cow yicky, come-a cow, cow yicky, yicky-yay" chorus. He and I began talking about forming an electric blues band with a guy named Sandy Bull. Sandy later came out with a few solo albums. Turns out he was a heroin user too. We listened to the new album by bluesman John Hammond, Jr., *Big City Blues*, on which the traditionally acoustic blues player was accompanied by an electric backup band.

I was not the only one whose imagination had been captured by The Beatles, The Rolling Stones, and the revolution in pop music that was now coming out of England. Many of us in the folk scene smelled big change in the wind, and we didn't want to be left behind.

* * *

Another act that played our venue was Banana and the Bunch, a group of guys about our age who played jug band and old-timey string band music with great aplomb. The leader was Banana, a multi-instrumentalist, whose real name was Lowell Levinger. I guess with a name like Lowell, you've got to call yourself something. There was also Rick Turner, who was not only an excellent guitar and mandolin player, but was an expert at repairing and building stringed instruments. There were a couple of other guys as well, whose names and faces have dissolved in the mists of time. They all worked in a musical instrument shop, which was housed in the same building as the Mooncusser. They lived in a big apartment above the store.

One night I awoke shortly before dawn to find that Jen was not beside me. She had disappeared without a word. I got up and decided to go look for her. I can't say exactly what made me go to the apartment above the instrument store. The door was not locked. The place was silent except for the sounds of slumber. I walked down the hallway. The door to Banana's room was wide open, and there they were: Jen and Banana, tucked in bed, sleeping soundly.

I guess I went a little crazy. The next thing I knew I had my hands locked around his throat, and I had pulled him out of the bed. They both awoke with me strangling Banana and Jen yelling, "Leave him alone! We didn't do anything! We're just friends! Nothing happened!"

Suddenly realizing what I was doing, I abruptly let him go. He dropped to the floor, clutching his throat and coughing, and I just walked out.

My head was buzzing like a hive of angry bees. Why had she gotten out of bed in the middle of the night to go be with him? If they weren't having an affair, what were they having? I was devastated. The pain was crushing. I guess I realized at that moment that I had fallen in love with Jen. I was eighteen years old, and I had been in what I thought was love before, but never in an adult relationship like this one, where you were actually living with someone, sleeping together every night. I walked back to Vineyard Haven and went to the hardware store. I bought a package of single-edged razor blades. I had decided to end my life by slashing my wrists. I went down to the beach, sat on the sand and held the razor to my wrist. I didn't want to leave a bloody mess for my friends to clean up. I sat like that for a good fifteen minutes. People would walk by me and give me queer looks. You'd think that, like in the movies, someone would rush over to me and say "Hey buddy, don't do it! You're young, you've got your whole life ahead of you!" But no one did. In the end I chickened out and went to my cubicle to lie down.

I thought about my relationship with Jen and concluded I had probably let her down sexually. Sex with her was not easy and carefree like it had been with Ginny Sue and others. I was desperate to please her, and by that very desperation perhaps I had lost her. She was not very open or communicative about sex—or anything else, for that matter; it was hard to know if I was making her happy or not. To make matters worse, we slept in a cubicle with blanket walls, right next to four other people, all of whom were sleeping alone, so we basically had no privacy.

Soon Jen came back, said she was sorry, swore again that nothing had happened with Banana and that they were "just good friends." I forgave her, but things were never the same.

The summer was drawing to a close, and it was time to say goodbye to the Café Moska and Martha's Vineyard and head on back to school.

Chapter Five

My Soul Is Psychedelicized

Even before the summer, Steve and I had started reading and talking about Aldous Huxley's *Doors of Perception* and his experiments with LSD and mescaline. We heard about what Timothy Leary and Richard Alpert were doing at Harvard. During the summer we'd heard an urban myth that, if taken in sufficient quantities, a cough remedy called Romilar would induce psychedelic hallucinations. We tried it with mixed results. A package held maybe two-dozen tablets. We each took a dozen, got very high, stumbled around on the deserted streets of Vineyard Haven at four in the morning, and puked our guts up for what seemed like hours. It was an experience, but not a psychedelic one.

That fall back at Goddard, Steve stumbled across a vial in the science lab containing a white powder. It was labeled 'Mescaline Sulfate – 1000 mg.' Steve did not hesitate. He removed the contents of the vial, replacing it with a like amount of sugar.

That night we enlisted Steve's roommate, Jeremy, to be our 'straight man.' Not knowing what the drug might do to us, we assigned Jeremy the task of preventing us from trying to fly off any rooftops, or similar foolhardy stunts. Then we divided the powder into two equal parts and downed it, dissolved in a little water. What ensued changed my life forever.

As soon as we felt the drug come on, we somehow knew it was going to be a good trip and that we would be in full control of our faculties. We were in Steve and Jeremy's dorm room, and I remember seeing the brightly colored book bindings on the shelf begin to shimmer and undulate. This was accompanied by a strange warmth—a kind of glow radiating from the core of my being. Steve and I smiled at each other, and I knew he was feeling the same thing.

With Jeremy in tow, we decided to go visit Steve's girlfriend, Sue, in her dorm room. When I walked outside, I looked down at the ground. The earth and the grass seemed to be teeming with life. I could see streams of energy coursing through the brown earth, like blood through veins, like sap through trees, through the rocks, through the grasses and weeds. It was like looking down at a network of superhighways at rush hour. "It's all connected," I kept saying, "and it's all connected to us."

Sue was there with her roommate, Phoebe, girlfriend of the late Wendy Jones. By now I was radiating pulsating waves of cosmic ecstasy and looking at everyone with unqualified love. I looked through their record collection, found an LP of Bach organ music and put it on the turntable. Steve and I were the only ones high, but somehow we got everyone in the room on our wavelength. We all sat in a circle on the bed in a 'group hug,' heads together, arms around each other and just listened in silence to the glory and majesty of J.S. Bach.

Then it was time for Steve and I to strike out on our own. This was a new world, and we wanted to explore it unfettered. Steve convinced Jeremy to lend us his motorcycle. I climbed on the back and, as dawn was breaking, we set out. We turned off the road onto a dirt trail through the woods. It was October in Vermont, and the dying leaves were aflame against the clear blue sky. *Going out in a blaze of glory*, I thought. *So that's what that means. Why can't we do that?* We wound our way up and up through the forest of maple and birch. "Wow," said Steve, "I'm Zen motorcycle-riding!"

At last we came to a clearing. A white, wooden three-rail corral fence surrounded a vast, green meadow, and in the meadow grazed a pure white horse. This was not a hallucination. The horse was real, and it was there in front of us. We puttered up to the fence, and the horse walked right up to us. He put his head over the top rail and gazed into our eyes with a look that told us he understood everything. Then he snorted, reared up and, mane flying, galloped away across the field, as if to tell us of the sheer joy of being alive in a way that words could never express.

I knew that the reality I witnessed on mescaline was ultimate reality, and that my everyday waking reality was filtered, so as not to hamper my ability to do whatever it took to survive in the world. The psychedelic reality is without filters—it's everything coming in at once, at full intensity—too much for a mere mortal to deal with on a daily basis.

Like my parents, I had always considered myself an intellectual and an agnostic. I always thought of religion as ignorant superstition and belief in a deity as a crutch that humans used to give themselves courage. On this day all that changed. I suddenly knew, without doubt, that an unseen force connects all things in the Universe, and that it is this force that people call God.

This experience became the keynote for all my beliefs, all my aspirations, and everything I did for the rest of my life.

Chapter Six

The Lost Is Found

I'd never stopped thinking about forming an electric band, and that fall at Goddard it all came together. I met four like-minded musicians who had either not been there the previous semester, or whom I had not met.

Walter Powers was a tall, skinny kid with shaggy brown hair and a boyish, freckled face that made him look like a 6'2" Tom Sawyer. He had a shy, soft-spoken manner and an archaic, literate speaking style that added to his charm. He almost never incorporated current "hip" jargon into his speech, but spoke like an aristocrat out of an F. Scott Fitzgerald novel. Once, when buying a dirty magazine at a newsstand, he said to the vendor, "I would like some smut, my good man." He played traditional blues on a funky, 7-string acoustic guitar and sang in a raw, fractured baritone. His style drew extensively from Koerner, Ray & Glover's *Blues, Rags & Hollers*, an album that had created a stir in the folk world the previous year. He looked good, was funny and smart, and he was up for starting an electric band.

Next, we recruited Willie Alexander. Willie played piano and an assortment of percussion instruments. He would make maracas out of pint wine bottles—you know, that cheap, sweet rotgut port, like Thunderbird—by filling them up with screws, nuts and bolts. Only trouble was, if he shook them too hard—and he almost invariably did—the bottles would shatter, sending a shower of glass and tiny hardware all over the place. Willie was absolutely one of a kind; he was a poet, artist, musician and the most original thinker I had ever met. His idols were Jack Kerouac, Willie Bobo (the Latin jazz percussionist) and James Dean. He had a unique image, which he went to some trouble to cultivate. His hair, though fashionably long, did not follow the current Beatles/mod trend, but was combed back, somewhat reminiscent of the '50s rocker look, but it was not slicked down, so it stuck out in a sort of studied messiness. People said he looked like Bob Dylan, but the fact was, he looked better; he was taller, cooler and he just oozed charisma. He didn't follow trends; he created them. His vocal style had not fully formed yet but, like Dylan, his delivery was unique, arresting and unlovely.

Hugh Magbie was another guitar player-singer with a folk blues background. Being the best guitarist, he became the de facto lead player, but he could also sing quite well. Hugh was a handsome, gregarious, extremely self-assured guy, always ready with a big smile and a bon mot. And he had one other valued credential: he was black. Even though Hugh did not speak or act particularly 'black,' his presence made us the very first interracial rock band in the world—as far as I know.

Walter volunteered to take up electric bass, which none of us had played before. I had my big Gibson jazz guitar, which I gave to Hugh to play, and we rented a second electric guitar, an electric bass and some amps from the local music store in town. The chairman of the music department, Ray McIntyre, was kind enough to let us use his large office for our rehearsals. We held the first rehearsal of the still-nameless band in autumn 1964. I soon convinced my long-suffering parents to help me get a Gretsch guitar, similar to the one George Harrison played.

At first we played folk blues and jug band songs from the repertoires of artists like Dave Van Ronk and the Jim Kweskin jug band, but we soon started adding some originals by Yours Truly, which also sounded quite folky. The only things that kept us from actually *being* a jug band were the electric guitars. We knew that the other thing we needed to make us a bona fide rock band was drums.

The search for a drummer was brief. There was only one drummer in the school, Tony Pfeiffer. Like Walter and Willie, he was tall and gangly, with longish sandy hair and sad, Ringo-like puppy eyes. All we had to do was convince him to join. He was very reluctant at first—worried the band would interfere with his studies—but we convinced him to get his drums from his parents' house outside Philadelphia and attend a rehearsal on a trial basis.

The first rehearsal with Tony on drums went better than any of us could have hoped and was just about the most fun that any of us had ever had (standing up). We were fairly quivering with creative energy. I immediately ran off and started writing more songs—rock songs. We started learning hit songs of the day by The Beatles, The Stones, The Animals, and some old R&B songs: "Searchin,'" the old Coasters classic, on which Walter sang a gritty lead vocal and "You're No Good" by Betty Everett, which had been a minor R&B hit that year and became a mega-hit a decade later for Linda Ronstadt, "Who Do You Love?" by Bo Diddley, on which Willie sang lead, and "Night Time Is the Right Time" by Ray Charles, on which Hugh got to tap into his inner soul brother.

Willie came up with the name. He told me he'd had a dream in which Ernest Hemingway appeared and told him we should call the band The Lost, after his "Lost Generation." It represented all those tortured, brilliant souls, the great artists and writers of post-World War I Paris.

In the earliest days of The Lost, I was still pining over Jen. We would pass each other in the hallways or on the campus, and I'd try to talk to her. But a wall had come up between us, and somehow we just could not communicate. That was when I wrote the song "Lookin' for a Reason." It was one of the very first original songs The Lost performed. It sounded a lot like a jug band song, and it got off my chest what I'd wanted to say to Jen:

> *I've been readin' books*
> *I've been thinkin' poems*
> *I've been lookin' for a reason*
> *Why I'm alone*
> *Lookin' for a reason*
> *Reason in blue*
> *Yes, I'm lookin' for a reason*
> *For losin' you*

We started performing in the common room for our fellow students and immediately received great encouragement. Suddenly we were catapulted to local celebrity, embodying the football, basketball and baseball teams all rolled into one—since Goddard had no sports teams. We became the de facto 'big Mmen on Ccampus.' This flood of approval was what I had been craving—what I had been starved for—all my life. To my parents, I was already a lost cause, an abject failure. They had no understanding or appreciation for the kind of music I was pursuing; they saw no value in anything I was doing, so the affirmation of my peers meant a lot to me.

Someone at Bard invited us to play down there, so we piled into a borrowed van and drove down to Annandale. We were well received, as crude and amateurish as we were, and we were encouraged to take it to the next level.

We auditioned at a club in Burlington, Vermont—the biggest town in the state—called The Cave and got hired to play every Saturday night. Since The Beatles had started in The Cavern Club, I took this to be a good omen. This was near the state university, and the audience at The Cave were, well, they were not as accepting as our classmates at Goddard. Instead of applause, we would often hear epithets, such as "Get a radio!"

Ridicule turned out to be a good thing because it improved us—fast. We redoubled our rehearsal efforts, we learned more popular songs of the day and I increased my output of originals. It was practically unheard of for a club band to play original songs in those days, but we managed to slip in a few.

It wasn't long before my new campus celebrity brought me a new girlfriend, Polly Gerhardt. She was sweet, quiet, kind, wonderfully calm and low-key. And the blondest blond I had ever seen. She had platinum blond hair—and it was natural. She had beautiful blue eyes and pink skin. She was of pure German extraction, my polar opposite (my revenge against the Master Race). But there was nothing Teutonic or domineering about Polly. She was all roundness and softness. She had no angles. She wasn't fat, but she had a round face, lovely round breasts, and hips that gently sloped outward into her ample thighs. It wasn't long before I was head-over-heels in love with her. But, at the same time, I couldn't help looking at other girls, and having the occasional tryst. Why monogamy did not suit me, I can't really say. Looking back, perhaps it was that I was so hungry for affirmation from the opposite sex, getting it from just one girl, even though I loved her, just wasn't enough.

A song I wrote called "Mean Motorcycle," was inspired by the motorcycle culture at Goddard—and my own wandering eye. It seemed that everyone there had a bike, and the most common kind were scramblers—off-road bikes. Guys (and some girls too) would ride these things up hill and down dale. And the one big hill, the one that had "The Hideout" on top, was one of the most popular places for the scrambler set. Now, when these bikes tried to climb a grass-covered hill, the wheels would often slip. No matter how powerful the machine, that slippery grass would win out. So the song is a narrative by a guy telling his girl he's incapable of monogamy. He says:

I'm a mean motorcycle on a grassy hill
A twenty-dollar wallet with a one-dollar bill
Everything I got is just not enough
To keep you from gettin' all hung up

The original lineup of The Lost. L to R: Walter, me (with my new
Gretsch guitar), Tony, Willie, Hugh (with my fat, black Gibson jazz
guitar). Photo: Don Guy

When fall semester ended, it was time, once again, for our off-campus
work semester. The Lost decided to go to Boston and work as a rock band.
Willie, Walter and Hugh all called Boston home, so that was the most logical destination.

* * *

Over the holidays, Polly invited me to her hometown, Philadelphia, to attend her friend's coming out party at a posh hotel in Rittenhouse Square,
the hub of Philadelphia Mainline society. I had to rent a tux and take
the train to Philly, where Polly met me and drove me to the beautiful
(but modest) suburban home of her parents. Realizing they were a part
of Philadelphia society, I was surprised at how cool and youthful they
were. They undoubtedly knew Polly and I were sleeping together, but
registered not a whit of disapproval. Nonetheless, I was given my own
sleeping quarters.

Once we arrived at the party, however, a much chillier wind began to blow. These upper crust society brats—especially the guys—were appalled that one of their own would take up with the likes of me. We weren't there long before three extremely clean-cut preppy boys—all much bigger than me, of course—accosted me in the plush-carpeted lobby outside the ballroom.

"Hey, what're you? You a Jew-boy... huh?" Another one spun me around.

"No, I think maybe he's a wop."

"Are you kidding?" said a third. "Look at that hair. He's a *Neanderthal*!"

They all laughed. I held up my middle finger, panning in a semi-circle, displaying it to all three of them like Vanna White on *The Price Is Right*. "Sit on this and rotate," I said, channeling Richie Downs, the toughest kid I knew growing up in New York. Just before it came to blows, Polly stepped in and whisked me away.

She bundled me into her powder blue VW Bug. We were both scared and enervated. I produced a neatly-rolled joint from my inside jacket pocket and we lit up. We each took a big hit, then burst into wild laughter.

"What a bunch of assholes!" she exclaimed.

"Yeah. Ruling class, my ass!"

"They'll be sorry when you're a big rock star and they're still assholes."

We drove through the streets of Philly getting higher and higher. We got so stoned we got honked at for standing still at a stop sign too long. We were waiting for it to change.

Chapter Seven

Boston

I rendezvoused with the rest of The Lost in Boston right after New Year. We found a large rambling apartment in what must have been the only run-down building in the posh enclave of Beacon Hill.

Our new pad at 104 Myrtle Street had a big living room, a good-sized kitchen, and three bedrooms. Hugh's parents lived in Cambridge, just across the Charles River, so he opted to bunk there. The rest of us moved into the apartment.

Boston was slow going at first. We pounded the pavements looking for work—music gigs, of course, but anything that would pay the rent. Tony, who was a nose-to-the-grindstone type of guy, answered a classified ad for door-to-door encyclopedia salesmen. They invited him to interview for the job, and I went along. It was a commission-only job, and we were both hired. We wore suits and ties and knocked on doors from dawn 'til dusk, but sold not one set of encyclopedias.

I made the rounds of local booking agents and one, a guy named Bob Penza, agreed to audition us. Penza booked some of the sleazy dives in Boston's famed Combat Zone, wherein all the city's sin was tightly contained within a twenty-square-block area. It was at one of these clubs that Penza auditioned us.

It was early on a weekday afternoon, so there were few customers. Penza, a short, portly fellow with greased-back dark hair, seated himself at a front row table, and we gave it our all. We avoided originals, instead belting out our versions of hits by the Beatles and the Stones. This strategy paid off, and Penza gave us a gig on the spot. We were hoping for something steady—even if it was a slot at one of these dives—but instead he offered us a one-off, a dance at a longshoreman's hall near the waterfront for a bunch of Navy guys. Oh well, we had to start somewhere, and this, at least, was a start.

The sailors were agog at how we looked. They had seen long hair on guys before—but only in photos of English rock bands. They had literally never seen anything that looked like us in person. And we didn't even have uniforms! They had uniforms, and we didn't! Heck, even The Beatles all dressed alike in those days. Bands were supposed to dress alike. We adhered more to the Rolling Stones model of attire, which was whatever we wanted. And we were quite inventive with it. Walter took to wearing his shirts backward, so that under a sport jacket it looked like a priest's collar. That went over big. But once we started playing, giving them the requisite "Louie Louie" and "Walkin' the Dog," and they started drinking, they kind of got past appearances and actually enjoyed themselves. And we actually got paid for playing music in a major metropolitan area.

Being ridiculed by total strangers on the street was something we came to expect, and Boston mentalities were significantly more provincial than those of, say, New York City. We were on the forefront of a fashion revolution, being among the first to carry the mod styles of England to US shores. Anything new scares people, and being scared they try to cover it up by being mean and derisive. Sometimes people actually threw stuff at us from passing cars. It always amazed me that, as long as we were on the stage, we were worshipped like gods, cheered for and screamed at, but once on the street like any common mortal, we were suddenly something alien—and a threat.

At the end of February, Goddard's work term came to an end. Willie, Walter and I had decided not to go back to school, but to try to make a go of it as musicians in Boston. Hugh and Tony elected to return to school. And so we were faced with the new challenge of having to find a new drummer and lead guitarist.

Chapter Eight

Hell No, I Won't Go!

Within weeks of notifying Goddard of my withdrawal from school I received a letter from my local draft board in New York City. I had been reclassified as 1-A and was cordially invited to report to the Manhattan office of the draft board on Whitehall Street in two weeks.

In the first months of 1965 the Vietnam War had ramped up to an unprecedented level. From what I had been reading in the newspapers and seeing on TV, I had positively decided that I wanted no part of this war. On the face of it, the war seemed utterly without merit. No one was threatening us (the US), and it was my opinion that, even if Vietnam went Communist, it would not have the slightest impact on my country. Americans were dying over there, all in defense of a corrupt, despotic regime that called themselves our allies on the sole merit of not being Communists. Besides, I was a lover, not a fighter.

I was freaked. One night, I consulted Willie and Walter. We smoked a joint and tried to come up with a way out of this. I got up and started pacing the room.

"What am I gonna do? If they draft me they'll put me on the front lines for sure. I'll last about twenty minutes!"

"I have this friend who took speed for a week before he went in," offered Walter. "They gave him a 4-F as a junkie."

"I'll try anything," I said.

"Fine. I know where you can score some Dexedrine."

"You should tell 'em you're a fag too… but you'd love to kill some people, and beg them to take you," Willie advised.

"Ah ha, reverse psychology. Sounds good."

The entire week prior to my appointment I popped these devilish little pills. I didn't sleep. I stayed up and yammered idiotically, driving my room-mates crazy. I didn't bathe or shave, or even comb my hair. I looked really scary.

When I entered the giant, institutional-green waiting room at White-hall Street, I was greeted with peals of laughter. The assembled multitude was composed mainly of teenage greasers from the slums of New York. These guys couldn't wait to turn in their zip guns for an M-16 and blow some gook's head off. They thought I was the funniest thing they had seen since Alley Oop, the time-traveling caveman from the Sunday funnies. I was sweating and grinding my teeth but gave no indication that I noticed their mirth. Everything was going exactly as planned.

On the questionnaire I had to fill out I came across as a suicidal, ho-mosexual junkie with a penchant for violence. The doctors didn't even make me pull my pants down and cough. I was sent straight to the psychiatrist. He grilled me for a while, and I stayed in character. I had known enough sui-cidal, homicidal, homosexual junkies in my time to act the part pretty well.

He stamped a few forms and signed something and told me to present it to the front desk. I did as instructed and fled out of there, with the derisive laughter and colorful epithets still ringing in my ears. "Hahaha, ya freako faggot!" They'd be laughing out of the other side of their faces before long. I rushed back to the safety of my childhood home and soaked in a hot bath until the speed wore off.

Lucky for me, it was still very early in the war and the draft. If I had been called a year later, those government doctors would have been hip to all my tricks and many more being tried by thousands of inductees all across the country.

Not long afterward I received my new draft card in the mail. I had been reclassified 4-F (not eligible for military service). The government made a few attempts to interest me in drug counseling and rehabilitation, but I never took them up on it.

Chapter Nine

The Missing Pieces

While in New York, the idea occurred to me that I might be able to find a replacement for one or both of our departed members. So, one blustery March day, I was wandering around on MacDougal Street, and I ran into David Cohen, a folk singer everybody thought looked like Bob Dylan, only taller. He later changed his name to David Blue and got signed to record for Elektra Records. After he died of a heart attack jogging in Washington Square at age forty-one, Joni Mitchell named her album, *Blue*, after him. I asked him if he knew anybody who could play rock 'n' roll lead guitar and he told me to go check out a guy named Kyle Garrahan, who was playing a solo gig at the Café Bizarre on 3rd Street.

The Bizarre was one of the bigger basket houses in the Village. I showed up right when it opened and had to sit through a succession of dreary folk singers singing the same repertoire we all sang back in '63: "Green, Green Rocky Road," "Baby Let Me Follow You Down," "San Francisco Bay Blues"… Then finally Kyle came on. He stood up at the mic and played an electric guitar—a red Gibson SG—with *fingerpicks*, those plastic and metal picks that a lot of folk players used for playing finger picking style. But Kyle was playing Chuck Berry licks. This was very unusual. He had a bluesy, soulful vocal delivery and a great look: long brown hair, blue eyes and a muscular frame. The girls would love him. *Yes*, I thought, *he'll do nicely*. He sang a couple of old New Orleans R&B tunes: "Ooh Poo Pah Doo" and "Certain Girl" (which he sang as "Certain Chick"), also very unusual—and original. Not the kind of thing you hear at a Greenwich Village coffee house. After his set I approached him.

"Hey man, nice set."

"Thanks."

"David Cohen said to check you out. I'm in this rock band up in Boston called The Lost. We're lookin' for a new lead guitar player who can sing. Interested?"

"I'm supposed to be starting a band in Providence with a guy named John Nuese. Ever hear of him?"

"Nope."

"I come from there, ya know."

"Providence?"

"Yeah."

"You should really check us out, Kyle. We've already done a bunch of gigs in Vermont and Boston. We have a lot of originals. Everybody says we're gonna make it."

"Uh huh…"

"We've got this huge, swingin' bachelor pad on Beacon Hill, man. You'd love it. What d'ya say?"

"Well, I'll give it some thought… I gotta check out this other thing, see…"

* * *

A week later, back in Boston, Kyle shows up on our doorstep. He pulls out his guitar and we all start jamming on old rock and R&B songs 'til the wee hours and the neighbors start knocking on the ceiling. He tells us his other project didn't work out, and asks if we are still looking. Yes we are, and he's hired! He is indeed an excellent fit for our rag-tag band of misfits.

Kyle and Walter immediately hit it off, so we acquire an additional mattress and he and Walter become roommates.

Now I have to find us a drummer. The only person I can think of is my old jazz drummer pal from high school, Fred Mason. I don't know if the idea of playing rock 'n' roll will appeal to him (he was somewhat dismissive of it when last I'd seen him, but all us jazz hippies were snobs), but I give him a call. He is attending Columbia University Business School in New York City, on track to become a pillar of society. In one conversation I convince him out of it. I guess my excitement at the lineup so far came across loud and clear. Fred tells me he's changed his first name to his middle name. He hated Fred, so now it's Lee. And so, Lee unceremoniously drops out of Columbia and, replete with full drum kit, moves in with us on Myrtle Street.

* * *

Lee Mason made no attempt to look the part of a rock musician. He was the ultimate non-conformist, refusing to conform to the non-conformists. While the rest of us all tried to outdo each other with outrageous clothes and hair styles, Lee doggedly stuck to his suits and ties. He even got more conservative than he normally would have been. He took to wearing three-piece banker suits. He slicked his hair straight back and kept it trimmed quite short. He was the contrarian's contrarian. But he played the hell out of those drums, and everybody in the band really liked him. In fact, he was just the finishing touch we needed.

The final lineup of The Lost. L to R: Kyle Garrahan, Willie Alexander, me, Walter Powers III, Lee Mason.

I had a vision for the band that pretty much mirrored The Beatles and some of the other mod English groups. I would have liked nothing more than a very homogeneous group of happy mop-tops, all harmonizing sweetly in voices as similar to each other as the Bee Gees. But that's not what I got. The Lost were a collection of very strong and disparate personalities, each very creative, very original, and anything but homogeneous. I was writing these sweet and tuneful songs, but the others delivered them with an edge that, with the clarity of hindsight, I now see is what really made The

Lost special and a local phenomenon. I started writing edgier, more raucous songs for the others to sing. But I'm getting ahead of myself…

Rehearsing with a full set of drums was not an option in that apartment, what with families living above and below us. At first Lee used practice pads while we all played our instruments either unplugged or very quietly. But that could not prepare us adequately for live performance.

We met some college guys on Beacon Hill: Don Law and Bert Yellen. They were roommates in a high-class bachelor pad on Pinkney Street, a couple of blocks away from our place. They were rabid music fans and invited us to a party with some other college kids at an apartment nearby. When we showed up at the door, decked out in our finest and most outrageous threads, the people who answered wouldn't let us in. Not even when we invoked the names of Don and Bert. We were crestfallen, to say the least. Humiliated is more like it—sent off into the night with our collective tail between our legs.

That night, Willie started scribbling the beginning verse of a new song:

> *I couldn't crash yer party*
> *So I broke down and I cried*
> *If I tried to hitchhike*
> *Yer the type don't give a ride…*

I started strumming some folk rock chords, and soon our first collaborative song, "Maybe More Than You," was born.

> *But I've got pride too*
> *I've been lied to*
> *Maybe more than you*
> *I'm the one you busted*
> *I'm the rider that you threw*

"Maybe More Than You" was a natural for Willie's snotty, punky voice. He had amassed a sizable collection of sound effects with which he would punctuate various songs. On "Maybe More Than You" he employed a little siren that you blew into. He hit the siren leading into the instrumental section. Bob Dylan, seemingly on a parallel track, used the same effect on "Highway 61," which was released in October of '65, the same month "Maybe More Than You" was released. So, of course, people thought we had copped the idea from Dylan. But, like Dylan, Willie was a true original. Besides, we had recorded "Maybe More Than You" a month earlier. But I'm getting ahead of myself again…

To make amends for the frat party debacle, Bert and Don soon took us to another party, this one at an MIT frat house on Beacon Street. This time it was a different story. The frat guys loved us, treated us like rock stars. There we met Ray Paret, the president of the fraternity. Like Don and Bert, Ray was an enthusiastic rock fan. I told him of our rehearsal problem and he invited us to rehearse right there in the rec room of the frat house.

We set up our gear the very next day. The frat guys loved having a rock band as their mascot, and we were grateful to say the least. With the addition of Kyle and Lee, the quality of our sound improved markedly, and we got better fast.

Chapter Ten

'The Rat'

It turned out that Bert was the manager and tambourine player of one of the leading bands in Boston—Barry & The Remains. One night he took us to see them at their regular gig at a club on Kenmore Square called the Rathskeller. The Rathskeller, or 'the Rat,' as everybody called it, was a basement beer dive where all the Boston University football jocks hung out. Some nights the crowd got pretty rowdy, and it was not uncommon for a fight or two to break out.

The Remains. L to R: Barry Tashian, Billy Briggs, Chip Damiani, Vern Miller. Photo: Remains Archives

There was a primitive wooden stage against the right wall, which was white brick adorned with a few neon beer signs. The stage had a waist-high railing around it. It was unclear whether the railing was to keep the band in or the audience out. Upstairs was a much more sedate restaurant/bar, catering to an older clientele.

Barry & The Remains were a great bar band, truly deserving of their stellar reputation. The leader and front man was Barry Tashian, who played guitar (lead and rhythm) and sang lead. Then there was Billy Briggs on electric piano and harmony vocals, Vern Miller on bass and harmony vocals and Chip Damiani on drums. They were a really tight unit, everyone disciplined and pulling more than his weight. On this night they did all cover tunes, but they did them superbly, and the crowd loved them.

After their set, Burt introduced us. Barry was one of the sweetest, most unassuming guys I'd ever met, mild-mannered, low-key, no ego—totally un-musician-like. The other guys were also really nice and friendly. They expressed interest in hearing our music, and Barry agreed to come to our rehearsal at the frat house the next day.

As promised, Barry showed up the following day. We played him some of our new originals, mostly ones I had written alone, plus "Maybe More Than You" and one that Willie wrote called "Everybody Knows." Barry was impressed. The Remains didn't have that many original songs. But he asked us to play some current hits. He said if we wanted to get club and college gigs in Boston, we'd need the crowd pleasers. And we had them. We played him our versions of "All My Lovin'" by The Beatles (with me singing lead), "The Last Time" by The Stones (with Walter singing lead), our very inventive arrangement of Bo Didley's "Who Do You Love" (with Willie singing lead), and Kyle's rendition of "Certain Chick," which, although not a current hit, showed off Kyle's impressive R&B vocal chops. Afterward, Barry got up and jammed with us. We had a great time, and he offered to arrange an audition for us at the Rat.

True to his word, a few days later we stood on the stage before Gene Brezniak, the owner of the Rathskeller. Gene was a tall lanky guy in his late thirties with receding reddish hair and a pleasant demeanor. He was unusually relaxed and friendly for a club owner. He told us we looked a lot wilder than any of the other bands he'd seen around Boston, but that didn't seem to bother him.

We followed Barry's advice and stuck to the crowd pleasers—and we got the gig. We were booked to play the Rat the following Wednesday night. If the crowd liked us, Gene said he might make it a steady weekly gig.

We spent the next few days rehearsing ceaselessly. We needed to come up with four forty-five-minute sets for our gig. When Wednesday rolled around we were ready. Barry and most of The Remains showed up to cheer us on, and they brought some other people with them.

I must say, we rocked the place pretty good. The football jocks seemed happy—as long as we played "Louie Louie" at least once every set. And we only had to duck a few flying beer mugs that crashed into the brick wall behind us and shattered into a million pieces. Just a normal Wednesday night, everyone assured us.

After our set, Barry introduced us to John Sdoucos (pron. 'Sudukis') of Music Productions, The Remains' booking agent. John gave me his business card and invited us to stop by his office on Boylston Street later that week. At the end of our first night, Gene offered us Wednesday night as our steady slot at the Rathskeller, and we were on our way.

The Lost 1965. Taken on the stage of the Rathskeller.

* * *

That same week we went up and saw John Sdoucos and his wife/partner Leah, who ran Music Productions out of an office at 739 Boylston Street. Sharing that office, and actually the proprietor of the suite, was Fred Taylor, head of HT Productions. Fred owned and booked two nightclubs, which were located side by side on the street level of that same building, Paul's Mall and the Jazz Workshop, which featured the biggest names in jazz when they came through Boston. John expressed an interest in trying to land us some gigs. He asked us if we would be interested in playing college dances and concerts—and, of course, some other local clubs as well. Also, there would be some out-of town gigs in places like western Massachusetts. and upstate New York. So, with nothing but a handshake, we were added to the artist roster of Music Productions.

After that, things moved fast. We suddenly had a full calendar of gigs coming up. We rented a used Dodge van. It was painted a hideous, two-tone aqua-green and white. We needed a manager/road manager—someone who could drive the van, help schlep equipment and make sure we got our money at the end of the night.

Guy Rupright lived just up the street from us on Myrtle Street with his wife, Susan, a singer. He had red hair, chiseled features and steely grey eyes. We all agreed that he looked a lot like Andrew Loog Oldham, the Stones' manager/producer. Well, that was good enough for us. He was into the idea, and so we hired him. The fact that he had no previous experience in the music business, in fact no apparent skills at all, bothered us not in the least.

Guy was very soft spoken. Although he wasn't tall or physically im-posing, there was something about him that said, "Don't fuck with me," a kind of Clint Eastwood-like glint in the eye that made people do what he wanted. This turned out to be his chief asset as our manager. He happily drove us and our equipment on long road trips to New Hampshire, western Massachusetts and upstate New York. And no one ever refused to pay us at the end of the night.

Many girls came and went from our apartment on Beacon Hill. With our growing popularity, girls became increasingly plentiful. Walter had vis-its from his girlfriend from Goddard, Amy, and Willie had a serious rela-tionship going with another Goddard girl, Susie. Susie would also visit as often as she could, but at the end of the 1965 school year she graduated and moved to Boston. Polly visited me once or twice after The Lost dropped out of school, but her visits became less and less frequent, and I eventually got word that she had taken up with a guy named Michael, who had a mustache, smoked a pipe and drove a little green English sports car.

This news hit me hard. I don't know what I expected. I mean, here I was becoming a local rock star in Boston, bedding a new girl every night.

Did I expect her to stay faithful to me? I guess I did; Polly was special. I really did miss her, and losing her was painful. And pain was song fodder. So I wrote two new sad songs: "I'll Let You Go" and "I Wanna Know." The latter sort of sounded like a bossa nova song, and Lee—with his jazz roots—put a bossa nova beat to it when we worked it into our repertoire. I think the lyric really captures the innocence of a nineteen-year-old guy who just can't understand women. Little does he know, he never will:

> *Why do they say they're sorry*
> *After they break your heart in two?*
> *Why do they say they love you when they don't*
> *And that they don't when they do?*
> *I wanna know, I wanna know*
> *I wanna know, I wanna know*

In February of 1965 we were booked to play a big concert at Boston University, opening for The Shirelles and Jr. Walker & The All Stars, who were riding on their first hit, "Shotgun." I thought it would be a good idea to smoke a few joints in the van on our way to the show. By the time we got onstage, we were all very stoned. This was the biggest audience we had ever appeared before. I remember standing on the stage looking out at that sea of faces, all looking at us expectantly. In front of us, Wildman Steve, Boston's top black DJ, addressed the crowd. "I'd like to remind you," he was saying, "there'll be no smoking... of anything!" The crowd laughed knowingly. We laughed nervously. "And now, to open the show a great local band, The Losts!"

But I saw there was a problem. Walter was plucking his bass frantically, but no sound was coming out. He checked his amp. Power was on, volume was up. But no sound. What could be the problem? The DJ stalled for time with some more clever patter (something about white people not knowing anything about machinery), but we didn't hear it. We were all scrambling to figure out why Walter's bass amp wasn't working. Then I saw it. It was just lying there on the floor—the jack at the end of his guitar cord, the end that should have been plugged into his bass. I pointed. He picked it up and plugged in. We exchanged looks that spoke volumes, but mainly said, "No more smoking dope before going onstage."

Other than that, our first big concert went pretty well.

Chapter Eleven

1965, Wow!

The sheer number of events and changes that happened in my life in 1965 is so voluminous that, looking back, I can't see how I was able to fit everything into just one year. The Lost were playing a lot of gigs: college dances, frat parties and many clubs.

Some of the clubs we played at included the Banjo Room, the Unicorn (a coffee house that had both folk and rock acts) and Club 47, a famous folk coffee house near Harvard Square in Cambridge that had started featuring rock bands around this time. Among the other bands that played there were The Chambers Brothers (later to score a #11 hit with "Time Has Come To-day") and The Trolls, which featured my old friend Banana from Martha's Vineyard. We would often play at a club in Kenmore Square, across from the Rat, called Where It's At. This was an all-ages club that did not serve alcohol and catered to teenagers. It was run by its owner, Ruth Clennet. Ruth was a middle-aged, uptight, brittle blond, who ran a tight ship—she wouldn't even let us smoke cigarettes backstage. We had to go outside (of course, this was when smoking was allowed everywhere and no one thought it was harmful). Kyle had a theory that she was secretly a bondage domi-natrix. He was sure that, somewhere in that club, was a false wall, behind which was a dungeon with shackles and chains.

We became quite visible around town, and people started recognizing us on the street, but, instead of throwing garbage at us, they would yell, "Hey, Lost!" It was like something out of *A Hard Day's Night*!

There were many girls and many new experiences. One event that stands out in my memory is my first sexual adventure with multiple partners.

I was having a casual affair with a pretty brunette named Cindy. One night I was at her apartment in the Back Bay with her and her roommate, Marianne. Marianne said it was her boyfriend's birthday and she wanted to give him a special present, and she asked my cooperation. The plan was this: when her boyfriend came over, both girls were to strip, and Cindy was to seduce Marianne's boyfriend. At the same time, I was to get naked and start making out with Marianne. Now, Marianne was sure that her boyfriend wouldn't let anyone make it with her right in front of him so, at the crucial moment, before any penetration occurred, we were all to change partners and get it on with our originally-designated lover. Well, I know it sounds goofy, but that's exactly the way it went down, and Marianne's boyfriend got the thrill of his life getting to fondle the beautiful naked body of Cindy.

Now that The Lost was gigging pretty steadily and earning some money, and being as the five of us were getting on each other's nerves all pent up together in that apartment, we decided to pair off and find separate apartments. Walter and Kyle found a place on Revere Street, Willie moved in with his girlfriend Susie on Phillips Street, and Lee and I found a nice two-bedroom on Joy Street. All three apartments were on Beacon Hill.

Shortly after I moved to Joy Street I started going with another attractive brunette named Susan. She had shiny, straight black hair and dark sparkling eyes. Her last name was Connell, so I guess maybe she was 'black Irish.' She lived in a funky apartment across town that didn't have any heat. It might have been that everyone in the building was squatting. It was still quite chilly, although it must have been early spring by now. One weekend my old pal from Goddard, Steve, came down for a visit. We had word that there was a guy on Beacon Hill named Osmo who was selling hits of pure LSD. After our epic mescaline experience in Vermont, Steve and I knew and trusted each other enough to want to trip again, and we resolved to now take it to the next level. LSD was supposed to be stronger and longer lasting than mescaline, and this was reputedly the best acid around. Susan had come over to my place, and we all walked down the hill, over to the address we had been given for Osmo on Revere Street.

Osmo was a soft-spoken skinny guy about our age with a permanent smile. He showed us his stash of 'Window Pane' acid. Each hit was on a tiny rectangular sheet of gelatin, supposedly containing 500 micrograms.

The mescaline we took had been 500 milligrams. We bought three hits for $15. Osmo invited us to drop right there in his pad and he would join us. We agreed. The stuff dissolved as soon as you put it on your tongue.

Before long we were tripping our brains out. At one point Steve disappeared into the bathroom for what seemed like a very long time. Osmo and Susan were strangely quiet. Since Susan and I had been sleeping together, I expected to feel a heavy rapport, an increase in chemistry with her on acid. But instead she felt quite distant. Osmo had the same enigmatic smile frozen on his face, but it told me nothing. At last I went into the bathroom to see what was happening with Steve. I found him staring intently into the mirror. By now he no longer had a beard, so his face was way more expressive. "Whoa, look at that!" he exclaimed as I walked in. I looked at his image in the mirror, but just saw him smiling back goonily. "See how many faces I have! They keep changing—maybe they're from past lives!" Then I looked at my own face, and it began to morph into a million other faces—beautiful women, old men... "Yeah, it's happening to my face too!" I said. "Past lives—definitely past lives!" He started to run the water in the sink. He scooped some up and threw it in his face, then laughed joyfully, like a child. Then he threw some water in my face. We both started laughing hysterically and throwing water at each other. We looked at each other and saw a true friend.

Back out in the living room, we tried to lighten the rather somber mood that had set in. We told Susan and Osmo about seeing our past-life faces. They were both unresponsive. I tried to draw Osmo out, asking what was happening with him, saying "let's be completely open with each other, let's 'lay our cards on the table.'" But all I got was an ironic, frozen smile. He was curled up in a big armchair, seeming to huddle there for safety. It made him look small and frail. In fact, he looked like he was dying. After a while I got up and said, "Well, I guess we'll get going. I kind of feel like getting some air." We thanked Osmo for his hospitality and got the hell out of there.

It was a short walk up the hill to my apartment on Joy Street. I'm not sure where Lee was that night, but I don't remember him being around. When we got to the front of the apartment building, Susan said she was going home. "Are you kidding?" I said. "It's late. There are no trains, no busses. How will you get home?"

"I'll walk," she said.

I couldn't believe she would rather walk halfway across Boston, high on LSD, on a cold, dark night to her freezing cold apartment than come up to my place and have a nice warm cup of tea with me and Steve. I thought she was nuts, and I told her so. She just shrugged and walked off into the night.

Steve and I had a fine trip together. I undertook to make us some tea, an operation which, on acid, seemed all but insurmountable. But at last I was able to figure out how to put the water in the kettle, the kettle on the stove, light the stove, find the tea, boil the water, find the cups... I considered it a great accomplishment when I was finally able to deliver the tea to Steve. But I kept worrying about Susan and asking him, "Why would she do a thing like that? Does she hate me? Is that normal behavior?"

Steve, being a psychology major, told me he thought her behavior was not normal at all. "In fact," he said, "to use a clinical term, I think she's bonkers!"

At some point—not sure if it was soon after this or months later—Susan began going with Lee, who was still my roommate, and they eventually got married!

* * *

I always associate places in my past with the music that was playing at that time in that place. We had a little portable record player on Joy Street and the records played nonstop. Lee was heavy into R&B, so Otis Redding's monumental *Otis Blue* album got a lot of play. Another favorite was Smokey Robinson & The Miracles, and we played his *Going To A Go-Go* album constantly, as well as *The Temptations Sing Smokey*. As a result of all this exposure to the great Smokey Robinson, he became one of my big influences in songwriting, and even my singing began to take on a more soulful bent. There was also a single by a guy named Eddie Holman, "This Can't Be True," on the Parkway label that I liked a lot. Eddie could hit notes that were downright stratospheric.

* * *

While living in that apartment I had a number of girlfriends, some of whom actually moved in with me. For a while I harbored a skinny blond urchin named Ruthie, who was seven months pregnant. She looked like a python that had swallowed a watermelon. She stayed for about a month.

When it was time to have her baby, she just disappeared, and I never heard from her again.

Barbara Gibson had been a girlfriend of Walter's from high school, I think. She had started coming around and hanging out at the Myrtle Street apartment. I found her very attractive, and when it became apparent that Walter wasn't really into her I kind of took her over. I remember her staying with me in the Joy Street apartment on a number of occasions. Her only apparent flaw was a penchant for heroin. One night I came home from a gig and found her passed out with a needle in her arm. I freaked. I considered taking her to the emergency room or calling the paramedics, but either scenario would undoubtedly involve police. So I started giving her mouth-to-mouth resuscitation. She was, at least, breathing and she had a pulse. Lee and I got her up and began walking her around the apartment. I made a strong batch of instant coffee and we started pouring cups of it down her throat. Finally, she came to. Breathing a sigh of relief, I made her promise never to bring that stuff into my house again. After a while she stopped coming around.

I had some friends who lived on River Street in Cambridge. One day after visiting them I was walking toward Massachusetts Ave. where I could get the train back to Boston, and a somewhat plump-yet-attractive girl with dirty blond hair and red cheeks stopped me. She literally grabbed me by the lapels right there on the street and told me to come with her. Intrigued, I followed. She said her name was Julie, as she took me by the hand and led me to her nearby apartment, which she said she shared with her sister. We started making out on the couch. I could tell Julie was a wild woman. She immediately started peeling off her clothes, and then started to unzip my fly. Now, I knew enough about myself to know that, being with a hottie like this for the first time, I was liable to 'go off half-cocked,' and not wanting to disappoint I excused myself and went to the bathroom, where I got myself off. It took less time than it would have to pee. As I exited the bathroom, the sister got home. She was a slim, cute brunette named Margo, who wore a saucy French beret and glasses. I went back to making out with Julie on the couch. Margo looked at us enviously. After a while Julie and I retired to her bedroom. Julie was a very loud love maker. And insatiable. It was lucky I had 'prepped' myself, because we just went on and on. You had to walk through Margo's room to get to Julie's room, and, on the other side of the door, I could hear Margo moaning in frustration almost as loud as Julie was fairly screaming with pleasure (perhaps hamming it up a bit for the benefit of her sister).

The next morning I left early. Julie was still fast asleep. Margo was not. She tried to drag me into bed with her, but I thought better of it. I gave her my address and told her to come over that night. And, that very night, Margo showed up at my door at Joy Street. We smoked a J and retired to the bedroom almost at once. I must say, Margo was every bit as much fun as Julie, and this time no fakery was necessary. She left the next day, and I never saw either sister again. That's the way it was in the '60s.

* * *

We had been hearing a lot of stories about the psychedelic culture that had sprung up in the Haight-Ashbury district of San Francisco. Apparently, ballroom-sized clubs were opening where they projected 'light shows,' elaborate slide shows that used moving film and manipulated abstract images on a screen above the stage while bands performed. Lee—The Lost's least psychedelic person—suggested putting colored lights inside his drums. On cue during our show, the stage lights would go dark and our 'light show,' accompanied by weird sound effects, would commence. We would insert this in the middle of an instrumental number to the delight of the crowd.

Fred Taylor took us under his wing, and before long Fred represented us for bookings, not John Sdoucos. When John and Fred went their separate ways, John took The Remains and Fred took us. And Fred did a really fine job for us, landing us some plum gigs at some of the best colleges in the country, as well as making us one of the most sought-after club attractions in Boston. He became something of a father figure for us, supplying knowledge and experience in the music biz that none of us had, least of all our de facto manager, Guy. And he introduced us to Al Coury, New England regional promo man for Capitol Records.

Al was a compact, dapper guy, fairly bursting with energy. He was always smiling, always very manic, and great with the bon mots. He used to tell us, "I love you guys. Y'know why? Because you're low, you're in there, and you're dirty!" And we would always laugh dutifully, as if this was the first time we had heard it. But he was a great guy and he really liked our music. Fred told us if we played our cards right, we would soon be signed to Capitol Records.

The possibility of being label-mates with The Beatles made my head swim. I had never stopped being a huge Beatles fan. I loved everything about them: their wit, their style, their vocal chops and, most of all, their incredible songwriting skills. By the spring of 1965 they had released five albums in the US and each one raised the musical bar a notch and upped the standard of pop music worldwide. In 1965 we were listening to *Beatles '65*, which at the time we had no idea was cannibalized from the British *Beatles for Sale* album, and various singles. Nonetheless it contained some of the all-time best John Lennon songs: "I'm a Loser," "No Reply" and "I'll Be Back." Of course, at that time we couldn't tell a John Lennon song from a Paul McCartney song. They were all credited to Lennon & McCartney, and we took that at face value.

And, oh yeah, The Beach Boys were also on Capitol. We liked them as well.

At that age, when a dream comes true, you start thinking that all you have to do is dream and it will come to pass. It had happened on Martha's Vineyard. We had done the impossible because we didn't know it was impossible. So, when Fred told us that Voyle Gilmore, the West Coast head of A&R for Capitol, was coming to our next gig at the Rathskeller, I wasn't all that surprised. I figured it was just another one of my dreams coming true. At that point I was sure we were destined for stardom, anointed.

And Voyle Gilmore did come to the Rathskeller. He liked what he heard and signed us on the spot. All thanks, of course, to Al Coury. But I thought, *Of course, this is the way I dreamed it—this is the way it's supposed to be.*

Fred was a great agent, but he was no manager and no lawyer. I suppose we had a lawyer look over the contract, but it was a mere formality. In those days, you just signed whatever the record company wanted you to sign. We gave up a hundred percent of our publishing, got a very small advance, and received a royalty of maybe two or three cents per record sold. This was a singles deal; we would not get to do an album unless we got a single on the national charts. When the contract came, I had to have my parents cosign it. I was only nineteen years old.

* * *

Kyle had been asked to play harmonica with Richard & Mimi Fariña at the Newport Folk Festival. So, on July 25, 1965 we all headed down to Rhode

Island to watch our boy onstage at Newport—and also Bob Dylan, who was headlining. Bob's new single, "Like a Rolling Stone," had just dropped, and everybody wondered whether he would play it with an electric band at Newport. While there, I got to meet some of the great luminaries of folk, including Peter Yarrow (who was the MC), Hamilton Camp and Bob Gibson. Then it was time for Dick & Mimi's set. Kyle acquitted himself with honor and we were all very proud of him. Finally Dylan came on wearing a green shirt with white polka dots. The Butterfield Blues Band, who had played earlier, backed him. He plugged in his Fender Stratocaster and launched into "Maggie's Farm," followed by "Like a Rolling Stone." I was so enamored with the music I was completely unaware that half the audience was booing (or that's the way the media reported it). Apparently by playing with electric instruments Bob had somehow betrayed the folk establishment. I just didn't get it. The people who I thought were so cool and so progressive just a couple of years before had suddenly turned into old fogies. We stood up and cheered for Bob after his set. Fuck those old folkies!

Dylan plugs in at Newport, 1965. Photo: David Gahr, Estate of David Gahr/Getty Images

* * *

Our first recording session for Capitol took place on August 31, 1965. We recorded at Capitol's famous Studio A in what used to be a church in the heart of Manhattan. Capitol had assigned us a producer—also a common practice in those days. His name was Marv Holzman. I'm not sure what his musical background was, but he was a nice enough guy and we assumed he knew what he was doing. Marv was what was called an A&R man. This stood for artist and repertoire, and the A&R man (there was no such thing as an A&R woman) was not only the person who produced your record, he was also supposedly the guy who chose the repertoire you were going to record. But I don't recall Marv giving us any input in this regard. The A&R man was never a recording engineer; there was always someone else with him in the studio to twist the knobs.

We recorded only three songs at that session and, looking back, I wonder why we chose these three: "Here She Comes" and "Always I Know," both written by me and with me singing lead, and "Certain Chick" with Kyle singing lead. Hardly our strongest material. And where was Marv?

So, no surprise when we received word from Capitol that there was nothing there that sounded like it could be a single. I agreed. We had absolutely no professional recording experience. At the time, the state of the art was three-track. You'd record all the instruments at once and they went onto one track, then you could record the vocals, lead and harmonies, usually all at once, but some overdubbing was possible with 'bouncing' all the tracks onto the empty third track. Frankly, our initial recordings sounded like shit. We didn't know what we were doing, and Marv Holzman did little to educate us. We were basically thrown into the pool at the deep end and told to swim.

I decided to hang around in New York for a while after our first session, as we had nothing planned in Boston for the immediate future and I could always stay at my parents' house. One day I was sitting in the Night Owl, a club on 3rd Street in the Village that had become the premier venue in New York for emerging rock bands. It was basically closed during the day, but apparently nobody cared if I sat there. Rehearsing onstage was a new band called The Lovin' Spoonful, featuring John Sebastian, who I knew by reputation as a harmonica player in the folk scene. He had been in The Even Dozen Jug Band with one of my heartthrobs, Maria D'Amato, before she became Maria Muldaur.

I'll never forget the moment John Sebastian picked up the electric autoharp, plugged it in and launched into the opening chords of "Do You Believe in Magic." Chills went up my spine. This was the coolest sound

I'd ever heard a live rock band make. Afterward I went up to them and told them that song was a hit. They told me they hoped I was right, as it had just been released as their first single.

* * *

Back in Boston, I was invited to a party on Hemenway Street in the Back Bay, over near the Berklee College of Music. Everyone was camped out on the floor, passing around a pipe filled with a new drug called DMT. It had a foul chemical smell when it burned, but it packed a powerful rush. I found myself sitting next to a beautiful blond with limpid green eyes named Ellen, who I later learned was one of the residents in this apartment. We each took a hit off the pipe and she swooned, dropping her head into my lap. I was in love! I remember giving her mouth-to-mouth hits of DMT. I got her number before the party broke up, and I resolved to go back and see her soon. But then things got busy…

Our next foray into the studio was scheduled for September 17th. This time we prepared rigorously. We did our own A&R, choosing our three strongest songs for the next session: "Maybe More Than You," "I Wanna Know" and "Back Door Blues," another tune I had written in the apartment on Myrtle Street.

I really wanted to see Ellen again before I left for New York, so I called her, and she invited me over. I was flushed with anticipation. This was by far the most beautiful girl I had met in Boston, and she seemed so sweet and kind. Upon walking into her apartment my excitement turned to a burning knot of disappointment in my stomach. There on the couch, looking as if he was all but moved in, was Jack, Ellen's new boyfriend. Jack was a sax player, a student at Berklee. To add to my disappointment, he was also incredibly handsome. But I covered my disappointment well, put a good face on it and pretended to be really happy for them. The next day I left for New York.

We made the most out of the trip to NYC by scheduling a gig at the Night Owl. Sharing the bill was The Blues Project. I really wanted to play acoustic guitar on two of the songs we were to record ("Maybe More Than You" and "I Wanna Know"), but I didn't own one. I had gotten friendly with Danny Kalb, the guitarist from The Blues Project, and he graciously consented to lend me his beautiful Gibson Hummingbird guitar for the session the next day.

Lower right: Danny Kalb plays the Gibson Hummingbird I borrowed
from him.

Our second session at Capitol was a vast improvement over the first.
We went in prepared, and we nailed it. Listening back on those big studio
speakers gave us quite a thrill. They sounded like real records.

* * *

In 1965 and '66 The Lost were getting quite a bit of publicity in teen fan
magazines like *16*, *Teen Talk* and *Tiger Beat*. *Datebook*, which was a cut
above most of them in terms of being less inane and dumbed-down, did a
rather nice piece on us. The guy who wrote that article was Danny Fields.
Danny was on the budding edge of what was to become a new branch of
literature known as Rock Journalism. When we were in New York for the
Night Owl gig, I hung out with him. He knew a lot of people, and he introduced me to quite a few New York movers and shakers. I spent one of those
nights on his couch with an attractive brunette named Hope Ruff. Years
later I saw that she was a backup singer on Todd Rundgren's landmark double album *Something/Anything?* Danny went on to become an executive at
Elektra Records, and to discover and manage The Ramones, arguably the
world's first punk band.

Danny Fields. Photo: Danny Fields Archives

Danny Fields' article in *Datebook*, 1966

Chapter Twelve

Eva

Wandering around the West Village, I walked over to look at the latest Carnaby Street styles in the city's hippest men's clothing shop, Paul Sargent on West 4th Street. I was feeling pretty good about the recording, and I decided to buy myself a new jacket. It was short and made of soft brown suede. Afterward, I crossed the street and found myself looking in the window of a ladies' dress shop—at the most beautiful girl I had ever seen. Talk about an emotional rollercoaster. I hadn't gotten over the disappointment of losing Ellen to Jack, and suddenly I was smitten anew.

I couldn't help myself; I walked in. She was sitting behind a sewing machine, doing some alterations, all focus and concentration. She had short blond hair, perfectly even features, and big amber eyes. In fact, her very skin seemed to radiate with a warm golden glow. She must have felt me staring at her, because she looked up. When our eyes met, she gave me a little smile. It was a clear invitation.

"What's your name?" I asked, too captivated to think of anything clever.

"Eva."

There was some serious chemistry going on here.

"I'm Ted. Are you the owner of this place?"

"No," she said, "it's just a job. Can I help you with anything?"

"Yes, you can come to dinner with me."

To my amazement she agreed, and once again my spirits soared.

Later in life, after becoming involved with yoga and meditation, I learned it's best for one to stay emotionally even; no big ups, no big downs.

"Make no appointments, get no disappointments." That's what Swami Satchidananda used to say, and that's the credo I've tried to live by. But that was later. I see now that, in those days, I was becoming addicted. Not to love exactly, but to the excitement, the anticipation of a new love, which I guess is why I was never able to stay faithful to anyone or be with one person for any length of time.

That night with Eva turned into a week. I had about that much time before our next gig in Boston, and I wanted to spend every minute of it with her. It was plain she was feeling it too. I had never felt this strongly about another person in my life. This was real love, something I had never felt before.

She had a small apartment on Thompson Street in Little Italy. It was a pretty shabby building, but she kept her place immaculate. She had painted the wood floors a shiny black and had colorful cushions and beautiful paintings and artifacts all over. Some of the paintings, I found out, were hers. I thought she was an incredibly talented artist, and I'm a tough critic. She also wrote poetry, played piano, picked up a little flute, and had acted in several repertory companies. She was almost four years my senior, and I was in awe. She also made a little extra money, modeling nude for art classes. She was not ashamed of her body—and small wonder; it was perfect. She had the most exquisite breasts I had ever seen. The nipples actually pointed up.

She was about 5'2" and couldn't have weighed more than a hundred pounds on her fattest day. Our bodies were a perfect fit, and making love to her was a transcendental experience. I moved all the clothes I had with me to her place, and we played house for that entire week. Then, one night, she brought home some acid. If I thought making love to her was transcendental before, making love on acid was—and is to this day—my idea of the ultimate experience in life.

During that trip I remember looking down at her face and seeing it as a stained glass church window, watching it turn into Jean of Arc, Cleopatra, Marie Antoinette, Helen of Troy and every iconic woman that ever reigned over the imagination of man. That a woman like this could be mine made my ego swell with pride. And pride goeth before a fall…

Eva turned out to be quite a few interesting people. I was young, stupid, cocky and overconfident. One night we went to the Café Au Go Go on Bleecker Street to hear a Village stalwart, Tim Buckley. I casually pointed out to her a girl I had slept with (Hope Ruff), thinking that would improve my cachet in her eyes. How wrong I was. When we got home, I was dealing with a new person. In a rage, she threw my clothes out the window and told me to get out and never come back. Close to tears, I rushed out of there, not knowing what else to do. I picked up my clothing off the street and went back to my parents' apartment. I tried and tried to call her, but her phone was off the hook. At last I went back and knocked on the door. It swung open. She was laying on the bed, unconscious, an empty bottle of sleeping pills in her hand. I called an ambulance. The paramedics revived her, but they had to take her to the hospital and pump her stomach. Then they took her to the psych ward at Bellevue. They wouldn't let me see her for forty-eight hours.

When I went into the women's ward to get her, it was like a scene out of *The Snake Pit*. I was immediately engulfed by mad women, all pawing and clawing at me. It was quite terrifying. As addicted as I was to the adoration of women, I discovered there was a limit, even for me. As I led Eva out of there, all the inmates applauded. In the taxi on the way home I swore I would never hurt her again.

But our relationship was fraught with pain. We couldn't live with each other, and we couldn't live without each other. We chased each other all over the country over a period of three years. But there I go getting ahead of myself again…

Eva

Chapter Thirteen

Maybe More Than You

Not long after The Lost's second session in New York, Al Coury came by our new rehearsal studio, which was over a drycleaners in Cambridge, to tell us Capitol had decided to release "Maybe More Than You," backed with "Back Door Blues" as our first single and that, in his opinion, it sounded like a hit. We were ecstatic. There followed a flurry of activity: We had new photos taken, which were printed up with the Capitol Records logo underneath. Flyers were printed up that said, "From the company that gave you... (small type) The Kingston Trio, (bigger type) The Beach Boys, (bigger type) The Beatles... and now have found (biggest type of all) THE LOST!" There it was in black and white (well, black and green actually): Capitol was going to make us bigger than the Beatles!

Next came the rather painful task of firing Guy Rupright. We all liked Guy, but he just wasn't pulling his weight. And he was beginning to act a little crazy. A cousin of Willie's, Dick Chandler, a mild-mannered bespectacled young man, offered to stake us to some new equipment. Apparently he was a trust fund kid and independently wealthy. And so Dick Chandler became our new manager. Still, no music biz credentials, no experience, no knowledge. I guess we were either slow learners, or we just would 'go with the flow.'

A whole series of gigs were lined up, including a mini-tour of Western Massachusetts and Upstate New York, including Troy, Albany, Utica and Buffalo. The single was released on October 18, 1965, a month after we had recorded it. This was an unusually long lag time for those days, but I guess we wanted time to prepare to promote it with gigs and stuff. We were even booked to appear on the *Stan Roberts Show*, a local TV show in Buffalo, hosted by WKBW DJ Stan Roberts. This was a teenage dance show in the mold of *American Bandstand*, where bands would come on and lip-synch to their latest record. After we performed "Maybe More Than You" Roberts interviewed us. He asked Willie, "So, how's your record going?"

Without missing a beat, Willie replied, "Forty-five."

While we were on the road, the radio started to play our single. Now, anyone that's seen *That Thing You Do* knows a musician never forgets the first time he heard himself on the radio. But I confess I can't remember exactly when we first heard "Maybe More Than You" blasting out of the ether. I'm pretty sure we were in the van, wending our way westward on Highway 90 through the bleak suburbs of Worcester, Albany, Troy or Utica. Of course, it was a jubilant moment. "Maybe More Than You" made it to #30 on the Boston radio charts and considerably higher in points west, such as Worcester, Massachusetts.

In Worcester we made it to #10 on the chart of their local Top 40 station. They asked us to play an outdoor concert for the radio station, right in front of the Worcester City Hall. When we got there, we saw that they had rigged a stage out of a flatbed truck, upon which we were to set up. It being a weekend, the lobby of the City Hall was to be our dressing room. There was a regal flight of marble steps leading down from our 'dressing room' to the flatbed truck and, as we descended the stairs, we saw a rabid crowd. The girls were screaming for us like we were The Beatles. And perhaps I was hallucinating, but it seemed to me that the boys were booing.

We mounted the flatbed and launched into our set. During the second song, the objects began to land on the stage: at first, girl's jewelry, candy and—underpants! But then pop bottles and cans, hurled by the jealous boys, filled the air. Lee got clipped in the forehead by an incoming bottle and started to bleed. That's when I decided it was time to pull the plug. We bid adieu to our enthusiastic constituents and hightailed it out of there.

Another memorable gig during that period was our second big concert. This time we were opening for Sonny & Cher at the Troy Armory in Troy, New York. Also on the bill was Len Barry, who was riding a big hit with "1-2-3." There were about six thousand people waiting to hear us. Lee was so nervous he opened the backstage door and threw up outside, just as we were about to go on. Although there were frequent concert events at the Troy Armory back then, the room was not designed for music; it was designed for tanks. And we had the 'tankless' task of opening the show. In those days, sound checks were a luxury, and we didn't get one. There were usually no monitor speakers on the stage, so you had to get used to singing and not hearing yourself. So when we started into our first number, a rousing original rocker by Yours Truly called "When I Call," we had no idea whether or not our voices were being heard. After the song I tapped on the mic. Absolutely nothing. I said, "Can you hear us?" Nothing. I looked up toward the sound booth, which was way up in the rafters. I couldn't see a soul. I turned to the band. "2120," I said. "2120 South Michigan Avenue" was a Rolling Stones tune, an instrumental, which we covered and could stretch for as long as was necessary. We launched into "2120" and vamped on those two chords ad infinitum. But when it was time for Kyle to blow his harmonica solo, there was still nothing coming out of the P.A. system. I looked up beseechingly at the sound booth, but there was no sign of life. We played that song as long as we could, then ended to scattered applause. I tried addressing the crowd again, saying, "Well, folks, looks like we've encountered some technical difficulties… " But no one heard me. I looked toward the wings. There was no one there. We were all alone out there and left to twist in the wind. Finally, we just left the stage. The gig was an absolute and complete disaster. There was never an explanation or an apology from anyone. We didn't stick around to see how Len Barry and Sonny & Cher fared, but I'd be willing to bet they got some sound out of those microphones.

Not long after that, in February of 1966, we were to open another big concert, this time for The Supremes at Brandeis University. Determined not to get caught flat-footed again, we decided to bring in our own sound system. We hired the Hanley brothers, who were on the cutting edge of live sound technology. Four years later they made their bones by doing the sound at Woodstock, but at this point they were known only to an elite few in the Boston area. The Supremes gig was in a big live gymnasium. By "live" I mean sound reverberated off the hardwood floors and walls, which made it loud and indistinct. The Hanleys showed up with speakers that looked like Godzilla's port-a-potty. I mean, these things were *huge*. We also got stage monitor speakers, and every amp, every drum was close-mic'd. We were *so ready*.

Backstage we got wind of the fact that we had been a grudging second choice for the gig. The hiring committee had tried to get our old friends, The Blues Project to open the show, as some of them had apparently gone to Brandeis (maybe even my friend, Danny Kalb), but they were unavailable. This sort of soured us on Brandeis right from the get-go.

We took the stage, full of confidence. This time we *would* be heard. Our first song, "When I Call," opened with a loud, sustained chord, a sort of "braaang!" The moment we hit that chord I saw the first three rows duck under their seats, clutching their ears. By the middle of the song, people were standing up with their fingers in their ears, booing, and yelling things like "get off!" I searched the horizon frantically, looking for one of the Hanleys to turn the sound down, but saw no one. We tried to turn down our amps, but it was to no avail. With each successive song the booing just got louder, and people down front were actually walking out. After three songs we fled the stage, flipping off the audience as we went. And so ended our third big concert.

86

Chapter Fourteen

1966, Part 1

On December 13, 1965 we returned to Capitol Studios and recorded three of our strongest songs: "When I Call," "Everybody Knows," a mid-tempo rocker by Willie that became one of our most requested numbers and "No Reason Why," a song I wrote after listening to Willie's Latin jazz records. The simple, bluesy melody was a perfect vehicle for the ragged voice of Walter Powers and the unusual, Afro-Cuban-inspired rhythm breaks made it the first rock song to be influenced by Afro-Cuban jazz, predating Santana by a good four years.

I stayed in New York after the rest of the band returned to Boston to be with Eva. We shacked up at her little apartment and lost ourselves in the delights of love. She turned me on to Eastern wisdom, showing me books like the *Bhagavad Gita* and *Autobiography of a Yogi* by Swami Paramhansa Yogananda. She showed me hatha yoga asanas and pranayama breathing techniques. She even showed me tantric sex techniques. It seemed to me she knew everything. I worshipped her; never wanted to be without her. Yes, I knew she had a crazy side; maybe I did too. But who wanted 'normal'? Extraordinary people demanded extraordinary considerations.

We spent Christmas together, then New Year's Eve. I resolved to get a place in Boston where we could live together. Eva could get a job anywhere, anytime. She was just one of those people. Employers took one look at her, and she was hired. So the idea of moving to another city daunted her not at all. In fact, she had lived all over: San Francisco, LA, Mexico. She was so much more worldly-wise than I was and had a gypsy soul.

When I went back to Boston, Lee wanted to move in with Susan Connell. So we gave up the apartment on Joy Street and I moved in with my friends in Cambridge. Barry Black had been a paratrooper in Vietnam, and Doc was an older guy in his forties who had been everywhere and done everything. Both of them were in the marijuana business and doing quite well. They had a huge three-bedroom apartment on River Street, off Central Square in Cambridge, and they let us move into the third bedroom. Doc lived with his girlfriend, Margaret. She and her sister, Diana Dew, owned a thriving dress shop near Harvard Square, which touted the most cutting edge handmade clothing anywhere. Margaret and Diana were Southern girls and expert seamstresses. Diana made me a cool shirt, white with big black polka dots. I'm wearing that shirt in the photo of The Lost in chapter nine, page 60.

To recount the number of crises and blowups Eva and I went through in our stormy relationship, the number of other guys she slept with and the number of other girls I slept with, would be enough to fill a whole other book, but not this one. After living together in Cambridge for maybe a month, Eva insisted we get married. This was not the first time for Eva; she had already been married and divorced from some guy in California. My instincts were all against the idea. I was for leaving well enough alone. Why do we need the state to validate our love? But it was all for naught. When Eva made up her mind, it was her way or the highway.

Just married. L to R: My tripping buddy, Steve, Dick Chandler, somebody else, Willie, Kyle, somebody else, Eva, Dr. Wu, me. Short brown hair on the right belongs to my mother.

Jim and Marilyn Kweskin (Jim was founder and leader of the Kweskin Jug Band) had been married by Dr. Wu, a little Chinese guy who spoke with a heavy Scottish brogue, and was a professor of English literature at Boston University. "That sounds cool," we thought, so we decided to get married there as well. And so, in January 1966, Eva and I were married. I bought Eva a genuine silk sari from India and Margaret and Diana made me a forest green velvet suit.

* * *

The Lost continued to gig constantly and thrive, still riding on our one single. One day in April 1966, Al Coury bounced into our rehearsal studio to tell us we were going on tour with The Beach Boys. At the time they were undisputedly the most popular American rock band, second only in the world to The Beatles. We were to do about eight or nine college concert dates all up and down the Eastern Seaboard. We were elated and incredibly grateful to Al and Capitol for pulling the necessary strings to get us this gig. But, like most feats of illusion, our attention was misdirected. Sure, it was a great coup for us to get this tour, but we had no second single to promote. I relate all this with the wisdom and clarity that only hindsight can provide. We knew next to nothing about music marketing—actually, make that 'nothing'—and, in those days, it was the artist's mindset to leave business to the businessmen. But there was nobody minding the store. Here was an opportunity for unprecedented exposure for us and our songs, and we had nothing new for the radio, which was, far and away, the driving force that either made you or broke you in music. The stokers of the "star maker machinery" were asleep at the shovel.

We had a fine time with the Beach Boys. They were all very pleasant, and Dennis Wilson was especially friendly and witty. Confidentially, I think he was probably the only stoner. One night he was 'too sick' to go on, and so Lee Mason filled in on drums. Lee played well but had to pull his punches to keep from drowning out the band (even then, we considered The Beach Boys 'rock lite').

It was a widely publicized fact that, after his breakdown, Brian Wilson would not be on this tour. Rumor had it that he was working on a new album that would put The Beach Boys on a par with The Beatles. We heard that Glen Campbell would be filling in for him on bass and vocals. On the first day I walked up to the bass player and asked if he was Glen Campbell.

He smiled and introduced himself as Bruce Johnston. Bruce turned out to be more than just another LA studio cat. He was a talented songwriter 'in his own write,' scoring a #1 hit in 1975 with Barry Manilow's *I Write the Songs*.

On several of the dates, a third act was added to open the show: The Goldberg-Miller Blues Band, with Barry Goldberg on organ and vocals, Steve Miller on guitar and vocals and Charlie Musselwhite on harmonica. Talk about diverse bills! Years later, Steve Miller would rise to stardom with a string of hit records in the '70s.

After one of the Beach Boys shows—I guess at a college in New England—I was supposed to meet Eva in the lobby of the auditorium. Without thinking, I walked out into the hall and up one of the aisles. I was immediately engulfed by throngs of rabid female fans. They were tearing at my clothes, my hair. I was terrified. *So this is what it's like to be a rock star*, I thought. To my surprise, I didn't like it much. Finally, Eva found me and, valiantly beating back the hungry hordes, spirited me out of there.

In May 1966 Brian Wilson unveiled his magnum opus, *Pet Sounds*. Frankly, I was blown away. I was a diehard Beatles fan, but this was, for me, the best work an American rock artist had produced to date; a true masterpiece.

The Beach Boys on tour, 1966. Photo: Balsa Bill Yerkes, Surf Chaser Publishing. From the book: *Surfboards, Stratocasters, Striped Shirts* by Bill Yerkes

* * *

That same month, The Lost did a two-week stand in New York City, opening
the city's first psychedelic ballroom, the Cheetah. We were finally able to
see a psychedelic light show first hand. We were the opening act; the headliners were The Capitols, an R&B trio out of Detroit, who were riding on
their first and only hit, "Cool Jerk." The woman who booked the club was
the charming and beautiful Pat Hartley. The thing I remember most (and
most fondly) about her was that she wore transparent blouses with no bra,
a fashion I devoutly hoped would catch on. Three years later Pat starred in
a documentary movie called *Rainbow Bridge*, the story of putting together
a Jimi Hendrix concert in Maui. Around the same time, she played a supporting role in the underground classic *Ciao! Manhattan*, starring Warhol
superstar Edie Sedgwick. Pat was definitely on the cutting edge of the psychedelic revolution.

Pat Hartley

Chapter Fifteen

1966, Part 2

The Lost returned to Capitol Studios in New York in July and recorded two more songs: "Violet Gown," a ballad with a catchy chorus I had penned and sang lead on, and "Mean Motorcycle," which had been written back in my Goddard College days. These tracks were produced by a friend of ours named Monty Dunn whose background was as a folk guitar player, having played with Ian & Sylvia and others. His main instrument was the twelve-string guitar, and he played it on this version of "Violet Gown."

While we were in New York, we decided to try recording at an independent recording studio, just for a change. I had written a song called "Changes," a Motown-flavored piece that sounded similar to The Temptations' "The Way You Do the Things You Do," written by Smokey Robinson. But, with Walter's raspy baritone singing lead, the song took on a very different vibe. The engineer at Regent Sound was Bill Szymczyk, a very creative guy. We had fun working with him on an arrangement that he contributed to substantially. Bill was one of a new breed of engineer/producers who were only just beginning to make their presence felt in the music industry, and would do so more in the years to come.

Meanwhile, our friends, The Remains, were moving up in the world. They had gotten with a new manager, John Kurland, who was based out of New York, and who, unlike the people we surrounded ourselves with, was well connected in the music biz. In December of 1965 they appeared on the fabled *Ed Sullivan Show*, a distinction shared by only a very few of the top names in rock 'n' roll. Ed had provided the launching pad to national exposure for no less than Elvis and The Beatles. And now, after only a couple of regional hits, The Remains had made it into that elite circle. But that was only the beginning. Through his connection to concert promoter Sid Bernstein, Kurland got The Remains the opening slot on the 1966 Beatles tour. We were happy for them… and a bit envious as well. But we got a great consolation prize: Barry got us all down front seats to the Boston show, which took place at a race track, Suffolk Downs, on August 18, 1966. At last I got to see my idols in person, and a good thing too, as this was The Beatles' last tour. The fact that The Remains could get that close to going all the way and still not make it, is yet another example of the cruel capriciousness of the business of rock 'n' roll.

The Remains open for The Beatles, August 1966. Photo: Ed Freeman, courtesy Ed Freeman Photography

* * *

Capital didn't deem any of the songs we recorded nine months earlier, after the release of "Maybe More Than You," worthy of release as a single. So, having missed the window of opportunity afforded by the Beach Boys tour, Capitol finally gave the green light to "Violet Gown" as a single. However, I was not pleased with the way it came out. Nobody in the band was. But Capitol went ahead and released "Violet Gown" backed with "Mean Motorcycle" in August. But then they succumbed to pressure from us to recall this version and let us go into a different studio with a different producer and record it again.

Since we had picked Monty Dunn as producer for our last session and he had bombed out, Capitol suggested we try a guy named Jerry Keller, who had written and sung one of my favorite records as a kid, "Here Comes Summer" (1959). I loved that record, and it had presaged one of the most important summers of my life (see Chapter One). So, okay, but we wanted to pick our own studio. We were tired of recording at Capitol and felt it was mired in old school values that were holding us back. We decided on AAA Recording in Dorchester, Massachusetts, one of a handful of up-and-coming, state-of-the-art studios in the Boston area that came highly recommended.

And so, to the great confusion of all the radio stations that had received the first version of "Violet Gown" and were now told NOT to play it and to stand by for a new version, we rushed into the studio to do the new version. We had worked out a really good arrangement, which included a cool piano part from Willie with Lee overdubbing woodblocks (an influence, I think, from the Beach Boys' *Pet Sounds* album).

There was some higher-up at Capitol whose name now escapes me who told us to record "No Reason Why" as an instrumental for the B side. His reasoning was that the vocal version of "No Reason Why" could possibly be used as an A side in the future. "Mean Motorcycle" was also jettisoned for similar reasons.

The new, vastly superior, version of "Violet Gown," backed with a frantically-paced instrumental of "No Reason Why," was released on August 29, 1966. But it was dead on arrival. Few radio stations played it. The confusion over the initial release, then the recall and rerelease was too much for commercial radio to tolerate from an unknown band. On top of that, "Violet Gown," a ballad with me singing lead, was a poor choice to follow up an up-tempo tune with Willie singing lead. The two records didn't sound similar or even like the same band.

With the help of Capitol, we had committed career suicide.

Certain issues within the band caused additional stress. Kyle and Walter had been into shooting up heroin almost from the beginning. I had always frowned on it, but didn't want to be a cop, and it hadn't really interfered too much with the functioning of the band—until now. Willie had gone through a heavy drinking period, followed by a trip to the hospital for pancreatitis. After that, he had to give up drinking—or else. So we got him into smoking pot. But now people were showing up late for rehearsals, or failing to show up altogether. At one gig, Walter lost his balance onstage and fell back into his amplifier. Rumors were spreading about us.

Then Lee announced he was leaving the group. He said he wanted to go in a different musical direction, and I'm sure that much was true, but we all knew there was more to it than that. We were starting to unravel.

Capitol assured us that they wanted us to keep recording. In fact, they wanted us to record with a new producer they had found for us *right away*. Why we agreed to go back to Capitol Studios in New York to record without a drummer is still a mystery to me. We certainly wanted to stay in Capitol's good graces and they told us not to worry, that our new producer, Dick Weissman, would get us a great studio drummer.

Dick Weissman was an ex-folkie, who had been a Capitol artist himself, as a member of The Journeymen, a Kingston Trio-like folk group that featured a very young John Phillips (who had, just a few months earlier, achieved mega-stardom as leader of The Mamas & The Papas). Dick came up to Boston before the scheduled session to meet with us and brainstorm about the tracks. He was an affable guy and I liked him. We played him some live demos of the songs we had made, and he picked three to record: "No Money in the Pocket," with Kyle singing lead, a cover of an instrumental written by Joe Zawinul for the Cannonball Adderly Quintet (originally titled "Money in the Pocket"), "Kaleidoscope," a new song I had written on which Willie sang lead and "Seven Starry Skies," another original by me, which was a love song to Eva that had some jazzy chords.

It must have been those chord changes that gave Dick the idea. When we got to the session, he had already charted, arranged and recorded a track for me to sing to. It featured syrupy girl backup singers doing oohs and ahhs and the wimpiest cocktail jazz bossa nova track I had ever heard. It made me sick. Why would Capitol want us to do something like *this*? But Dick said it was just an experiment and, still quite anxious to stay in Capitol's good graces, I went along with it. As far as I was concerned this totally massacred my song, and I would never have allowed this version to be released. But it never came to that.

The thing about these 'producers,' who were blindly assigned to produce groups like ours, was that they didn't have anything invested in the artist, and visa-versa; but, being creative types, they wanted to contribute something creative to the music. The creative process is supposed to go something like this: The producer sits with the artist, makes a suggested change. The artist considers it and, if it has merit, tries it out. If both parties agree, the idea is incorporated into the music. If either party feels it doesn't work (usually the artist), it's scrapped and we move on. But that's not the way it worked in the '60s. These "A&R men," who wanted to play producer, vented their 'creativity' by simply rearranging the artist's work, without consulting the artist. This happened to me throughout my career, as you will see.

So we only actually laid down two tracks with the studio drummer. He turned out to be a jazz cat with no feel for rock whatsoever. We were pretty devastated with the results. Dick played a banjo part on "Kaleidoscope" and, with a decent rock drum track, this could have made a great follow-up single to "Maybe More Than You," as it was up-tempo, folk rock and featured Willie's voice. But it was too late for wishing. Soon after we returned to Boston, the option on our contract came up and Capitol did not renew it.

Despite our disappointment, we had gigs to play, so we set about auditioning drummers. George Papadapoulos, owner of the Unicorn, let us use his club to hold the auditions. We did them during the day when the club was closed. We ran an ad in some of the underground papers and anything that musicians might read, and we got quite a few responses. There were only two guys, however, that we felt were good enough. First choice was Rick Shlosser, a really exceptional player, who was studying at Berklee. As soon as we heard Rick, we told him he had the gig. But ultimately he declined, saying he needed to stay in school and finish his education. (Rick went on to a stellar career as a studio drummer all through the '70s and played on some of the decade's most memorable records). Second choice was John Ferro, a blue-collar kid from Dorchester, also an excellent drummer, but lacking the flair and personality of either Lee or Shlosser. So we hired Johnny Ferro and continued to gig around Boston and environs.

* * *

Meanwhile, Eva and I had become one of the 'happening couples about town' (when we were together), making the scene in every Boston venue that mattered. We bought a car, a 1959 Saab. It was silver and had Pirelli snow tires. I thought it was a thing of beauty. I had never owned a car; in fact, I had never learned to drive. Unlike the West Coast, there was no car culture where I grew up; we took public transportation. When I got into the band, there was always someone who could drive us around. I considered it an advantage not to have a license as I could never be called upon to drive. In fact, the only person in the band who had a license was Lee. But now I wanted to learn, and Eva set about teaching me. One day, we were driving around a big empty parking lot. She was at the wheel, and we got into an argument (one of the many). In a blind rage, she floored it and started careening crazily around the parking lot, almost colliding with the few cars that were parked there. I was about ready to jump for it when she finally relented. Anyway, I (sort of) learned to drive.

At some Boston club we ran into Ellen and Jack, who were now also married. Seeing kindred spirits, we became good friends. Eva even tolerated knowing that I had been attracted to Ellen before I met her. Ellen was a rare beauty, inside and out, and it was hard for anyone not to like her. Similarly, Jack was incredibly charming and also a first-rate woodwind player, having a good command of flute as well as sax. He was starting to get some fairly substantial gigs, mostly with jazz artists. Eventually they moved to New York, and we lost track of them for a while.

* * *

One night we went to see a new band called The Youngbloods. My old pal Banana had disbanded The Trolls and had thrown in with Jesse Colin Young, a well-established folk singer with a soaring tenor voice. Jesse had become well-known in the folk world for his excellent solo album, which he made for Capitol in the early '60s. Like just about every other Greenwich Village folkie, Jesse was not about to be left in the acoustic dust as everyone else plugged in. In The Youngbloods he eschewed his acoustic guitar for an electric bass and drafted Banana on guitar and keyboards, Jerry Corbitt on lead guitar, and Joe Bauer on drums. Although the band formed in the later part of 1965, their first album didn't get released until January of 1967 and didn't chart until March. They released a couple of singles, "Grizzly Bear," a Jerry Corbitt original that made it to #52 on the *Billboard Hot 100* and "Get Together," a folk standard that had been written by the mysterious Chester Powers (a.k.a. Dino Valenti), who was to reemerge a few years later as a member of Quicksilver Messenger Service. "Get Together" had been recorded by Hamilton Camp, We Five and, that same year, by Jefferson Airplane. But Jesse's voice and that song created a recording that was a crystalline masterpiece. When I saw them perform it live I told Eva it was a hit. But "Get Together" only made it to #62 on the charts. That was in September of 1967. Two years later it was used in a nationwide public service TV ad. RCA decided to rerelease it and, as a result, it made it to #5.

I recount all this as yet another illustration of how capricious it all is; how a tiny twitch of fate can massively alter a music career. The Lost failed to come up with a follow-up single when it counted the most, and we ended up as a footnote in the also-ran column of rock 'n' roll. The Youngbloods' career was flatlining when fate stepped in and administered an unexpected (and well-deserved) jolt that made enough of an impression to give Jesse Colin Young's career the juice it needed to carry him on to eight charting solo albums through 1978.

One night in late 1966 Eva and I were at the Club 47. I think the headliners were The Chambers Brothers. As we walked to our seats, I chanced to see Peter and Edie. Wow, what were the odds? She was still at Windham College. He had moved to Boston, changed his name from Peter Blankfield to Peter Wolf and was now the lead singer of a new band called The Hallucinations. Edie was as beautiful as ever and I was glad I had Eva on my arm to suppress any thoughts of our triangular past. The Lost had just been approached to headline at the opening of Boston's first psychedelic ballroom, the Boston Tea Party. I wanted to help Peter out with his new band (who knows, maybe it was out of guilt), and I told him I would try to get them on the bill with us. The club management agreed and The Hallucinations were set to open for The Lost at the Boston Tea Party for three consecutive weekends in January and February of 1967.

I never saw Edie again. It wasn't until the early '70s that I heard she had been killed in an auto accident. The news hit me pretty hard. I can't even imagine how Peter felt. It isn't often in life you meet someone that pretty and also that sweet.

Peter Wolf went on to team up with blues guitarist J. Geils to become the lead singer of the J. Geils Band, soon to become the top blues band in Boston and eventually a nationwide phenomenon. Sometime in the '70s I caught them at the Whiskey A Go Go in LA, where he embarrassed me by making me stand up in the audience and take a bow. By then he was married to movie star Faye Dunaway.

The Tea Party was a huge success, quickly becoming Boston's top rock venue. Soon afterward, others would try to imitate it and cash in on the psychedelic experience, like George Popadopoulos, who opened the Psychedelic Supermarket in late 1967. Bert Yellen's old college roommate, Don Law, started his meteoric rise that made him Boston's most successful concert promoter by becoming manager at the Boston Tea Party in 1968. Among the amazing acts I saw there were: Led Zeppelin in their first US performance (as 'The New Yardbirds'), Terry Reid (who turned down Jimmy Page's offer to be lead singer for that band) and The Velvet Underground.

In early 1967, The Lost decided to call it quits. Lee leaving, the record company dropping us, and the hard drug use, all added up to an avalanche of adversity that we could not overcome. The Tea Party turned out to be The Lost's last gig except for a frat party at New England College in Henniker, New Hampshire. I'll never forget driving back to Boston after that gig. Eva had come up with me in the Saab. We'd stayed overnight in a motel, and she let me drive part of the way back the next day. I remember watching the two-lane blacktop unwind before me and thinking, *That was the last gig; The Lost is no more*.

But we did do one more thing: a recording session that was funded by a couple named Pat Hall and Ken Manley who had written and recorded a kid's play called *Space Kids*, for which they needed music. The idea was to sell this as a breakfast cereal premium. We had a lot of fun creating original music for the project, in spite of how incredibly corny the acting and plot were. I wrote one song with vocals called "Rocket Ship," which kind of sounded like something by Curtis Mayfield & the Impressions played by a white rock band. *Space Kids* was never sold and never released until Erik Lindgren released it on his Arf! Arf! Records reissue label in 1993.

Looking back, I'd have to say The Lost had the most potential to break through to the big time of any of my bands. One big reason for this was that we were on the forefront of a new movement in pop music. We were in on the ground floor, ahead of the curve, before the floodgates burst with thousands of long-haired boys with guitars all vying for the same forty slots on the charts. If only I knew then what I know now: you have to develop and establish an identifiable sound. The Lost had a wonderful cast of diverse and colorful personalities, each with his own strong artist identity, but we did not have a strong identity as an act. Our music ranged from my pretty ballads to rough-and-tumble R&B to folk rock to jazz. None of our records had 'Hit Record' stamped all over it. At this writing I am still in touch with all the members of The Lost and I love them all like brothers. We shared an amazing journey in an amazing time and I will always cherish those memories.

It was the end of an era, but I was not sad. I didn't think in terms of 'eras,' nor did I dwell on the past. I was still very young—I had just turned twenty-one—and I eagerly looked forward to the next chapter.

Chapter Sixteen

New York Again

I decided I needed to be where the action was. In order to break through in the music business, one needed to be where the business was, and New York City was one of the two spots in the US (the other being Los Angeles) where the music business was. I guess you could include Nashville if you were into country, but I wasn't.

So Eva and I moved back to New York. With the help of my parents, we purchased an artist-in-residence loft at 76 Jefferson Street on a desolate industrial block right by the East River and within sight of the Manhattan Bridge. When you moved into an A.I.R. loft in Manhattan, you had to reimburse the previous owner for the amenities that the first owner had installed, such as a kitchen and bathroom. The owner of the building only rented you the space; you had to buy the amenities and resell them when you moved out. We paid the previous tenant $750 for the kitchen, bathroom facilities and appliances. Our monthly rent was $75. That's right, no typo here, $75! And you wonder why art and music flourished in the '60s and not today.

Soon after arriving in the Big Apple, we sold the Saab, which was breaking down with alarming regularity (but I'll spare you the Saab story).

Our loft was a big open room, about thirty by forty feet. We painted the brick walls white and the wood floor glossy black. It had twelve big windows on two sides. The bathroom was a corner that was completely partitioned off. Next to that, the kitchen was kind of an alcove. We set up the bed not far from the kitchen, which left the rest of the vast floor space open for Eva to paint and a band to rehearse. But I had no band as yet.

The building was all artist lofts. On the first floor (one flight up from the street) was a guy named Steve who had Chiron Press, a silkscreen studio that created limited edition prints for artists. I asked if I could help out, and so was hired (for little or no money), and Steve taught me how to do silk screening. This was a technique that involved filtering each color through a silk screen to create a print, one color at a time. It was very painstaking and precise. We did work for some of New York's leading artists of the day, including Robert Rauschenberg.

On the second floor lived Bobby Neuwirth, a folk singer and songwriter, who became Bob Dylan's main confidant and road manager. Bobby is best known for his appearances with Dylan in D.A. Pennebaker's documentary *Don't Look Back* and Dylan's film *Renaldo and Clara*. The Pennebaker film didn't play in New York until September 1967, and this was several months earlier, so I didn't know what a celebrity he was until I saw the movie. I remember Bobby as a really nice guy who let me borrow his acoustic guitar on more than one occasion (I still didn't own one). One day I happened in on him and he was shooting photos of Ramblin' Jack Elliott sitting in an antique bathtub in the middle of the floor (nothing risqué—Jack was fully clothed; in fact, he was wearing his cowboy hat).

On the fourth floor, directly above us, was a really huge loft owned by Tony Murad, a young artist, and sort of building caretaker. Tony's place opened onto the roof, which he had fixed up as a garden—a secret Eden in the dark heart of the city.

* * *

I was never much for political activism. Looking back, I think my attitude was rather snobbish about it. I thought I was too hip for that sort of thing. I thought protests were clichéd and corny. The incredible bravery of the freedom riders in the South was lost on me. The horrific murders of James Chaney, Andrew Goodman and Mickey Schwerner was a testament to their inspiring commitment and courage, and it makes me feel ashamed now that the young me distanced himself from all that.

But I did attend the historic anti-war march led by Martin Luther King Jr, which took place in Manhattan on April 18, 1967. About 125,000 of us followed MLK east on 42nd Street from Central Park to the UN Building. I confess, I was surprised at how swept up I was with the emotion of that day, and hearing MLK in person was an inspiration. Even so, I never attended another demonstration.

Eva and I were hanging out in some club or restaurant one night and met a guy named Ken Joffe. We had a few drinks and Ken got very friendly. He told us he owned a concert production company called Aurora Productions with his partner, Don Friedman. Don was a veteran concert promoter in New York, having been involved with many icons of the early '60s, including Lenny Bruce. At Ken's invitation, I went to see them at their office, which was actually Don's apartment on the Upper East Side. I played them some of my songs, and they offered to sign me to a publishing deal for a small weekly stipend. I was also asked to help out with promoting the concerts, putting up fliers and handling some of the details at the shows. Of course, I agreed.

The first show I was involved with was the initial US appearance of The Who. I had only heard "My Generation" at that point, and it bowled me over. John Entwistle's bass solo on that track alone was enough to sell me, not to mention Roger Daltrey's cheeky stuttering vocal. It was only later that I realized that the true genius behind The Who was always Pete Townshend.

We had arranged to present The Who on Friday night at the Malibu Shore Club on Long Island, which was actually a country club with a make-shift outdoor stage, and again on Saturday night at the Village Theatre on Second Avenue and 6th Street in Manhattan. The Village was an old movie house that had recently been converted into a concert venue, and Aurora Productions was the exclusive promoter for that venue. A year or so later it would be taken over by Bill Graham and renamed the Fillmore East. We paid The Who $1,500 for both shows.

Looking back, I can't believe I did this, or that Don and Ken allowed me to do it: I actually brought a reel-to-reel tape recorder to the Malibu Shore Club and set it up backstage so The Who could hear some of my songs. I played a few of them for Roger and John. Pete and Keith Moon were occupied elsewhere. They listened politely and asked me if I had heard Tim Rose. So they were hip to some of the Greenwich Village folkies. I told them the only Tim Rose story I knew: that he didn't really write "Morning Dew." It had actually been written by a Canadian girl named Bonnie Dobson and Rose had claimed authorship illegitimately. Because she was Canadian, there was some technicality that enabled Rose to get away with claiming co-authorship. This interested them greatly. Then Roger and I hung out in the bar before the show. We had a few drinks and he gave me a set of Indian dancing bells, which had a lovely jingle. I used them on my next recording and treasured them for years. He told me that it was The Who that had turned The Beatles on to feedback, the effect The Fab Four had used to open "I Feel Fine."

When The Who took the stage, I was blown away by what I saw and heard. The sheer power of the performance and the music was something neither I nor anyone else had seen from a rock band on American shores until that night. And it was mostly wasted on a crowd of upper crust adolescents, who were more interested in schmoozing with their friends than listening to some British band that no one had ever heard of. But the last number got their attention. It was "My Generation," reaching a climax when Pete Townshend raised his Fender Stratocaster over his head and smashed it to pieces on the stage, ending the show with the guitar howling feedback and everyone else kicking over their equipment. This was the most exciting rock show I had ever seen—and I got to see it again the following night in Manhattan, where there were people who were actually listening.

In researching these dates, subsequent to writing the above, it looks like these may not have been the very first appearances by The Who in North America. Wikipedia shows a series of dates at the RKO Theater in Manhattan, hosted by 'Murry the K,' which took place in late March 1967. As best as I can remember, the weekend at the Malibu Shore Club and The Village Theater took place in April.

The Who, 1967. Photo: Ray Stevenson, Rex Features

The following weekend we presented The Young Rascals (who dropped the 'Young' in their name the following year). They were local Long Island boys who I had heard a lot about going back to my days in The Lost. Even before their first hit in December of 1965, people were comparing The Lost to The Young Rascals. "Who would be the first to make it?" they conjectured. But when I heard "Good Lovin'" in March 1966, there was no doubt in my mind. The Rascals put on a great show. I was especially impressed with the singing and organ playing of Felix Cavaliere, who I had the pleasure of meeting and working with when I worked on their Anthology at Rhino in the 1990s and again, years later, at Concord, when Felix made a new album with guitar legend Steve Cropper on our newly-resurrected Stax imprint.

Other artists Aurora Productions presented included: Blue Cheer (the loudest band I had ever heard), Iron Butterfly (the second-loudest), and Richie Havens. I really loved Richie. I had been a fan since the early '60s when I would hear him at the Café Wha on Sunday afternoons. On one of the many occasions when Eva broke up with me and moved out, I wrote a song to her called "Now Is Just a Time." The music was written in an open G tuning on guitar. Richie used an open tuning (although not the same one, as I learned later), and I was thinking at some level that maybe he might cover this song. The first verse started with a haiku poem I had written years earlier in college. I'd read somewhere that the correct form for a haiku is seventeen syllables, and this was:

My hands across the darkness face
A flock of moments from me to you

I didn't record the song until the opportunity to get it to Richie had passed, but many years later, when I worked with him on his "Best of..." CD at Rhino, and when he appeared at a folk festival I organized in 1993, I did actually send him a recording of the song. Never heard anything back, though.

* * *

Eva was always moving out. She also had the infuriating habit of sleeping with my friends. Nobody really close; she was careful not to fuck anyone in any of my bands, for instance, but members of other bands were fair game.

I won't go into too much detail here, but she would always tell me when I saw her again who she had fucked when I was gone or she was gone. One time she came back and told me she had been with Ken Joffe. That ended my association with Aurora Productions. Ironically, I was crashing at Ken's apartment when Eva and I were on the outs, which is how he knew he could move in on her. But I really can't blame Ken. She was always the one pulling the strings, and no man could resist her. I slept with some of my friends' girlfriends, too. Sometimes I'd meet a girl who was with someone I knew, and I would get clear signals from her. Then I'd call her afterward, and would always score. I never attempted to resist these opportunities. Such was the morality of the '60s.

One time, when Eva and I were separated, I looked up Diana Dew, who had moved to New York City and become a fashion celebrity. Very recently she had appeared on the *Johnny Carson Show* modeling her invention, the Electric Dress, the first piece of apparel to light up. Diana had a loft in the East 20s, close to Andy Warhol's Factory. In fact, she was part of that crowd, and she took me to Max's Kansas City, the new 'in place to be.' I didn't care much for the people I met there—cold fishes, I thought. But Diana herself was extremely warm, and we spent a pleasant few days together. This time it was my turn to come home with a story for Eva.

Diana Dew (R) models the Electric Dress, 1967. Photo: Ed Pfizenmaier, courtesy of the Pfizenmeier Family Archive

Chapter Seventeen

Chamæleon Church

Knocking around New York, I was now without any visible means of support. Somewhere I ran into Chevy Chase, the tall guy I had met four years earlier at the funeral of my college roommate, Wendell Jones. Once he learned my history, he enthusiastically asserted that he was a drummer and we should start a band together. He was a very charming and funny guy, but I really didn't know how good a drummer he was, and I was still not certain that I wanted to start down the band road again.

Meanwhile, my old friend Ray Paret, the MIT frat boy who had let The Lost rehearse in his frat house, had become the manager of Ultimate Spinach, a Boston band in the mold of the San Francisco psychedelic movement, which was enjoying widespread popularity in Boston. Ray said he wanted to introduce me to Alan Lorber, Spinach's record producer. Lorber had a respectable New York pedigree, having worked with the likes of Neil Sedaka and Jackie Wilson, mainly as an arranger. In the '50s and early '60s the title of 'record producer' was not yet in common usage.

Ray brought me up to Lorber's office/apartment in the East 50s. I brought Bobby Neuwirth's acoustic guitar, and I played him "Now Is Just a Time," the song I had just written for Richie Havens. Lorber was a short, Napoleonic figure with a gruff, no-nonsense New York attitude. He offered me a deal on the spot. He would be my publisher and pay me an advance against future royalties of $75 a week. Furthermore, when I got another band together, he was ready to cut an album with us. It was an offer I couldn't refuse. I asked Ray to be my manager, he accepted, and we were off to the races.

Tony Scheuren was Ultimate Spinach's road manager. He was a bit halting and lacked social skills, but was extremely talented, as it turned out. He played me a few of his songs on guitar, then a few more on piano. He could play just about any instrument he picked up. He had a good voice and was conventionally good looking—straight blond hair, blue eyes, Nordic features. He could've been a model. We started to collaborate, and it turned out our songwriting talents complimented each other, as did our singing voices. Tony had an idea to write a song about a chameleon-like girl named Camellia who wanted to blend into her surroundings. We called the song "Camellia Is Changing," and almost as an afterthought we decided to call our new band Chamæleon Church (with that antiquated Greek character in there to boot) even though we didn't have a band yet.

Chevy was still vigorously lobbying me to start a band so he could be the drummer, and we had him come to my loft with his drums. He wasn't a great drummer, but he wasn't bad, and the material Tony and I were working on was not that challenging for a drummer. Chevy was also a decent jazz piano player, at least on one song, Bill Evans' "Waltz for Debby." Besides, he was a fall-down-on-the-floor riot, so we hired him.

Tony was ready to get a bass and add that to his already considerable arsenal of instruments. But what we really needed was a lead guitarist.

Amazingly, soon afterward, I was walking along MacDougal Street, and who should I bump into but Kyle Garrahan, my lead guitarist from The Lost. Unbeknownst to me, he too had moved back to New York. So here we were, almost in the same spot where we had first met three years earlier. I asked him what he was doing. He was looking for a gig. I told him about the new band I was forming and about the sure-thing album deal with Lorber and invited him over to the loft to see if he might be the missing piece for this band. Kyle and Chevy got on famously, and Kyle always liked my songs, so he was in.

Kyle was Chevy's greatest audience. Everything Chevy did cracked Kyle up. It cracked all of us up, actually; the guy was insanely funny. The high-jinx continued, regardless of location. We'd be on the subway, and Chevy would sit down next to an attractive woman and, in the impaired voice of a slack-jawed imbecile, would say to her: "Miss, would you please kiss me? I'm dying." Then he would drool a little. We would be watching from across the aisle, trying not to fall on the floor with laughter, as the poor girl would slowly get up and then streak in terror to the other end of the train.

Chevy was involved with an off-off-Broadway repertory company called Channel One. It was the brainchild of a guy named Ken Shapiro, who had been a child TV star in the '50s. They operated out of a small theater on East 4th Street and Second Avenue. The theater was set up with seats in a semi-circle opposite three huge TV monitors, each aimed at a different angle, so everyone in the audience could see at least one of them. In a loft above the theater comedy skits were videotaped—a brand new technology at the time—and the audience would be shown a program of various bits that came off like a live television show. After Chamæleon Church was up and running, Chevy brought us up to the Channel One loft to participate in one of the skits. We played a naked rock band—and we were stark naked, except for our instruments—backing up an over-dressed lead singer, played by Ken, who was decked out in over-the-top fringes, lace and love beads.

One night a bunch of us were at the Channel One theater after it closed. We had been smoking some weed and may have had a few drinks and decided to play hide and seek. There was me, Chevy, Ken and Lane of Channel One, and Chevy's girlfriend, a sweet young actress named Blythe Danner. When Chevy was "it," we all scurried to hide between rows. Blythe and I were huddled on the floor an aisle apart. When Chevy yelled "Ready or not, here I come!" Blythe and I found ourselves holding hands under the theater seats. I can't say what impelled her to reach for my hand under the seat. It was certainly nothing romantic. I think it was more the nervous excitement of being hunted and of hiding, the camaraderie of being the prey, or maybe it was just, like, "Hi, who's that in the next aisle?" Of course, Blythe went on to a stellar career on stage and screen, spanning four decades that continues at the time of this writing. Her daughter, Gwyneth Paltrow, was born five years later and inherited the 'thespian gene,' matching her mother in skill and eclipsing her in fame.

Channel One steadily gained in popularity and eventually moved to a more deluxe location uptown and changed its name to The Groove Tube, which, in turn, was made into a feature film called *The Groove Tube* in 1974, with some of the 1967 bits still intact.

One bit that didn't make it into the movie was "Mr. Happy." Mr. Happy was a little puppet on a kid's TV show. He had two bulging eyes and a round, red nose and he jiggled a bit when he spoke in his high falsetto puppet voice. It usually took the audience about thirty or forty seconds to realize that what they were watching was an upside-down penis with eyes painted on the balls.

* * *

Unlike The Lost, Kyle, Tony and I had a good three-part vocal blend. Tony and I worked up some really beautiful melodic songs that employed a lot of harmonies. I wrote quite a few new ones by myself as well. My new material was softer and more tuneful than most of what I had done with The Lost. As always, The Beatles were chief among my influences, especiallty their softer, more melodic side. Another big influence was the psychedelic experience, a factor that permeated much of the music of that time. But for me, it expressed itself as spirituality and trying to make the world see that we are all one.

"Off With the Old" is an example of this. I wrote it in an open tuning I had discovered that kind of sounded like an Indian sitar and, when we recorded it for our album, there was a sitar on it:

> *Off with the old, on with the new*
> *I've asked for gold, but then I never really knew*
> *That there are some things that shine more than the stars*
> *And we own everything 'cause nothing's really ours*
> *And if you wish for anything that's true*
> *Off with the old, on with the new*

One day Kyle showed up for rehearsal with Joe Butler, the drummer of The Lovin' Spoonful, in tow. Joe jammed with us, at first just picking up a cowbell. But then Chevy moved over to piano and Joe got on drums, and we started to sound really good.

Chamæleon Church in our loft at 76 Jefferson St., NYC (1967). L to R: Tony Scheuren, me, Chevy Chase, Kyle Garrahan.

I was more the boss of Chamæleon Church than I had been of The Lost. I had a vision for this band, and in retrospect I think I may have imposed my will on the others somewhat heavy handedly. I took everyone shopping for clothes. I had us all dressed up in long Edwardian morning coats. Chevy's had a Nehru collar and looked like it was made out of brocaded upholstery fabric. I think he hated it. But everyone went along with my grand design.

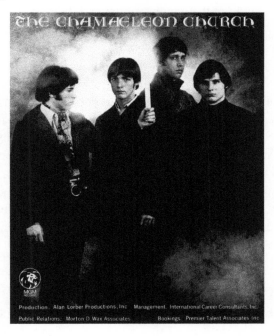

Chamæleon Church in our foppish finery (1968). There is no 'the' in the name of the band, but people put one in anyway.

At this point Eva had moved out of the loft and gotten herself a new office job and a nice one-bedroom apartment on East 7th Street, between Avenues A and B. This block was the southern border of Tompkins Square Park, and the apartment overlooked the park. There were few nicer locations on the Lower East Side. I ostensibly went to see the apartment, and we wound up in bed together. We just couldn't stay away from each other.

Eventually, I moved in with Eva on 7th Street and Kyle stayed in the loft with his girlfriend, Vera, a very smart and beautiful girl, who had been the roommate of a girlfriend I once had in Beacon Hill. I thought a lot of Vera, and she seemed to exert a good influence on Kyle. There were no drug issues in Chamæleon Church, and I attribute this partly to Vera's influence and partly to the fact that none of the rest of us were into hard drugs.

At the apartment on 7th Street Tony and I continued working on writing the album. One grey day we wrote a song called "Tompkins Square Park" while looking out the window at the park below:

> *Lazy day haze, staying indoors in the dark*
> *Watching the maze out there in Tompkins Square Park*

There was one line in the song that mentioned "kids on a bench getting high," but when it came to recording the song, Alan Lorber forbade us from saying the word "high," and we had to change it to "getting by," which made absolutely no sense. This was just one of the many things about Alan Lorber that infuriated us.

Around this time I finally acquired my own acoustic guitar, a Gibson J-50, and what a beautiful-sounding guitar it was. I still have one just like it, and it sounds just as good, but I've played other J-50s that did not sound remotely as good.

* * *

I became quite a scenester in New York, especially during the times when Eva and I would be split up. I met a pair of self-proclaimed groupies, a blond named Cleo and a brunette named Cookie. They made no bones about being groupies, and wouldn't fuck anyone who was not sufficiently famous, and that included me. But they were very friendly and always invited me places. One day in July 1967 they told me about a new club called Salvation that was opening on Sheridan Square in the West Village. It was a scene I just had to make. As it turns out, I'm glad I did, because the band was a new group just over from England, fronted by a black American guitarist named Jimi Hendrix. The Jimi Hendrix Experience made their US club debut that night at the short-lived Salvation. I had never heard electric guitar played like that in my life. My mind was seriously blown. It was all I could talk about for days. Soon afterward Cleo and Cookie made a spoken word album called *The Groupies*, produced by none other than Alan Lorber, which consisted of excerpts from interviews of the girls describing their many sexploits with famous rockers in their comical, Judy Holiday New York voices.

Another place I would hang out was Steve Paul's The Scene on West 46th Street. The house band there was The McCoys, who were managed by Steve Paul, the club's owner. The McCoys were comprised of singer/guitarist Rick Derringer (nee Zehringer), his brother Randy on drums, Randy Hobbs on bass and Ronnie Brandon on keyboards, all very good musicians. They had had a #1 record in 1965 with "Hang On Sloopy." I had actually seen them open for the Rolling Stones in the Boston Garden at that time. Steve Paul also managed a spectacular blues guitarist—an albino named Johnny Winter. The Scene was famous for its spontaneous jam sessions, and one night I stumbled in there just in time to see Johnny Winter, Jimi Hendrix, and Peter Green of Fleetwood Mac, all jamming together onstage. As if that wasn't enough, John Lord of Deep Purple was sitting in on organ.

One night at The Scene, someone pointed out Dino Valenti, the elusive Chester Powers, who had written the song "Get Together," and who was currently singing with Quicksilver Messenger Service, one of the new crop of San Francisco Bay area bands that were making a splash at the time. But what interested me about Dino was the beautiful fringed jacket he was wearing. It was adorned with authentic Indian beadwork and a silver concho with a turquoise in the middle. I had to ask him where he got it. He told me a man named Frank Berry from Sausalito had made it for him.

In my many travels around New York in 1967, my path often intersected with that of a young photographer named Lee Kraft. One night he offered me $50 to pose for a cover photo he was shooting the next day for a book. It turned out to be a pulp fiction novel about working class teens in London called *Up the Junction*. So, at the appointed time, I showed up in my flashiest flowered shirt and posed in a doorway with a red-haired girl who was as cold and unfriendly as she looks in the picture.

My modeling debut (and swansong), 1967. Photo: Lee Kraft

* * *

Procol Harum, a new band from England, was playing a concert in our neighborhood, at the Anderson Theater, another old movie house that had begun presenting rock concerts. It was on Second Avenue, a few blocks south of the Village Theater (soon to be the Fillmore East). I went over there early and, looking like I belonged, just strolled in during the sound check and took a seat. Procol Harum was onstage setting up. And then the most extraordinary thing happened. The road manager yelled out to the scattered group of spectators out front: "Does anybody have a set of drums?" I raised my hand. "I do," I said, without thinking. Chevy's drums were set up in our loft. So I got into a station wagon with the road manager and we drove down to Jefferson Street. We disassembled Chevy's drums and loaded them into the station wagon. I didn't call Chevy and ask permission, for fear he'd refuse. It was too late to back out now. I wondered if Procol Harum relied on being able to borrow a set of drums at every stop on their tour.

Naturally, I got to witness Procol Harum's first appearance in the United States without having to pay. The performance was impressive, especially the epic "A Whiter Shade of Pale," which was beginning to climb the charts at the time. The lead guitarist, Robin Trower, did an interesting thing: to give his guitar a distorted sound, he put it through 2 amps, a small one and then a big one. This created distortion and sustain without excessive volume. After the concert, we loaded Chevy's drums back into the station wagon, along with me, the road manager, and all five members of Procol Harum, and drove back downtown. I did my best to set up the drums like they had been but, alas, some pieces of hardware were missing. Procol Harum had departed without one single word of thanks. Needless to say, Chevy was furious at me for pulling this stunt, but I replaced the hardware and he eventually got over it.

Procol Harum, 1967 (note the foppish Edwardian coat). Photo: IPE Collection

* * *

The best hangout spot in the Village was the Tin Angel on Bleecker Street. One night there in 1968 I kept meeting Canadians. First, I hung with David Clayton Thomas, a singer. He was a cool guy and, although I hadn't heard his music, I got a good feeling about him. A year later he replaced Al Kooper as lead singer for Blood, Sweat & Tears. The first album they made with David won the band the Grammy® Award for Album of the Year. Later that same night I found myself chatting up a tall blond Canadian named Joni Mitchell. She told me she was invited to a rent party and did I want to come along. For those who don't know what a rent party is, it was an old New York tradition. If you were hard up for the rent, you'd throw a party and charge the guests a dollar or two admission so you could raise the rent for that month. Joni and I went to an apartment somewhere in the depths of downtown Manhattan and paid out two dollars each to drink cheap wine and schmooze with a lot of strangers. Joni casually let it drop that one of her songs, "The Circle Game," was the title song on Tom Rush's new album, which also featured two other songs by her, one of them titled "Tin Angel," as well as songs from other undiscovered songwriters like James Taylor and Jackson Browne. I had heard the album and I was duly impressed. This Joni chick was the real thing.

Across the street from the Tin Angel was the Garrick Theater, which was owned by Howard Solomon, who also owned the Café au Go Go, which was right next door. In 1967 Frank Zappa & The Mothers of Invention played a six-month residency at the Garrick. When The Mothers' debut album, *Freak Out!* first appeared in 1966, we played it over and over in the apartment on River Street, so I had to take this rare opportunity to see them live. Zappa was amazing, which I expected, but the opening act was a petite 19-year-old singer-songwriter Zappa had dubbed 'Uncle Meat.' Her real name was Sandy Hurvitz and she was a genuine prodigy. She wrote memorable songs and sang and played piano with a skill way beyond her years. A couple of years later she re-christened herself Essra Mohawk. Talk about near misses, Essra's career reads like a roadmap of 'almost-made-its.' In 1969 she was signed to Reprise Records by Mo Ostin, the original stoker of the "star-maker machinery" Joni Mitchell sang about in "Free Man in Paris." But, in spite of being named by *Rolling Stone* as one of the twenty-five best albums ever made, Essra's first album for Reprise, *Primordial Lovers*, never even made the charts.

After the gig, I walked Uncle Meat (Sandy) home to an apartment in the West Village. I wished her luck and fell out of touch with her for thirty years.

In 1999 Essra visited me in my office at Rhino, hoping to get us to release her long out-of-print Warner Brothers albums. Of course, she had no recollection of me back in 1967, but we renewed our friendship and I lobbied to get Rhino to release those albums and, in 2000, Rhino Handmade, an 'elite' division of Rhino that specialized in limited releases of collectible rarities, released Essra's first three albums.

Sometime in early 1968 Tony bought a 1937 Plymouth. It was navy blue and in cherry condition. Fortunately, Tony had the mechanical skills to keep it running, but I had concerns that he might injure a hand with his constant tinkering, and indeed he did suffer a couple of mishaps that threatened his ability to play. We would tool around New York in this elegant machine, attracting bemused attention wherever we went.

One day, driving around the Village, who should I spot but my junior high first date, Carla Wise. She was all grown up and looking quite pretty, having found a way to manage that unruly hair. We offered her a lift and drove her home, back to Stuyvesant Town, our childhood home, where she had now acquired an apartment of her own near that of her parents. She told us she had become a teacher at the local high school, the same one she had attended. As she got out of the car I thanked her.

"What for?" she asked.

"If you hadn't taken me to that Dick Clark show I might have ended up a bank teller."

* * *

Eva and I explored various spiritual practices. Someone even convinced us to check out Scientology, which was brand new. They gave me a test with two tin cans they called an E-meter. I later learned that it was simply a galvanic skin response test, like a lie detector. They asked me a series of questions and concluded that I was a "socially destructive personality." However, I was not beyond help. For a substantial fee, they were willing to fix me. Did people actually fall for this tripe?

Eventually Eve and I found Swami Satchidananda. He had recently arrived from India, and his supporters had set him up in a large apartment on West End Avenue that was devoid of furniture, except for a few cushions and a raised dais where Swami would address the assembled aspirants. They called it Integral Yoga. 'Swami Satch' was the real deal. This was a man who was a truly evolved spiritual being. No hidden agendas, only bound-less, non-judgmental love for all who approached. The weekly meetings would consist of a short talk, then chanting and meditation. There was never a charge, only a dāna (donation) bowl where people could leave whatever amount they could afford, or nothing. No one was monitoring it.

Being in his presence was a transformative experience. I witnessed firsthand what a human being could attain through the practice of yoga and meditation. I was completely sold and determined to achieve the highest state of consciousness possible for me in this lifetime. Eva and I went to see him as often as we could. One evening Swamiji said he would be giving out mantras and, in an intimate ceremony in a tiny room the size of a closet (in fact, it was intended to be a closet), Swami Satchidananda gave me my personal mantra and told me never to share it with another living soul. I have chanted it every day since, and I have never revealed it to anyone.

Swami Satchidananda. Photo: Dan Nadel

* * *

Eva had introduced me to an ex-boyfriend of hers, Carl Esser, and we be-came friends. Carl was an incredibly creative guy: he was an actor, a writer and played and composed music as well. In 1967 he wrote and recorded an album called *Hip Alice*, an updated version of *Alice in Wonderland*, which retold Lewis Carroll's classic through the comedic lens of the current world of hippies and psychedelics. He got me to play the part of the hookah-smoking caterpillar, who spoke kind of like a stoned Lord Buckley.

Carl lived in a building on 6th Street near Second Avenue, right around the corner from the Fillmore East. One day, coming out of his building, who should I run into coming in, but Ellen and Jack Schroer. It turned out they lived with Jack's brother in the same building. And so Eva and I renewed our friendship with Ellen and Jack.

Not long after this, they moved to Woodstock, a hip, artsy town about a hundred miles north of New York City that was home to many musicians, Bob Dylan among them. Jack had gotten a gig with Van Morrison, who, after the demise of his Ireland-based band Them, had embarked on a solo career in the US. He lived in Woodstock and wanted his band to be located there as well. Van had hit pay dirt right out of the box with his first solo single, "Brown Eyed Girl," which made it to #10 in late 1967. Now Van wanted to form a permanent, working, touring band, and Jack was to be the horn player.

One of the many times Eva and I split up, she went up to Woodstock and stayed with Jack and Ellen for a few days. I followed her up there. We took a long walk, deep into the woods, and there we reaffirmed our love on a bed of leaves. After that we fell out of touch with Jack and Ellen, and I lost track of them for quite a while.

* * *

Alan Lorber lent Chamæleon Church a reel-to-reel tape recorder, which we set up in the loft. As Tony and I would write a new song, we would arrange and rehearse it with the band and then lay down a live demo on tape. I would take the tapes up to Lorber's office, and he would pronounce the songs suitable or unsuitable for inclusion on the album. It was becoming evident that he and I did not see eye-to-eye creatively. I wanted to get an agreement from him that the band—or at least I—would have an equal say in the production of the album. I got a verbal agreement from him that I would be included in all creative decisions, but he would never put anything in writing.

Toward the end of 1967 pre-production was done, and we were ready to begin recording. We recorded at Mayfair Recording Studios at 701 Seventh Avenue, near Times Square. It was Lorber's studio of choice and, at the time, was the only studio with eight-track mixing capability in New York

City. Lorber's recording engineer was Eddie Smith, a jovial, good-natured guy in his mid-fifties. He was a veteran of decades of recording. There was nothing innovative about his engineering. He never tried to get creative; he just did what Lorber told him to do. The best I can say about him is that he was a nice guy and knew his way around this studio. But Lorber and Eddie were both essentially old school. They were trying to transition to the new psychedelic modality in music, but only because they saw dollar signs attached. They were the last gasp of a previous generation of pop music progenitors. They were about as psychedelic as Wayne Newton.

Chamæleon Church recorded twelve tracks, eleven of which appeared on our eponymous debut, all of them written by us. The twelfth track, "Your Golden Love," appeared as the B-side of our first (and only) single, "Camillia Is Changing." At last I had created a full-length album, realizing one of my biggest life goals. Lorber promised to let me know when he would be recording the orchestration and doing the mix. We had vaguely talked about adding some orchestral arrangements—Lorber's specialty—but, obviously, I needed to hear what he had in mind. After all, these were my songs—my best songs ever. I waited by the phone for a couple of weeks, calling and leaving messages for Lorber at frequent intervals. At last Lorber called me back. "Your album's done. Pick it up from my doorman," he said.

"Huh? But you said I would be included in the arrangements and the mix!" I was beside myself, close to tears.

"Don't complain until you've heard it. This is the best work I've ever done," Lorber said, and hung up.

I went uptown to his building and picked up an acetate (an individual vinyl pressing) of the album from his doorman. I assembled the band and, tremulously, we put it on the turntable. What we heard made us all physically ill. Everything was mush. There was no clarity, no edge, no punchy bass, almost no drums at all. Practically every sound on the recording was washed in deep echo and reverb. There were weird, repeating echo effects and backward envelopes—Lorber's idea of psychedelic effects, but they sounded random, external, done without purpose or understanding. To us, it just sounded like mush. There was all kinds of orchestral instrumentation, but none of it resembled any of what I or Tony had in mind for our songs. All I could think was: *There go twelve of the best songs I ever wrote, down the drain.* Lorber had betrayed us, and there was nothing we could do.

We beseeched him to go back in with us and redo the mix, but he wouldn't hear of it. This album had cost a whopping $25,000 and not a cent more would be spent. He was sure we would eventually grow to appreciate the great job he had done.

The album was released in April 1968 to tepid reviews. All *Billboard* magazine, which never pans a record, could muster was to call it "pleasant."

Lorber had gotten us a spot on a TV special called *Preview*, which starred Dionne Warwick and some other new music acts. We went to ABC studios to tape the show the first week in April. We lip synched "Camellia Is Changing" and we got to watch it at Vera's parents' house in New Jersey when it aired on Easter Sunday, April 14, 1968.

Tony and Chevy, wearing makeup bibs, set up on the set of ABC TV's
Preview, April 1968

Many years later, I was interviewed on an Internet radio show called *Now Sounds*, hosted by Steve Stanley. This show caters to a growing niche audience of '60s psych fans. This is a relatively small group, but very passionate about the music of that era. *Now Sounds* targets an even smaller subgroup of fans, who are into the softer, loungier psychedelic rock and pop of the late '60s. Steve told me he thought *Chamœleon Church* was one of the greatest albums of the decade.

Trying to listen to it through his ears, and with the added objectivity that time affords, I think I can see some of what Lorber might have been going for. The excessive echo and watery instrumental tracks give the album a dreamy, ethereal quality, which is consistent with a lot of the songwriting. Tony and I had a strong preconception of what we wanted the album to sound like: we wanted *Sgt. Pepper's*. But we didn't play like The Beatles, and we didn't sing like The Beatles, and we could hardly blame Lorber for that. Instead of going head-to-head with The Beatles, Lorber went in a completely different direction and, although heavily flawed, the album does sound quite unique. It's very hard for an artist to remove himself and his ego from his work, but after all these years, I've tried to do that with my early work, and I've achieved some level of reconciliation with it.

At the time, *Chamœleon Church* received no traction from radio and got little-to-no support from MGM Records, the label on which Lorber released all his productions. It sank like a stone upon release.

Meanwhile, Ray Paret's other group, Ultimate Spinach, also produced by Lorber, were doing great. Their debut album had reached #34 on *Billboard's* Top LPs chart in February of 1968 and had reportedly sold in the neighborhood of 100,000 albums. I was really happy for my friend Ray, but frankly the music of Spinach was not really my cup of tea. While I was very much of the British Invasion school of melodic songwriting, Ultimate Spinach was more in the mold of the San Francisco psychedelic sound, with a lot of classical references and long, rambling instrumental sections. The music sounded very cerebral to me and, frankly, somewhat pretentious.

In early 1968 Ray invited me to the studio of none other than Richard Avedon, the world's most celebrated photographer, having achieved widespread fame for his series of portraits of The Beatles. He was shooting the album cover for the second Ultimate Spinach album, which was due to come out later that year.

Ray told us he could get us gigs in the Boston area and suggested we move up there. I was on the outs with Eva and saw New York as turning into something squalid and horrific in 1968. Violent crime and hard drugs were on the rise. The Lower East Side was going to hell in a hand basket. Tony and I both wanted to move back to Boston. Kyle and Chevy were not enthusiastic about the idea, but we talked them into giving it a try.

Chapter Eighteen

Boston Again

Ray Paret lived in an elegant, three-story wood frame house on Eastman Circle in Wellesley, Massachusetts, a suburb about fifteen miles southwest of Boston. It was one of those big, gabled affairs that had been constructed in the early '20s and had once been a sorority house for a now-defunct girls' boarding school. Wellesley College, of course, was a famous girls' college that was still going strong, but apparently there had been another school, a secondary school for girls in Wellesley, that had gone belly-up. Eastman Circle was a little, one-way horseshoe road that entered and exited onto Worcester Street, a main thoroughfare. There were only a few houses, and all on the right side of the street. On the left, in the center of the horseshoe, was a modest green with a few stately old oak trees.

Ray shared the house with Richard Griggs, a songwriter, guitarist and sometime-member of The Ill Wind, a psychedelic folk rock band signed to ABC Records that had the rare distinction of being produced by Tom Wilson, a legendary record producer whose production credits included Bob Dylan, Simon & Garfunkel and The Mothers of Invention. In fact, in May 1968, just before I left New York, Ray and some of the Ill Wind brought me up to a studio to witness a Tom Wilson mixing session. He was a very affable guy, friendly and happy to show me some of his tricks. They were mixing "Sky Pilot," which would be the last hit single by The Animals. The engineer was creating an amazing effect by manipulating the tape as it passed through the playback head. It was a pleasing 'whooshing' sound, like wind whistling through a mountain pass. They called it 'flanging' or 'phase shifting' and it would eventually become a ubiquitous sound used on many recordings in the future, but this was the first intentional use of it on a record.

There had been some previous roommates at Eastman Circle who had moved out, so Richard and his girlfriend Ellie were Ray's only roommates in this mansion-sized dwelling. Ray invited all the members of Chamæleon Church to move in there with him, but only Tony and I took him up on it. Chevy and Kyle opted to get accommodations in Boston. Other members of The Ill Wind lived in a similar house next door. It was a little hippie colony tucked away on this secret horseshoe lane in white-bread, straight-laced Wellesley.

Chamæleon Church played several live gigs in and around Boston. The first one was a three-night stand at a club on Boylston Street called the Catacombs. I recall the sets going painfully slowly, because everyone but me had to change instruments practically between every song. Tony played guitar on some songs, keyboard on some and bass on some. Kyle rotated between all those and also played drums on one song. Chevy went to keyboards on one song and stood up and sang lead on one as well. While an impressive display of virtuosity, this proved incredibly ungainly for live performances.

Our second show was at a love-in on Cambridge Common in June of 1968. Another band that was produced by Alan Lorber, Orpheus, shared the bill with us. Their single, "Can't Find the Time," was getting a lot of airplay on Boston radio and was currently 'bubbling under' the *Billboard Hot 100* chart at #111. In yet another quirk of music biz fate, it would reach #80 more than a year later, in August 1969. But even odder was that the song was covered by Hootie & The Blowfish in 2000 and appears on the soundtrack album for the movie *Me, Myself and Irene*. Now if that isn't pure capricious serendipity, I don't know what is.

I remember that concert as a celebration of peace, love and flowers, even though it was the summer *after* the Summer of Love. I took a snapshot of my friends Woody and Renee and their baby that day that epitomizes the loving vibe of the time. Rumor had it that Renee was the girl who had inspired the hit song "Walk Away Renee" by The Left Banke and, upon subsequent research, I was able to confirm that it was true. Not hard to believe, looking at her...

Woody, Renee, and baby, Cambridge Common, 1968

Chamæleon Church played one more gig. This was well into the summer of 1968. It was an outdoor concert in a high school football stadium in Waltham, Massachusetts, a town a few miles north of Wellesley. We were starting to get more confident about our live presentation and had the changing instruments thing pretty much down. One of the high points of our show was when we let Chevy step out front and take the mic as lead singer. Kyle got behind the drums, and the rest of us vamped on a simple R&B riff that sounded kind of like "Hip Hug-Her" by Booker T. & The MG's, while Chevy just took off, saying whatever came into his head, and believe me, it was funny. Only sometimes it was also kind of outrageous, and this small town was not ready for what Chevy was about to put down that day…

> *I would really like to smell your… underpants*
> *I would like very much to smell your… underpants…*
> *You spilled my grass; I'm gonna make you eat it!*

…and so on. After that, the town fathers of Waltham made it clear we would never play their town again. The fact was, we would never play any town again. Shortly after that, Chevy and Kyle decided to move back to New York, effectively disbanding Chamæleon Church.

Tony and I stayed on in bucolic Wellesley and kept writing songs together.

Chevy, of course, went on to fame and fortune as a member of the original Not Ready for Prime Time Players on the first season of *Saturday Night Live* and then a lucrative film career. I ran into him again in the early '70s when I moved to LA. By then he had a successful career, writing comedy material for the likes of the Smothers Brothers, but he was not very friendly to his less-successful comrades of days gone by. It was as if lack of success was a communicable disease and he was scared of catching it. One time I asked him to read a script I was working on—he flatly refused. In a further display of mean-spiritedness, when interviewed in 1990 by Barbara Walters after the Oscars, she asked him about the rock band he had once belonged to. He replied, "We wore faggy little suits and sang faggy little songs."

Wow!

* * *

In the summer of 1968 we watched the riots at the Democratic National Convention on TV, with the Chicago cops bashing in the heads of peaceful student demonstrators, while the kids chanted, "The whole world is watching, the whole world is watching." And Tony and I wrote "The World Has Just Begun." In the opening scene we depict a victory parade for a political candidate (we were picturing Nixon)…

> *I can hear the cymbals crashing*
> *As the brass plays down the street*
> *I can see the waves of people*
> *Reaching out to touch his feet*
> *And as the wave comes crashing down*
> *To drown the noonday sun*
> *No one can deny it now*
> *The world has just begun*

When we recorded the song it ended with the sounds of a riot and people chanting, "The whole world is watching."

During my time in Wellesley I had been in fairly constant touch with Eva. We had been apart for a few months and that was about as much as either one of us could take. I told her about the beautiful house we lived in and how peaceful our life was, and I finally convinced her to come up there. After a couple of exploratory visits, she moved back in with me.

L to R: Tony, me, and Eva play *Bonnie and Clyde* on Tony's car, 1968.

Chapter Nineteen

Ultimate Spinach

Ultimate Spinach was the brainchild of one Ian Bruce-Douglas. After the success of their debut album and extensive touring, the band went into the studio to record their second album. At this point Ian fired his drummer, replacing him with Russ Levine, but kept the rest of the personnel essentially intact. I guess it was during the making of *Behold & See*—the somewhat redundant title of their second album—that things started to unravel. According to Ray and band members, Ian was spouting off with inappropriate and embarrassing diatribes during gigs. Russ remembers him as "the most egotistical maniac I have ever come in contact with." During the *Behold & See* sessions Ian created such bad feelings within the band that some members started cracking up. The guitarist and the bass player were next to leave. But Ian kept on. He hired Jeff "Skunk" Baxter on lead guitar and Mike Levine on bass. His erratic behavior continued and ultimately (pun intended), Ray, Alan Lorber and the new lineup of the band decided Ian had to go. In September 1968 Ian was fired by his band. He was last seen going down the elevator at Amphion Management, hurling abuse and nasty epithets at his former bandmates.

Tony and I, who were now gigless and living with Ray in Wellesley, suddenly became the logical candidates to replace Ian because: 1) we were still under contract to Lorber, with an obligation to deliver at least one more album, 2) Tony played keyboards (Ian's main instrument), 3) we were both competent lead singers and 4) we both wrote prolifically—and a new album's worth of material was what they needed. And so, less than a week after Ian's departure, Tony and I were inducted into Ultimate Spinach, to form the third and final permutation of the band. We set about rehearsing with the latest lineup and writing material that would comprise the third album. The only member of Ultimate Spinach who survived all the purges was Barbara Hudson, a soft-spoken, shy girl with long dark hair and a sweet if innocuous soprano voice. She played rhythm guitar.

Ultimate Spinach III in our rehearsal studio. L to R: Tony Scheuren, Russ Levine, Mike Levine, me, Jeff "Skunk" Baxter, Barbara Hudson

As soon as we started rehearsing we learned that we had a gig at the Commodore Ballroom in Lowell, Massachusetts that was coming up in just one week. We had to rehearse several of Ian's songs off the first album along with the new crop of originals. The night of the gig, all the band members, along with our roadie, Kelly (Bob Keleher) and assistant roadie, young Billy Pollard, piled into a van with all the equipment. There wasn't enough room for all of us, so Russ Levine and I volunteered to drive up in Russ's car.

When we arrived at the ballroom, Russ and I were told there had been a serious accident with the van, and were directed to a nearby hospital. There had been a blowout in one of the front tires at high speed and the van had flipped over. Several of the band members were injured, though none seriously. But twenty-one-year-old Billy Pollard, who had been riding shotgun, was thrown through the windshield and paralyzed from the waist down for the rest of his life.

* * *

For me and Tony, going back into the studio with Alan Lorber was a case of "once bitten, twice shy." Before we even agreed to join the band, and with Ray Paret backing us up, we had extracted some very specific conditions from Alan Lorber: 1) the drums would be properly recorded and present, 2) likewise with the bass and 3) we had approval of the mix. If we didn't like it, he would have to go back and do it again with us present.

We recorded the third Ultimate Spinach album at Mayfair in New York from December 2 to December 11, 1968. We didn't encounter the same production conflicts we had on Chamæleon Church, but there was another problem. Mike Levine was not cutting it on bass. This was something that had been apparent to me from the first rehearsal, but as the new member of the band I was loathe to say anything. However, as we got into recording the basic tracks, it became plain to everyone. It was a shame, but it couldn't be helped; we had to let Mike go, and we needed a new bass player pronto! It just so happened that our new assistant roadie, Tom Caulfield, was also a bass player. We tried him out and he was amazing. So Tom was hired on the spot and it's his bass we hear on the album. There were a few good songs on that album, but to be perfectly honest, I never felt this band was truly my baby, the way I had with my first two bands. I think, to both Tony and me, this was really more or less a 'bread and butter gig,' something we did to pay the bills.

When the album was completed, I suggested what I thought was a great title: *A New Leaf* (the first Spinach album had a big spinach leaf on the cover). But, in their infinite wisdom, Lorber and MGM Records decided to simply call the album *Ultimate Spinach*, which was the same title as the first album. Maybe they were hoping that people would buy this one by mistake.

Sometime in early 1969 Eva took off again, this time for the West Coast, a scene I was dying to make. But Spinach had a series of local gigs in the Boston area lined up, followed by a tour. In January 1969 we all piled into a station wagon and, towing a U-Haul trailer loaded with our gear, drove almost the entire length of the East Coast to St. Petersburg, Florida.

The weather in St. Petersburg was a lot balmier than it had been in Boston, but it was overcast and muggy. We played at the biggest club in the Tampa-St. Petersburg area, and there were girls, lots of them, clustered around the stage. After the gig we were besieged by tempting offers. I took off with an older one (she was at least out of her teens), who drove a Thunderbird and had a nice house she had won in a divorce settlement. When I rendezvoused with the rest of the band at the motel the next day, I was regaled by outrageous tales of women invading their hotel room and waking them up in the middle of the night by some unique means—which I will leave to the reader's imagination.

The next stop on our winter tour was Wichita, Kansas. I'm really not sure who planned the logistics of this trek, but I was pretty sure it was not anybody who was on it. By now it was very clear that we were not going to drive the station wagon pulling the trailer from St. Petersburg to Wichita, so we put the equipment in a truck and had Kelly—who was the quintessential road manager, always professional, always cheerful, never complaining— drive the equipment while the band took the train. We were booked to open at the Municipal Auditorium for The Ohio Express, a bubble gum group who were still riding on their hit of the previous spring, "Yummy Yummy Yummy."

We arrived in Wichita on the heels of their biggest blizzard in twenty years. The streets were waist deep in snow, and it was nothing short of a miracle that we were able to make it from the train station to the auditorium. Even more amazing was that Kelly was also able to get there with the equipment. Less surprising was the fact the The Ohio Express had cancelled because of the extreme weather. But we soldiered on. There were about fifteen people in the audience in a hall that held 3,000. We got up there and played our set anyway. We made it into a party for the few brave souls who had come out by inviting them up onto the stage and having them sing along and play tambourines and shakers.

The next stop on the tour was a two-week residency at a club in Aspen, Colorado, winter playground of the jet set. We took another train from Wichita to Denver, and then a small plane for the final leg into Aspen. I had done something to my back throwing a suitcase up onto the train, something

I had never experienced before. My first ever taste of physical vulnerability. The Aspen gig was cool, but would have been a lot cooler had I not thrown my back out. It gave me unending trouble. One thing I remember about Aspen was that there was another band playing up the street whose male lead singer went under the odd moniker 'Alice Cooper.' Rumor had it that Frank Zappa had dubbed him 'Alice,' and, after 'Uncle Meat,' nothing that Frank came up with would surprise me.

I was disappointed that we came that far west and didn't get to the West Coast. Of course, stories of the hippie explosion in California had been filling the media, both underground and mainstream. I was dying to check it out, especially San Francisco, before the bubble burst. And San Francisco was where Eva was.

PART 2 – WEST COAST

Chapter Twenty

Can't Keep Tomorrow Waitin'

Not long after we got back to Boston, several members of Ultimate Spinach—Jeff Baxter, Kelly, Tom and Barbara—were busted for pot in an apartment on Beacon Street. In those days in Boston it was a big deal even if you were merely present where pot was being smoked and, in fact, they were charged with "being present where narcotics were found." There was rampant publicity and a major legal kafuffle, the ripples of which spread far and wide.

'Spinach' Members, 9 Others Held in Back Bay Drug Raid

Four members of the well-known rock group "The Ultimate Spinach," plus nine other persons including three girls were held in $1000 bail each on arraignment in Roxbury District Court Wednesday as a result of a drug raid at 907 Beacon st., Back Bay.

All pleaded innocent to charges of possessing marijuana and other drugs or being present where Boston and MDC police confiscated an estimated $5000 worth of contraband.

Judge Charles I. Taylor continued the cases for hearing on March 24.

Members of the Ultimate Spinach group charged with being present where narcotics were found were Robert F. Kelleher, 22, of 65 Moreland st., West Roxbury, identified as the manager; Thomas G. Caulfield, 17, of Revere Beach Blvd., Revere, bass player; Jeffrey A. Baxter, 20, a tenant of the raided house, a guitarist, and singer Barbara J. Hudson, 19, of Malden st., Everett.

Charged with illegal possession of amrijuana were Mark A. Lockwood, 22, of Van St., Worcester; Brian Stevens, 18, of Brush Hill Rd., Milton, and Alan Rotman, 25, of the Beacon St. address.

Others charged with being present were Michael O'Connor, 18, of the Beacon St. address; Donald W. Ballam, 22, giving an address in Essex, Eng.; William Madison, 24, of Kingston, R. I.; Harriet Meeker, 20, of 901 Beacon St., and two juveniles, including a girl.

I took this as a sign. It was time for me to check out the West Coast. And so, with nothing but my acoustic guitar and one suitcase, I grabbed a plane for San Francisco. I told Ray and Tony I would be back in about two weeks. The last song I wrote before my departure was a country rock piece called "Ballad of a Naked Loser":

> *Can't keep tomorrow waitin'*
> *Leave this life behind*
> *Colors that will blind you 700 times*
> *I wish that I could circle 'round*
> *And catch it from behind*
> *But when I looked to find you were gone*

* * *

Aside from Eva, the only friend I had living in the Bay Area was a girl named Judy Miller. Judy was a folk singer with long dark hair who played and sang in the style of Joan Baez and whom I had met in Cambridge in 1966. She was living in Berkeley and said I was welcome to stay at her apartment. So, in mid-April 1969, I landed in Oakland and headed for Berkeley.

Berkeley was one of the hippie epicenters in the Bay Area, the others being Haight-Ashbury and Sausalito. Telegraph Avenue, a bustling artery lined with quaint shops and cafés, ran south from the campus of U.C. Berkeley. This was the street where everyone congregated: street people, vendors, buskers, college students, drug addicts and mimes. After taking in the sights, I meandered over to Judy's house a few blocks away.

From the very first, I loved the free and easy vibe of California. You could hitchhike anywhere, and people would always pick you up. It was open, friendly and laid back. The weather was beautiful and I was eager to explore. My first foray was to Marin County to find Frank Berry, the leather craftsman who had made Dino Valenti's fringed jacket. He had moved from Sausalito to Fairfax, where he had a store and workshop in a little wood frame cottage. All his jackets were made to order, and to have one made cost a fortune, especially one like the one I wanted, with beads and a concho. But, as luck would have it, Frank had one jacket that he had made for someone who had not picked it up. It had the requisite beadwork and concho. I tried it on and it fit me perfectly. Mine for $50. My California trip had begun auspiciously.

That night I went to San Francisco to the Avalon Ballroom and heard The Grateful Dead and saw a spectacular light show. Out on the dance floor people were passing around a hash pipe and I joined one group of merry-makers that included a beautiful blond flowerchild named Star who couldn't have been out of her teens, a blue-eyed hippie princess if ever there was one. She gave me some acid and told me to come along with her tribe. They piled into a car and, late that night, I found myself tripping my brains out, wandering through the wooded hillsides of Mill Valley with Star. We lay on the ground, staring up at the sky and swearing undying love until the stars faded. At dawn some people drove me back to Berkeley, and I never saw her again.

Later that day I wrote my first song in California. It was called "Let It Shine." I wrote it with Star in mind (knowing I would never see her again), but I based the lyric on an old Irish folk blessing I had seen on bus placards in New York City that starts: "May the road rise up to meet you, may the wind be always at your back..."

May the sun shine warm upon your face
May the stars shine brightly all your days
And seasons spin madly on bands of time
And take good care to let it shine

Judy Miller was a nice person; very smart and quite attractive. But we were not cut out to be lovers. As soon as I did it, I realized that sleeping with her was a mistake. I stayed with her just a couple of nights, but after our one sexual encounter, it became uncomfortable. I thanked her for her hospitality and moved out.

The Berkeley Inn was a low-rent hotel at the corner of Telegraph and Haste in the heart of the hippie zone. It was a big, old brick building that was probably unchanged, inside and out, since the 1940s. It was populated by a colorful assortment of characters from transients to artists to writers. Mrs. Radcliffe was the day manager, a thin, arid woman in her mid-fifties with died brown hair and a brusque-yet-friendly manner. She showed me to a third floor corner room that had windows on two sides looking out at a vacant lot across the street where the street people had started cultivating vegetables, trees and flowers. They called it the People's Park.

Soon after I checked into the Berkeley Inn I met Ron, a tall guy in his late twenties from Brooklyn, New York. Ron was ensconced in a room just down the hall. He had long, thinning black hair and olive skin, and a slightly droopy posture that made him look like a giant question mark. He liked to dress all in black and wore a broad-brimmed black hat, perhaps because he was self-conscious about his balding. He was extremely near-sighted and wore prescription shades with coke-bottle lenses that made his dark eyes look huge. His manner of speech and sense of humor reminded me of my New York City roots and made me feel right at home. He told me he had dropped out of the University of Chicago post-graduate program after getting a Masters in psychology. He had changed his mind about being a shrink; he now had decided to write children's books and song lyrics. He was collaborating on songs with a folk/country singer/guitarist at the inn named David Novo, a son of migrant Mexican farm workers from a small town in the San Joaquin Valley. I found out Dave had a reel-to-reel Wallensak tape recorder, and he offered to let me borrow it to record a few of my latest songs.

By the time I had been at the Berkeley Inn a week, I had written several more songs, plus I had a few I had written back east that I hadn't recorded yet, so I holed up in my room and laid down track after track. California was stimulating my creative juices, and I decided to stay a little longer than the originally planned two weeks.

Ron and Dave were duly impressed by my output, and Ron privately asked me if I might want to try to put music to some of his lyrics. "Why not?" I quipped. "This is California!" And so Ron DeZure and I began a personal and professional collaboration that was to last many years.

I don't know why I hadn't called Eva yet. I had now been in Berkeley for more than three weeks, and even though she was just across the bay in the City, it seemed like too huge a gulf to bridge. Maybe I was thinking of the old Albert Einstein quote that says insanity is when you do the same stupid thing over and over again, each time expecting a different result.

On May 15, 1969 the street outside my window exploded in a maelstrom of tear gas, rocks, bottles and gunshots. The People's Park riots had begun. It seems this large vacant lot across the street belonged to the University of California. It had become a wasteland of abandoned cars, garbage and homeless squatters. Then the street people decided to clear away the unsightly debris and cultivate the land. Now it had trees, flowers and vegetable gardens. The Telegraph Avenue merchants were delighted; a neighborhood blight had been replaced with a lovely garden. But the UC Regents threatened to shut it down. There were meetings and discussions. The Regents agreed to do nothing for now. Then Ronald Reagan, the Governor of California, saw a chance to play to his far-right constituency. He preemptively had the park bulldozed, put up a chain link fence and called in the state troopers and county sheriffs to keep the hippies out. To him and his crowd, the hippie takeover of the park smelled way too much like communism, a blatant assault on the sacred American right to private property.

On May 15th there was a rally attended by about 3,000 people in Sproul Plaza on the Berkeley campus. The original purpose was to discuss the Arab-Israeli conflict, but when somebody yelled, "Let's take back the park!" an army of students started south on Telegraph, heading for Haste Street.

In the resulting melee, a couple of students were shot, one fatally, one person was permanently blinded and more than a hundred people were admitted to the local hospital with injuries. It was reported that the cops were out of control, shooting at people who posed no threat. There were news camera crews filming it all—from my window! For days afterward, no one in the Berkeley Inn could go out and come back in without showing a room key to the military guards that had the streets cordoned off in every direction.

The People's Park Riots

All of this brought home to me the eerie reality that, in California, there were radical extremes living in close proximity to each other and the whole place could go up like a powder keg at any moment. Living in a place like Berkeley, or anywhere in the Bay Area for that matter, one could easily get lulled into the belief that everyone in California was cool. But nothing could be further from the truth; it was a majority of right wing voters that put Reagan in office, and he ran on the platform of zero tolerance for demonstrators.

In the end, the People's Park was restored and given back to the people of Berkeley, although it took nearly a decade.

For maybe a week, Berkeley became a no-man's land, with police and soldiers everywhere, harassing and attacking citizens. I decided this would be a good time to visit Eva. When I heard her voice on the phone, my whole being was instantly flooded with that warm heroin rush of unreasoning love. She told me to come over right away.

Eva had a knack—and great karma—for finding great apartments. Her place on Douglass Street in the Castro was no exception. It wasn't large, but like all her places, it was immaculate and beautifully appointed. It was high on a hill overlooking Market Street. There was a nice view of the hills to the west that lit up and twinkled at night.

As soon as we saw each other that overpowering chemistry kicked in and we fell into bed. Another cycle had begun.

I moved out of the Berkeley Inn and in with Eva. We tried to start anew as a married couple. I even got a job with a private mail delivery service that picked up mail from the post office and delivered to some of the big businesses downtown who needed to get their mail earlier than the post office would deliver. I worked for Mr. Clemens, a sinewy old man with white hair and pink skin. He was one of those stoic old Americans who say little and are the opposite of obsequious. I schlepped the huge mail sacks from the truck to the various mailrooms cheerfully, but after a couple of weeks, Mr. Clemens told me my job was over. It seems I was just filling in for his regular helper, who had been on vacation—a minor detail he had not explained to me.

I brought Eva over to Berkeley to meet Ron. The three of us went tripping around together on several occasions. Once we went to the Fillmore to see The Who. They were performing excerpts from Pete Townshend's new rock opera, *Tommy*.

The Who at the Fillmore West, June 17, 1969

Eva and I also witnessed an early demonstration of the Moog synthesizer by Dr. Robert Moog at a San Francisco theater that spring. It had massive patch bays that looked like the switchboards used by telephone operators. Although it had been used on a few rock recordings, I had never really been aware of the vast range of sounds this machine could produce.

Moog even showed a sequencing feature that enabled the thing to play a sequence of notes over and over automatically, while another melody was played over it.

Ron was not favorably impressed with Eva. To him, she seemed abrasive, pushy and overbearing. As a psych major, he thought she was unbalanced. Seeing her through his eyes, I began to think he might be right. All these years I thought I was the crazy one who couldn't sustain a relationship, or at least I was as much to blame as she for our failures. I realized I was probably incapable of monogamy, but I wasn't psychotic. Next to Eva, I began to feel downright sane. And I began to move away from her.

While in San Francisco and Berkeley I played a couple of live acoustic gigs in local coffee houses, my first solo acoustic performances. I mostly performed songs from my new acoustic repertoire, which was growing rapidly. I made an appointment to see a record producer named David Rubinson, who was running Bill Graham's Fillmore Records. I played him my tape and he started "correcting" my chord changes: "Oh, now, you see, that one's wrong..." WRONG? How can somebody tell you the chords are wrong in your own song? Well, obviously this was not the company for me. But it turned out they were the only game in town. Pretty much all the record companies and all the music publishers were in LA. San Francisco had lots of bands and performance venues, but really no music *industry*. I discussed this with Ron and we decided to make a preliminary reconnaissance mission to LA with an eye toward possibly moving there.

Once again, I moved out of Eva's. But this time it was somehow different. I felt free of her spell. For the first time I could imagine the rest of my life without her. I snuck back into the Berkeley Inn. Dave and Ron somehow got me a key to a vacant room without the knowledge or consent of Mrs. Radcliffe. There was a night manager; a slinky mustachioed little guy named Greg, who was cool—or who, at least, would not give me away. I holed up in this clandestine chamber for several days, occasionally adding more songs to my ever-growing collection of demos.

Chapter Twenty-One

Goin' South

The first place Ron and I went in SoCal was to visit a girl I had met in Boston named Anita. She was a friend of Ray Paret's and was one of two people in Southern California whose number I had. I called her and she said, "Sure, c'mon down!" She lived in Santa Ana, Orange County. We took a couple of buses, the second of which deposited us in the middle of what appeared to be an endless shopping mall. There were low, non-descript buildings along wide noisy streets seething with traffic in every direction. We looked at each other. "This is a *city*?" We had never seen anything like this in our lives. The air was gray with smog and smelled like exhaust fumes and burnt rubber. And there were no people walking on the streets.

Anita finally came and picked us up at the bus station. She was a pudgy girl with straight blond hair cut short. She had to go right home, as she and two of her friends were going to a big concert that night at a local stadium. I think it was Creedence Clearwater Revival. Ron and I didn't have tickets and Anita wasn't going to leave us alone at her place, so we got to sit in her car outside the stadium for four hours while she and her two friends went to the concert.

The next day we got Anita to drive us to Hollywood. We had no idea about the vast distances that encompassed Southern California, and now we realized just how far from the mark we really were. Once in Hollywood, we drove up and down Sunset Strip and spotted several big record companies and music publishers right away. So we had Anita drive us to a motel on Sunset and we checked in. Over the next two days we were able to walk into the offices of no fewer than four music publishers and two record labels. We had no appointments; we just said we were in town for two days only and we needed to see so-and-so to play him our tape, and most of the time, someone would see us. And he would sit and listen to my tape right then and there. One of the people we saw was Jimmy Webb's father, who ran the office of his publishing company on the Strip.

Nobody offered me a deal, but we knew our chances of getting a deal were better here than up north. We headed back to Berkeley and started packing. We realized we would need a car. Ron had a few hundred dollars saved and he agreed to spring for the vehicle, although neither one of us had a driver's license. I had driven the Saab and some other vehicles back east a few times, so I would be the designated driver. But first we needed a car. We checked out a few possibilities and settled on a black 1962 Morris Minor in immaculate condition. The body was, anyway. We bought it for $400. I took the driving test at the DMV and passed. I had to hole up in hiding at the Berkeley Inn for the week or so it took to receive my license and the registration for the car, but as soon as we got it, we crammed everything we owned and then some into that little car and hit the road for LA.

On arrival we went straight to the UCLA campus. A guy in Berkeley had told us that, given that it was summer, it should be easy for us to get free accommodations at UCLA by going to Weyburn Hall, a large student housing facility, and telling them we were visiting students from UC Berkeley and we were considering transferring to UCLA. We parked the car at Le Conte Avenue and Westwood Boulevard, the entrance to the UCLA campus, and decided to get out and find someone who could direct us to Weyburn.

No sooner did we emerge from the Morris, than I heard someone call Ron's name. She was an attractive blond in her late twenties, not slim, but pleasingly buxom. She looked like a farm girl from Michigan, which, as it turns out, is exactly what she was. Ron couldn't believe his eyes.

"Diana!" he cried.

"Ron DeZure! What are you doing here?"

Ron introduced me to Diana as a former classmate of his at the University of Chicago—a sociology major—and we explained to her our decision to move to LA.

"I'm just on my way to Warren's office," she said.

Warren was her husband, also a former classmate of Ron's and now a professor of sociology at UCLA.

"Why don't you come with me? I know he'd love to see you."

"Yeah, that sounds great," Ron said. "We're trying to find Weyburn Hall. Know where it is?"

She pointed to a tall, nondescript modern building, looming over all the others, about a block away. This was working out well.

We walked across the campus, which was quite large and impressive. Warren's office was in one of the older, more stately halls that lined a wide promenade that also contained Royce Hall, a large auditorium where they frequently held concerts.

Warren was a quirky guy. He was thin and taut, sharp as a tack, but with an odd sort of wit that not everyone appreciated. He was very pale, about thirty, but looked thirty-five, with brown hair and eyes and he spoke with the short, clipped accent of the Midwest. Diana had it too, but not as pronounced.

"Holy shit, Ron DeZure!" he exclaimed upon seeing Ron walk into his office. Diana introduced me, and we filled him in on the circumstances surrounding this colossal coincidence. We told him of our plan to obtain free accommodations by impersonating Berkeley students. Warren laughed. He heartily approved of anything flaunting the establishment. Politically he was somewhere to the left of Che Guevara.

Diana suggested we have dinner with them. We readily agreed, still amazed at our great good fortune to have run into these two amiable and well-established people when we knew absolutely no one in LA. Diana told us they lived in Laurel Canyon and wrote out driving directions.

Our next stop was Weyburn Hall, where, as predicted, we obtained first class accommodations rent-free. We moved all our stuff up to the spacious double room and got cleaned up for our evening out.

As we wound our way up Laurel Canyon Boulevard, I immediately fell in love with the Hollywood Hills. What a contrast from the rest of ugly, smoggy LA. The winding, hilly maze of narrow streets looked to me like something out of Disneyland. I kept thinking of that Mammas & Poppas song: "Young girls are coming to the canyon..."

"This is it," I said, "This is where we're gonna live."

Warren and Diana's house was way up Lookout Mountain Avenue, a street that branched off Laurel Canyon Boulevard about a mile up from Sunset. It was modern and beautifully designed, straddling a steep hillside, as were many houses in the canyon. It had a living room, kitchen, master bedroom and bath as well as a big outside balcony on the top level where you entered, and two smaller bedrooms, a bathroom and a lower balcony on the floor below. On the lowest level, nestled in a hollow in the canyon, was a big yard, which had been cemented over and made into a basketball court. It had been designed by a fairly well known California architect, whose name now escapes me. Diana and Warren had a little boy about two, but he was already asleep by the time we arrived.

Besides being an excellent cook, Diana had a sweet, warm, welcoming quality that immediately put us at ease. The preamble to dinner was a couple of joints of high quality marijuana. Oh yeah, maybe LA was gonna be okay after all.

Dinner was *coq au vin*, one of Diana's specialties. I had brought my guitar and, after dinner, played them a few of my original tunes. That went over well, and I felt we were now being welcomed into a warm familial circle.

The very next day we set about trying to find a place to rent in Laurel Canyon. After a few days of driving through the labyrinth of streets, trails and cul-de-sacs of the canyon, we found the perfect place: it was a cute one-bedroom house on Kirkwood Drive, about a half-mile south of Lookout Mountain. The house had just a single bedroom, as well as a living room, kitchen and two bathrooms, but there was a two-car garage and a big backyard and—behind the garage—there was a long narrow room, just big enough to be Ron's bedroom. I got the bedroom in the house and Ron was happy to have his little hideaway, separated from the house. Ron was a bit of a recluse at heart. The rent was $175 a month. A bit steep, but we managed to scrape it up.

The problem with owning a car was that you had to keep putting stuff into it. Gasoline I knew about, but *oil*? Unbeknownst to us, the Morris Minor was leaking oil badly. It leaked out just about as fast as we put it in. Trouble was, we didn't know to put it in. So, one smoggy day, the engine seized up on the freeway and Morris was no more. We had it towed to an English car mechanic named Penny. Actually his name was Mr. Pennington, but everyone called him Penny. Penny really liked our car—the body was in perfect condition—so he traded us a beat up 1959 Renault Dauphine for it. The Renault didn't look like much, but it ran. And now we knew to check the oil.

* * *

The other person whose number I had was Peter Tork of The Monkees. For some reason, Ray Paret knew him and told me to look him up. I called him, told him a little about who I was and what I'd done, said I was completely new to LA, and he very graciously invited us out to visit him in Topanga. We followed his directions to the wilds of Topanga Canyon, a much more rural version of Laurel Canyon. Our sputtering little Renault made it valiantly up hill and down dale, until we found our way to Peter's rustic retreat.

Peter Tork, 1969, Photo: Henry Diltz, henrydiltzphotography.com

It was hardly what I had pictured as the residence of a rock star. I kept thinking: *these guys were the American Beatles, the 'Pre-Fab Four,' and this is all he wound up with?* Turns out he didn't even own the ramshackle bungalow where we found him. He was renting this place, with some roommates to boot. But he was cheerful enough; he had let his hair and beard grow and had started a new band with his girlfriend on drums and some other people. I guess those were the people that were living there with him. He had some good weed, and we hung out on the back porch overlooking some pristine woodland, but as the conversation progressed, it became more and more apparent that Peter Tork was a bitter man. He felt like he had gotten a

raw deal. Now that the sun had set on the Monkees' TV show and their recording career, Peter realized that a lot of people had reaped big profits from
the Monkees phenomenon, but not him. In fact, the only member of the band
that had come away with any significant financial rewards was, ironically,
Michael Nesmith. That was because he was the only one who had written
a significant number of songs. It was ironic because Michael Nesmith was
independently wealthy. His mother had invented Liquid Paper, commonly
known as white-out, the revenues for which far eclipsed any potential income from the band and set Michael up for life. So I sat on Peter Tork's back
porch, passing a J with Ron and Peter, and pondered the vagaries of fame
and fortune and how many ways things can go wrong. *Rock Star Etiquette,
Lesson #1: Fame is fragile—and you can't take it to the bank.*

* * *

At about this time, it became pretty obvious to me that my two-week trip to
California was going to go on considerably longer than that—like, forever.
I didn't miss the East Coast, I didn't miss my parents or sister, I didn't miss
the humidity or the snow. I wanted to stay here in Lala Land forever. I called
my sister and asked her to go to Wellesley and collect my stuff. I called Ray
and Tony and told them I was not coming back, and that they should come
out here. One big casualty of the move was my Gretsch electric guitar. It had
somehow 'disappeared' from the Ultimate Spinach rehearsal room. But I
did not mourn this loss for long. I was sure a new electric guitar would come
my way when the time was right.

We hadn't been in our new digs two weeks when I heard from Eva.
She had been given an airplane ticket by some guy and was about to leave
for Europe for an indefinite period. Her flight was leaving from LA and she
wanted to come over and say goodbye to me. She showed up with bag and
baggage and stayed with me for a couple of nights. Only she was never
there. As soon as she arrived she dashed off to see some other friends. I had
no idea where she was or if or when she would be back. Except that her stuff
was in my house. Her behavior was nothing short of bizarre.

Chapter Twenty-Two

V

The following night, Ron and I went over to hang out with Warren and Diana. They were having a small gathering at their house and our presence was requested. Of course, I was asked to bring my guitar.

As we rounded the bend on Laurel Canyon Boulevard, we were confronted by towering flames coming from the ruins of the Houdini Mansion, which had once stood at the foot of Lookout Mountain. The mansion had famously been used as a location for James Dean's 1955 film debut, *Rebel Without a Cause* and had burned down in 1959, leaving just the foundation and some ruined stonework. But it had become a Mecca for squatters and transients and I guess someone with a penchant for arson decided to burn the place down a second time, although I'm guessing that all those flames and smoke could only have been produced by dry brush.

There were a few people gathered at Warren and Diana's, but I only saw one. She was a vision in white: blond hair, plain white pullover top, white lace pants, white bikini underpants, which were clearly visible through the transparent lace pants, and white, open-toed platform shoes. Her body was as lithe as a wood nymph. I could see she was a few years older than I. Her face was a beautifully sculpted rendering of some goddess of myth and legend—the high cheekbones, the alabaster skin. She wore big round sunglasses tinted pale blue. When she took them off, revealing her chocolate-brown eyes, I gathered that her hair was probably dyed. If there was such a thing as "spiritual glamour," she was it. Her name was Valeriana, but she said to simply call her "V." She was about the coolest looking thing I had ever seen. When our eyes met, something happened.

After the usual niceties, I learned that she lived next door. She asked me to play something. I took out my guitar, my mind racing for a song that would suitably impress. I decided on "Now Is Just a Time," the song I had written for Richie Havens that had almost made it onto the Chamæleon Church album:

> *My hands across the darkness face*
> *A flock of moments from me to you*
> *I'll hold your soul for all my days*
> *And I'll go the ways you taught me to*
> *Now is just a time and here is but a place*
> *The only other face belongs to me*
> *And this is just a rhyme that fills a space*
> *Like the space you filled for me*

At the end, amid the applause and oohs and ahs from the other guests, I heard an audible gasp emit from her lovely, sensual lips. I knew I had her.

We spent the evening in rapt conversation. The sound of her voice was like nothing I'd ever heard, sort of breathy and melodious, and her pronunciation was kind of like some of the old movie stars, maybe a little like Garbo, but with not a trace of affectation. She was shy, evasive and didn't want to talk about herself (how refreshing!). Instead, she asked me questions, getting me to talk about myself (my favorite subject). I got that she had been born in Spain and grew up in New York City. She was married to a guy who was away on business for the better part of a year, but would be returning soon. They did not live together.

She had strong opinions about music and was heavily into both rock and classical. We both agreed that Led Zeppelin was the best new band since The Beatles, but she passionately defended The Doors, a band I had dismissed as lightweight. I had seen them live in Boston in 1967 and was not impressed. She insisted that Jim Morrison was a god. She invited me next door to her house to play me some Doors music. I was starting to like them already...

Her home exuded peace and spirituality. She told me she was into yoga and meditation, interests we had in common. Not unlike Warren and

Diana's, the upper level of the house, where we entered, had a spacious living room, a kitchen, and a workroom off the kitchen, which was cluttered with books, papers and artwork in various states of completion. Downstairs was a large bedroom and bathroom and outside deck. The living room had a comfortable couch and many plants. She lit candles that sat, in art nouveau frosted glass candle holders shaped like leaf clusters, on all the window sills, which ran along two sides of the room. She opened a carved rosewood box with abalone elephants and produced a beautifully-rolled joint, lit it on one of the candles and passed it to me. I took a big hit and took it all in.

She had a state-of-the-art stereo with Macintosh components, a Technics turntable and JBL speakers. She put The Doors' "Moonlight Drive" on the turntable. The music filled the room with a fidelity and presence I had rarely heard anywhere outside the recording studio. Immediately she leapt to her feet and was whooping and whirling around the room with wild abandon. She was something to behold. "Listen to his words," she was saying, "it's poetry. He's sublime!"

I saw her point. Jim Morrison certainly had something. It was the rest of the band I had a problem with. That whining Farfisa organ, the wimpy guitar, the keyboard bass, the jazzy drums. Compared to The Who, or Zeppelin, or any of the British bands, they sounded mild as milk toast to me.

Then we switched to Led Zeppelin. Now here was something on which I could wholeheartedly agree. The magical combination of Page and Plant was a match made in heaven, and the songwriting was bold, innovative and fearless. Here were master musicians who were making music exclusively for themselves, with no attempt to pander to popular tastes and succeeding commercially in spite—or perhaps because—of this.

I queried her about her husband. He was in Europe producing a major motion picture and would be back in a few weeks. They did not have a romantic/sexual relationship. She said they were "like Hansel and Gretel." He did not live with her in this house, but would show up often and without warning when he was in town. This was his house; he came and went as he pleased. She was his bird in a gilded cage. She had been celibate for years, perhaps not by choice but by circumstance, and she was going to use this hand that life had dealt her to elevate her spiritual consciousness, to lift herself out of the carnal gutter and toward The Light. She had everything she needed and did not need to work. It's hard to imagine what she would have done if she did. She was a divine eccentric, a rock 'n' roll angel in white, a hothouse flower, and was not equipped for survival in this cruel and wicked world.

We sat and talked 'til nearly dawn. As we said goodnight at last, there was a moment when we faced each other, eye-to-eye, and we fell, effortlessly and without intent, into a kiss. This was a kiss the like of which I had never experienced before and probably never will again. When it was over we looked at each other like two people who had been struck by lightning. A new era had begun in my life.

When I got home, Eva was in my bed. Her flight to Amsterdam was that morning. I barely said two words to her. I didn't ask her where she had been; I didn't weep or beg her not to leave. I was strangely beatific, compassionate, and forgiving, but also quite distant. I had an enigmatic, Buddha-like half-smile on my face that no doubt caused her some little consternation. She no longer wielded any power over me. The spell had been broken forever. I got into bed with her and quickly fell sound asleep. In the morning, I was awakened by her getting ready to leave. When she made her exit, I sleepily wished her luck without getting out of bed.

Chapter Twenty-Three

Season of the Witch

We had not been ensconced in our Kirkwood Drive abode for more than a month when Ron's old friend, Tony Kutner, arrived. Our living room would now be Tony's bedroom. Tony was a guitar-playing songwriter and singer and had collaborated with Ron on some children's songs while they both lived in Chicago. Tony was a short, facile guy with blond curls, sleepy blue eyes and a relaxed, easygoing manner that could charm the fleas off a dog. He carried with him a nylon-stringed guitar on which he was quite proficient. Tony's arrival was something of a relief to me, firstly because it loosened the pressure to come up with the rent every month (as Tony would now be paying a third) and secondly because, while I had been extremely prolific in cranking out my own songs, I had not gotten around to actually putting music to any of Ron's lyrics—although we were now hard at work, getting stoned every day, writing a wacky screenplay.

Our landlady was a French actress named Lilyan Chauvin. She was a striking brunette in her mid-forties who had obviously been a great beauty in her youth—and she wasn't so bad right now. She had appeared in numerous movies and TV shows, but usually in supporting roles. She was well known in Hollywood as a highly respected acting coach.

For some reason Lilyan took a shine to us. Seeing we barely had any furniture in our place (our décor was 'orange crate moderne'), she was always bringing us little household things: dishes, sheets, towels… One day she showed up with a set of three of the strangest looking coffee mugs I had ever seen. They had faces, each one more malevolent than the last.

With some of the events that had been happening that summer—the big fire at the Houdini place and then the Manson murders and subsequent capture of this evil hippie cult—we were already a bit jittery. The whole Manson episode had, in one terrible stroke, permanently perverted the hippie counterculture in the eyes of the world and cast a stain on all of us. Those maniacs had confirmed the worst suspicions of the extreme right-wingers, who were, after all, running things in this country. The cops were prowling Sunset with renewed, unbridled viciousness. We got rousted and searched on numerous occasions. The Age of Aquarius had dawned and set in barely two years, and we were now in the Season of the Witch.

We took it into our heads that Lilyan Chauvin was a witch, and that these mugs were like voodoo dolls, representing the three of us. Were they there to spy on us? Would they put a hex on us? Would they take us over, like *Invasion of the Body Snatchers*? Nervously smoking joint after joint, we pondered these questions and what to do with the mugs.

I decided to make a little house for them out of a shoebox. I cut a window for each one, so they could look out. Then I placed the shoebox on a pedestal in the back of a clothing closet. You had to peel the clothes back but, when you did, there they were, looking out at you. If we were trying to scare ourselves, we were doing a damn good job.

* * *

A few days earlier, we had picked up a teenage girl hitchhiking. Her name was Darlene, an aspiring porno actress. She gave out blow jobs like party favors. Like a fool, I availed myself of one, and she instantly became our new best friend. She would show up at our house unannounced at all hours of the day and night, often crawling into bed with one or another of us, and staying over. While Darlene's blow jobs were a wonderful sleep aid, her constant presence and completely inane conversation soon became unnerving.

One day, shortly after our receipt of the mugs, Darlene showed up at our front door. She and a seedy-looking guy stood before us, propping up a tall skinny guy with a scraggly mustache, who appeared to be passed out. Behind them a car stood in the street, motor running. They led him right up to our front door and then released him. He fell, face first, right through our open door. Darlene introduced the body on the floor as "Ruda," a local junkie, and told us he was dying of a heroin overdose. We had to help him, she said, we were his only hope.

Having some experience with these things in the past (I recalled the Barbara Gibson episode on Joy Street), I stepped up like the good Boy Scout I was. "Get him on his feet," I said. "We can't let him lose consciousness." When I glanced out the door, Darlene and the guy she was with were gone. I went into emergency mode. It wasn't that I was so concerned for this guy's wellbeing, it was more like we really did not want to have to explain a dead junkie on our floor to the cops. I told Tony to get some water boiling for instant coffee, while Ron and I draped his arms over our shoulders and walked him around the living room, all the while talking to him, occasionally slapping him on the cheek, trying to get him to wake up. This went on for a good long time. We forced cup after cup of black coffee down his throat, and finally he seemed to regain consciousness. "Hey, buddy," I said, "You okay?" He opened his eyes, focused on me, and nodded. We let him sleep on our couch, and in the morning he was gone.

Two days later, Ruda knocked on our front door. I answered. "Hey, man," he said, "I just came by to thank you for saving my life."

"You're welcome," I said, and started to close the door.

He stuck his foot out to keep it open. "Can I say thanks to the other guys?"

"They're out," I lied.

All the while, Ruda was peering into our house, looking around. At last he withdrew. "Let's hang out some time," he said in parting.

"Yeah, cool," I said and closed the door hastily. This whole exchange gave me the royal creeps.

Two days later we came home, and our house had been broken into. My guitar was gone. This was unacceptable. This, my only guitar, was my means of livelihood, the essential tool I needed to get where I needed to go in this town. There was never a question in our minds as to who had done it. We reached Darlene and she told us Ruda and his junkie pals all hung out in a vacant store underneath the Canyon Country Store, which was located right at the foot of Kirkwood Drive. Tony had a hunting knife and so, armed only with that and insane determination, the three of us headed down the hill.

We barged into the musty basement without knocking. There were three or four guys assembled in there. Ruda was not among them.

"Alright," I said, brandishing the knife, "your pal Ruda ripped off my guitar. Where is he?" I got right in the face of the smallest guy among them and held the knife to his throat.

"Wait a minute, man, I'll tell you!" the guy squealed. "He'll take it to Gabor's Pawnshop on Western Avenue. That's where he takes all the shit he steals."

"That was easy," Tony said as we got into the car.

"These California junkies. What wimps!" I said, still pumped up with adrenalin.

"Lucky for us," snorted Ron.

It was now quite late in the day—rush hour—so we decided to go there first thing in the morning.

* * *

Early the next day, still packing our collective blade, we were sitting in the Renault across the street from the pawnshop on Western Avenue. The plan was to wait until Ruda showed up, then pounce, reclaiming the guitar before he had a chance to hock it. But what if he had already been there and gone? While that possibility certainly existed, we resolved to wait awhile and see if he turned up. By noon we got tired of waiting and decided to go into the shop and ask.

As we walked through the door, we were immediately aware that the two guys behind the counter had us in the sights of two very large guns. *Oh shit*, I thought, *they spotted us staking them out and they think we're here to rob the place!* Hands in the air, I explained the reason for our visit. "It's not what you think," I said, "this guy named Ruda, a skinny guy with dark hair, stole my guitar. They said he'd take it here. A Gibson J-50, early '60s?"

One of the guys turned and brought it down from a shelf behind him. "You mean, this one?" he asked, opening the case.

So Ruda had beaten us there. Not that big a surprise, given that he had the entire previous day. "Yes," I said, "that's my baby."

"Well," said the proprietor, you can pay us the forty dollars we gave Ruda and take the guitar now, or file a police report and wait six or eight months while your guitar is impounded as evidence."

I chose option A. I went to the bank and got the cash—it just about drained my account—and we left with my guitar. A major bullet dodged.

* * *

156

Other weird shit happened during those few weeks. One night, Ron got a phone call from himself.

"Hello," he said.

And in his exact voice and tone, the voice on the other end said "Hello."

"Who is this?" asked Ron, becoming unnerved.

And in an ominous tone, the voice at the other end—his own voice—said, "You know who this is," and clicked off.

We were thoroughly creeped out. We attributed all this negativity to the mugs. They were almost certainly putting the whammy on us. I knew a girl named Isis who was into witchcraft, and I called her and asked her advice. She gave me the number of a guy who was a bona fide warlock. If anybody could tell us how to reverse this evil spell, Bernard could.

We called Bernard, and he agreed to come over and check out our mugs. We told him we had no money to pay him, but promised to give him an OZ (ounce) of primo weed.

Whatever comes to your mind when you think of a warlock, Bernard was not it. He was a small, frail, nerdy guy with thinning brown hair, an over-sized nose and wire-rimmed glasses. No beard, no robes, no magic staff. I brought out the mugs, still in their shoebox house. He sat at our kitchen table, ceremoniously put on a pair of white cotton gloves, and picked up each one, examining it thoroughly. "Yes," he said at length, "these objects have been forged in evil. If you keep them, they will bring ruin on you." At least he talked like a warlock.

"What can we do?" I asked.

"There is only one thing you can do. You have to bury them at least two feet under fresh earth at dawn on the first day of the dark of the moon…"

There was more, but I don't remember all of the instructions. They were very precise. We had an incantation in ancient Druid or something that we had to recite. The mugs were to stay in their box while we buried them. Ron dutifully wrote everything down. In hindsight, this all seems completely ridiculous, like a B movie, but for us it was genuinely scary. I felt fear churning deep in my guts. Bernard took his ounce of grass and left.

The calendar on the wall told us that the new moon was two days away, Thursday. On Thursday at dawn, with the mists appropriately hovering in the hollows of the canyon, we dug the hole in our backyard. We had a tape measure and were careful to follow the precise dimensions. Then, we ever-so-carefully lowered the mugs, still in their box, into their grave. As we covered them with earth, we muttered the prescribed words with each shovelful of dirt. When the deed was done, we went back into the house in silence, each of us praying that this would work.

I won't say that nothing bad ever happened to us again, but after that, life seemed to regain its normal ratio of good luck to bad. I have to say, though, that for the whole time we lived on Kirkwood Drive, I was conscious of those evil beings silently lurking below the surface of our backyard.

Chapter Twenty-Four

The Brief Career of Silly Willy

I was dying to see V again. I was sure the next time would be 'it.' I called her numerous times, but she didn't pick up the phone. At last, she answered. She was afraid to open the Pandora's Box that she knew would be our relationship. The husband would be back soon. He was extremely jealous and a dangerous man. I was not to call this number anymore. "I can't let you go," I said. "Please, just call me from time to time to let me know you're alright." She said she'd try, and hung up. I was desolate, my hopes suddenly and unexpectedly dashed.

* * *

On the home front, Ron, Tony and I came up with a new Christmas character to supplant Rudolph, the Red-Nosed Reindeer. He was an elf in Santa's workshop, who had such a silly face that the other elves ostracized him (yeah, I know, it does sound a lot like 'Rudolph'). Our new Christmas story was titled *Silly Willy, Christmas Elf*. We wrote a treatment for an animated TV special. To be fair, the Silly Willy story had a lot more gravitas than the Rudolph story. In Rudolph, all that was at stake was Santa not being able to see through the fog on Christmas Eve. In our story, Silly Willy, as a well-meaning idiot savant, cures Santa of major depression, brought on by the sorry state of the world and humanity in general. Ron and Tony wrote the title song, which, speaking from a fairly objective standpoint, was incredibly cute. We pooled all of our money and went into a recording studio on Sunset to record it. It came out surprisingly good. I revived my art skills and made a rendering of Silly Willy on a large sheet of poster board.

Tony's father was a high-powered lawyer in Chicago, and he gave us two contacts: Sid Sheinberg, the top guy at Universal/MCA and Rudy Vallee (yes, that's right, the guy who sang through a megaphone before microphones were invented). We decided to try to get Vallee onboard first, as our token star. Tony, who had more chutzpah than P.T. Barnum on steroids, got on the phone with Rudy and got us an invitation to his villa on Mulholland Drive. We piled into the Renault with our poster, the script and a reel-to-reel tape of the Silly Willy song and headed into the hills. We took our guitars as well, just in case Rudy had not heard of the tape recorder.

Rudy Vallee. Photo: Freetown Photos

Rudy's mansion was a vestige of old Hollywood splendor. It was perched on a ridge above Mulholland, with the whole city spread out below. We snaked our way up a narrow driveway, which ended in a turntable. The only way to turn your car around to leave was to have someone flip a switch, and you'd do a 180. It was a Spanish style, pink stucco villa with maybe forty rooms, each appointed in priceless antiques—all bought brand new, no doubt. It sort of looked like Norma

Desmond's place in *Sunset Boulevard*. Rudy himself was a priceless antique. Now almost seventy, he was a trifle crotchety. He wore a burgundy satin dressing gown over baby blue silk pajamas, and he would huck up phlegm and spit into a handkerchief every few seconds. "Okay, boys," he said, "(huck, tooey) tell me your tale o' woe." We gave Rudy the pitch. We were right to bring our guitars, because Rudy did not have a tape recorder. The live performance of the Silly Willy song cinched it. Rudy was thoroughly entertained. He was also flattered that people our age would even know who he was, let alone seek him out. So, on a handshake, Rudy Vallee was 'attached' to our project.

Next, we called Sid Sheinberg's office, used Tony's father's name, and got an appointment. We drove out to Universal Studios with our presentation. Sheinberg was genuinely impressed. The fact that *Silly Willy* was pretty much a re-casting of *Rudolph, the Red-Nosed Reindeer* bothered him not at all. He was impressed that we had already gotten Rudy Vallee attached, but said we could probably do better. He was acting like this was a done deal! We were dizzy with the elixir of victory. Sid picked up the phone. "Get me Russ Regan," he said. Russ Regan was president of Uni Records, the predecessor of MCA. "Russ, I'm sending some guys over to you with an idea. This is either the biggest Christmas idea of all times or—'duck, incoming!'" Hmmm, well, maybe he wasn't *completely* sold on the idea, but we went right over to Russ Regan's office and were ushered in immediately.

Russ Regan listened politely to the pitch, asked to hang onto the tape and told us he would get back to us. A far cooler reception than we had received at Chez Sid. On our way out, he stopped us. "Hey, I want you guys to listen to this new kid from England and tell me what you think." He dropped the needle on an acetate and played us "Your Song" by Elton John. I told him I thought it was a really good song and the guy could really sing and play well. He seemed reassured, and we left. We never heard back from him or Sid Sheinberg, in spite of numerous attempts to follow up with phone calls. *Hollywood Etiquette, Lesson #1: "I'll get back to you" does not necessarily mean "I'll get back to you."* R.I.P. Silly Willy.

Silly Willy

Chapter Twenty-Five

Joni

I really needed to get some connections in the LA music industry. I called Elliot Roberts' office at Lookout Management. Elliot was, among other things, the manager of Joni Mitchell. I was hoping I could get a message to Joni, that she would remember me from New York and that she might help me out in some way. I got an answering service operator. Elliot was not in the office. I explained that I was a friend of Joni Mitchell's from New York and needed to get in touch with her. "Oh," said the operator, "Elliot's at Joni's house right now. Why don't you call him there?" And she gave me Joni Mitchell's home number. I wrote it down and hung up, not believing my luck—or her incompetence.

I called Joni and reminded her of our night out in New York, the Tin Angel, the rent party… I told her I lived in Laurel Canyon, and she said she did too. It turns out she lived on Lookout Mountain, the same street as Warren and Diana and V. She gave me the address and invited me over. I wasted no time.

Her house was close to the bottom of Lookout; just a few houses up from the legendary Tom Mix log cabin at the corner of Lookout and Laurel Canyon Boulevard, now occupied by Frank Zappa and the Mothers. Local legend had it that Tom Mix had buried his beloved horse under the floor of that house.

Joni was warm and welcoming. I didn't have a good enough tape to play her, but I played her a couple of songs on my guitar, and she played me some of the new stuff she was working on. One, I remember, was about a street musician called "For Free." An unexpected treat was meeting her boy-friend, Graham Nash. I had been a Hollies fan for years, so I was completely enthralled to be with both of them. And they were so sweet and kind. Graham seemed really interested in me. He asked me what my favorite Hollies songs were. "Clown" and "Pay You Back with Interest," I said. Fortunately, he was a writer on both.

Crosby, Stills & Nash were going to be headlining their first LA con-cert at the Greek Theatre, with Joni as the opening act, and they gave me two backstage passes to attend. I was what you might call 'stoked.'

One of the first things Joni told me was "If you really want to be a singer, you should quit smoking cigarettes." I took this very much to heart. I had been breaking into fits of coughing on the high notes lately anyway. So I locked myself in the house for four days and chain-smoked joints of bad homegrown marijuana. After four days I had such a bad sore throat and headache, I didn't want to smoke anything. Within a few months I was cigarette-free.

* * *

I had met a pretty young redhead, a singer-songwriter named Rachel Perry. So far, we had only enjoyed a single one-night stand, but I liked her, and she looked good, so I took her to the concert at the Greek Theater. As we turned off Los Feliz Boulevard, heading up to The Greek, we were greeted by a spectacular aerial phenomenon in the western sky. I still don't know what caused it, but there was a swirling pattern of cloud-like vapor trails, forming a sort of helix, tinted brilliant pink by the setting sun. I took this to be a portent of good things to come.

Of course, the concert was brilliant. Crosby, Stills and Nash brought Neil Young out as a surprise special guest, and we got to hang out backstage afterward with Joni and C S N & Y. Rachel was duly impressed, and after-ward she took me back to her place in the Hollywood Hills and showed me her full appreciation. She also let me borrow her high-end reel-to-reel tape machine, which I used to record my next few songs. She never made it as a singer-songwriter, but she founded a successful business, Rachel Parry Cosmetics, which pioneered all-natural skincare products.

* * *

Joni and I continued to see each other intermittently all through the rest of 1969, and right up until the end of 1970. I know this because I still have a Christmas card she made me with crayons that said, "Kick out the stops in '71." As a joke, she first wrote the year backward, then crossed it out and wrote it correctly. Before she got her sky-blue Mercedes convertible, I used to drive her down to the Canyon Country Store for groceries.

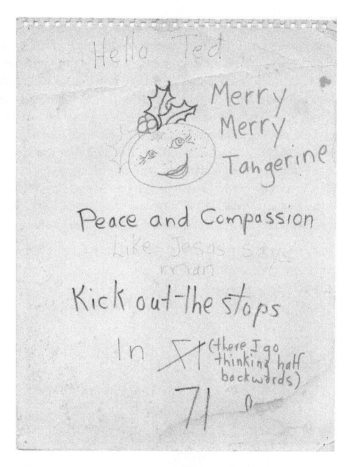

One night, late in the summer of '69, not long after Woodstock and the CSN concert at The Greek, I dropped by her house at around ten at night. This was the kind of thing people did in those days, and it was apparently acceptable behavior. Joni was at the piano, but very gracious as always. "You can't stay," she said in a hushed voice, "I'm writing. But listen to this…" She began to sing:

> *I came upon a child of God*
> *He was walking along the road*
> *And I asked him 'where are you going?'*
> *And this he told me…*

She sang the entire song and then said, "Well, what do you think?"

"Wow… great!" I stammered, agog. I was, for once, at a loss for words. I genuflected and kowtowed out of there.

For many years I believed I had witnessed the birth of the song "Woodstock" that night. Then I saw a documentary in which David Geffen said Joni wrote "Woodstock" in a New York City hotel suite where they were both staying during the Woodstock festival. Michael Walker, the author of the book *Laurel Canyon*, told me the same story. I had no explanation for what I know I experienced. Then I saw another documentary, *Legends of the Canyon* and Graham Nash cleared it all up: He said that she wrote "eighty percent" of the song in New York City. The night I dropped in on her was right after the festival, so what I witnessed was her adding the last twenty percent. So, technically, I was the first person to hear the final, finished version as she recorded it on her next album, *Ladies of the Canyon.*

Joni Mitchell – Taken in that "very, very, very fine house" where I used to visit her. Photo: Baron Wolman, Iconic Images/Baron Wolman

Joni's Laurel Canyon house was a Mecca for fellow musicians, song-writers, and all manner of itinerant freaks, and she was always gracious and welcoming. Once, as I was leaving, I ran into my old friend David Blue from the Village. He said hi to me and walked past, as if we had just seen each other on MacDougal Street yesterday. Another time I knocked on her door and James Taylor answered. It seems a big yellow taxi had taken Graham Nash away and my protégé J.T. was the new boyfriend. James looked odd and disoriented. He looked at me long and hard, but I knew he couldn't place me. I reminded him of the Café Moska, summer of '64. He nodded, still looking distracted. He said Joni was not at home. I felt I was intruding, so I left. I didn't have an explanation for his odd behavior, but later I heard that he had been shooting up heroin and figured maybe that had something to do with it. The last time I saw him, in 2007, he was a different person. He was smiling and friendly and he remembered me, the summer of '64, and the Café Moska perfectly.

Chapter Twenty-Six

In Love Again

Meanwhile, I was still longing for V. She was all I could think about. She had told me not to call her again, and I had honored that request, but one balmy Laurel Canyon night when the air was filled with the scent of jasmine, almost in a trance, I found myself at her front door. I knocked, swallowing hard. I didn't know if I would be greeted by her or her husband, or what, but I was willing to chance it. After an endless moment she opened the door and gasped. I loved to hear her gasp; it meant I still had her. We just stared at each other for another long moment, and then she stepped back and let me in. She closed the front door, double-locked it and put the chain on.

All the candles were burning and J.S. Bach floated majestically out of the JBLs. "You shouldn't have come here," she said, breathless.

"I couldn't help it. I don't even remember driving up here."

"My husband just left a half hour ago!"

"So he's back?"

"Yes… but he won't be back here tonight," she said.

And suddenly we were kissing, wrapped tightly in each other's arms, bodies melting together, forming one thing. The next thing I remember, we were downstairs in her bedroom. I threw her down on the enormous bed, and I was alternating between peeling her clothes off and my own.

At last, we were naked and in each other's arms. My heart was pounding, but at the same time I was somehow calm. This was all so familiar. I was completely relaxed. It was like she was literally the 'other half' of me that I had been missing my entire life. She was like *home*. After thoroughly exploring each other all over, we were inside each other. Bam! It was like a circuit suddenly completed. As soon as I was in her, a warm, glowing flow of energy began to rise inside me, first in my loins, then rising into my abdomen, and then my heart. It could only be described as pure, inexorable love.

We were perfectly in synch. There was no need for words, no external gyrations. No phony moans. A porno fan watching us would have fallen asleep. We barely moved. Later, we decided our lovemaking should be called *sans movement*. Everything I was feeling I knew she was feeling. In all the times we made love over the next fifteen years, there was never a time when it wasn't perfect.

I was in deep trouble. I was hooked—and hooked good—on a woman who would never be fully mine. Our love was a high wire act, all predicated upon a delicate balance. She couldn't leave her husband because she was not equipped to deal with the world. I couldn't take care of myself financially, let alone anyone else. And, besides, I was still addicted to the affections of every woman I could attract. I was incapable of monogamy. So, somehow it was perfect. And scary as hell.

And V was scared too, and guilty—scared her husband would find out and guilty for betraying him, although it wasn't a betrayal from where I sat; I wasn't claiming anything that was ever his. At the same time, she was as hooked on me as I was on her. It was another 'can't live with and can't live without' situation, something I thought I was finally free of when V broke Eva's spell. It was weeks before she let me see her again, although I was sometimes able to get through on the phone. We developed a signal: I would call and ring her phone once; if she was alone she would call me back.

Chapter Twenty-Seven

A New Deal

The beginning of the '70s signaled the era of the singer-songwriter in pop music. I had heard a preview of Elton John over at Universal, Lou Adler was making a solo album with hit songwriter Carole King that was to reign as the best-selling album of all time, and my protégé, James Taylor, had become Paul McCartney's protégé and broken big with his debut on Apple Records. Not to mention Jackson Browne, my pal Joni, and a slew of others. All I had was an acoustic guitar, so solo seemed like the natural direction for me to go, as opposed to trying to form another rock band.

I also seemed to be at the forefront of a westward migration that put me back in touch with several of my East Coast music buddies and was gradually shifting the epicenter of the music business from New York to LA. One day, right on Kirkwood Drive, I ran into an old friend from New York, John Boylan. John had been in a Greenwich Village band with his brother Terry called The Gingermen. He had been the first musician I knew to go to work for 'the man.' He got a job working for Koppelman & Rubin, the firm that managed The Lovin' Spoonful. Once, when I still lived in New York, I visited him at his office and played him some songs for an artist he was representing named Teddy Neely. Now he was living right up the street from me with his girlfriend, Linda Ronstadt, whom he also produced. I was already a fan of Linda, who had scored a hit single with her group The Stone Poneys with Michael Nesmith's song, "Different Drum." While in Ultimate Spinach I had shared the stage with them at a college concert back east. More recently, she had released her first single as a solo artist, "Long, Long Time," which was currently on the charts.

"Linda's looking for songs," John told me. "Have you got anything she might like?"

"I don't know. Maybe," I said. "I've got a lot of new songs."

"We're playing the Troubadour tomorrow night and rehearsing in the afternoon. Why don't you come down and play her a few songs?"

Linda Ronstadt, 1969. Photo: Henry Diltz, henrydiltzphotography.com

Linda was one of the very few in the new crop of California artists who was not a songwriter. To her credit, she didn't try to be one. She had one of the greatest sets of pipes in the business, and she was a brilliant interpreter of other people's material. To get her to cover one of your songs was a major coup.

The next afternoon I showed up at the Troubadour with my guitar and played her some of my songs live. She was rehearsing for her show that night with her backup band, which consisted of future-Eagles Glen Frey and Don Henley, among others. She was very friendly and sweet, but none of my songs were right for her. I wasn't surprised. I wasn't writing country rock these days, and that's what she seemed to be into. My one country rock song, "Ballad of a Naked Loser," was lyrically inappropriate for a girl singer, so I came up empty.

Then I drove Linda to a nearby Taco Bell to get lunch for the band. She impressed me as a very nice, down-to-earth girl. I don't really remember our conversation in the car; it was pretty mundane. But I remember feeling like I was hanging out with a peer, someone sweet and totally unpretentious.

John Boylan went on to a stellar career, producing artists like Little River Band and Boston and becoming West Coast VP of Epic Records.

* * *

A recording engineer named Mic Leitz took me under his wing. Mic (pronounced 'Mike,' but also short for microphone) was the epitome of the California cool guy; he was about thirty, tall, with long brown hair, all-American good looks and amber tinted aviator shades. He drove a new Corvette. Mic owned a nice house in a well-manicured part of the Hollywood Hills. He was the first-call engineer for producer Mike Post, who was riding on some pretty big radio hits at the time. He also did a lot of film score work. I didn't know how much recording engineers made, but from the looks of Mic's setup, they did pretty well.

Mic's girlfriend was a Georgia peach named Brooks Hunnicutt, lead singer of a band called The Doppler Effect. I don't remember what the band sounded like, but I'll never forget the name; it's one of my all-time favorite band names—it's the word for the auditory illusion you experience when a train blowing its whistle speeds past you. The pitch seems to lower as the train gets farther away, even though it stays the same. Brooks' younger brother, Greg, came out from Georgia and joined them right around the time I started hanging out with Mic.

Mic had a nice 15ips tape machine and some good mics and he had me over to record guitar-voice demos of some new songs. Greg, who was about twenty-one, was an extremely handsome, outgoing kid, and eager to get into the music business. With Mic's help, he was hired by Tom Johnson, a fellow southerner, who had just opened the West Coast branch of Tree Music, a well-established music publishing company based in Nashville that had published many big country hits over the years. I gathered that branching out to LA and hiring this very young kid as their first A&R scout indicated that Tree was also thinking of branching out musically.

Greg played Tom some of my tapes, and I was offered a deal, which included a weekly draw against royalties of $75. It did not represent a bump up from what I had gotten in New York from Lorber, but it was sorely needed income. Besides, they were ready to get me a rehearsal space, pay a band, and take me into the studio. But there was one major wrinkle. I was still under contract to Alan Lorber. Mic told me he was going to send me to the best lawyer in the business, Al Schlesinger.

Mic did not exaggerate. Al Schlesinger was an unassuming, soft-spoken man. He was bald, had glasses and wore gray business suits. His offices were at Crossroads of the World, a quaint cluster of buildings near Sunset and Las Palmas that was America's first outdoor shopping mall in 1936. The mix of art deco, Tudor and Mediterranean architecture has been preserved as a historic monument. I showed up at the appointed time, bringing along my contract with Lorber. Al was extremely friendly and optimistic. He made a copy of the contract and told me he would write Lorber a letter. Two weeks later, I was out of my contract, free as a bird. At the time I had no idea how impressive Al's roster of clients really was. In addition to legally representing many of the biggest recording acts of the day, including The Beach Boys and The Doors, he was the personal manager of Bread, who were then at the height of their success. I told Al I had very little money, but that I would gladly pay him in installments if he would just send me the bill. I didn't dare ask how much it would be, and I never found out, because Al Schlesinger never sent me a bill. This guy was unique in the entertainment business, and he is still beloved by all who knew him.

I had no shortage of songs to offer Tree. Greg Hunnicutt and I went through my tapes and narrowed the list down to ten songs we wanted to record for openers. Tree's first LA office was in a cavernous building on Sunset near Gower Street that had been the headquarters of the now-defunct Republic Pictures. The building had few tenants, and there was a huge empty room right near Tree's office that looked like it had once been the studio cafeteria. This would be our rehearsal space. We got a P.A. system and some amps. Now all we needed were musicians.

I had run into a bass player named Jack Conrad a few times at the Canyon Country store. He was a big burly guy with shoulder-length brown hair who always wore a broad-brimmed black hat with an Indian concho hatband and a feather. He lived with his big dog in a tiny cabin that was perched precariously on the steep hillside that was the eastern wall of Laurel Canyon, just a few hundred feet north of the Canyon Country Store. He told me that he had done a lot of session work and had toured with some big names. One day I climbed the 200 steps that led up to his aerie with my guitar. We sat and jammed on some of my tunes and the bass parts he came up with spontaneously blew my mind. This was the first musician I had ever played with who came up with parts that I could not improve upon.

SEASONS GREETINGS

Jack Conrad

I told Jack about my publishing deal and he agreed to rehearse the songs and do the recordings with me. Tree was offering the musicians $15 each for each rehearsal and another $15 for each song recorded. Jack knew a guitar player and a drummer I could get as well, and he said they were good—very good.

I called the guitarist, Ted Greene, and the drummer, Don Murray, and they both agreed to show up at the first rehearsal. They would sign on if the project felt right to them.

What a revelation and what a pleasure it was to play with first-string pro musicians. My songs were not simple or predictable, but these guys picked up on them right away and could augment my arrangement ideas with ideas of their own that were as good or better. Ted Greene was a shy, retiring guy with an Abe Lincoln beard and rimless glasses. He said he was getting tired of doing rock sessions and was thinking of just teaching, but he liked me and my songs, so he agreed to play on my sessions. He had written a book called *Chord Chemistry* that was starting to take off as a chord guide for guitarists. It eventually became a staple and sold steadily for the next twenty years. I had never heard anyone get sounds out of a guitar like Ted Greene. Some of his licks were so fast and fluid, it was like hearing Coltrane blowing his 'sheets of sound.' Don Murray did a great job on drums. At the time I had no idea he had been the original drummer with The Turtles and had been the first white drummer to play the 'fatback' beat on "You Baby," which got the attention of many of us who were in bands back in 1966. (The Remains used it later that same year on their single, "Don't Look Back.")

We couldn't afford to spend enough time on rehearsals or in the studio to make my songs sound like masters, but most of them turned out as good song demos, and the playing on them was pretty spectacular. We brought in Craig Doerge on piano and organ for a few of the tracks, and he was every bit as brilliant as the other players. I was lucky to get him; this was just before his rise to legendary status as keyboard player for The Section, the cadre of LA studio players who famously backed up James Taylor and Jackson Browne, among others.

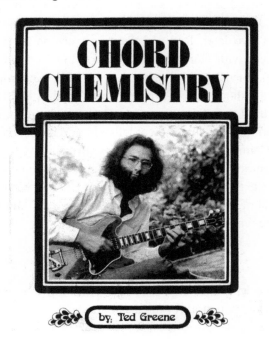

We did these sessions in a studio called Quantum Audio in Torrance, California in the summer of 1970. My car was on the fritz, and Warren was kind enough to lend me his new car. Well, it was not exactly new, but newly-acquired. It was a 1959 Porsche Roadster, already a classic in 1970.

We did the last of the instrumental tracks on a beautiful warm Sunday. I remember we finished recording early that day, and I gave Ted Greene a ride home to Reseda in the West Valley, so I thought I'd take the Porsche for a spin through Topanga Canyon.

* * *

Every Sunday there was a big swap meet in the parking lot of the Topanga Center, which had a post office, café and general store. It was a combination of flea market, art show and be-in. I decided to stop and hang out there for a while. I was struck by some artwork on display by Camilla Hall, a sweet, chubby girl with short blond hair and glasses. Her work featured a collection of fanciful creatures one might see in a Dr. Seuss book. The illustrations were bright, humorous and colorful, as was Camilla. I immediately thought of the children's books my roommate Ron had been writing. I got Camilla's number and resolved to put her and Ron together. They did wind up collaborating, with Camilla doing a series of illustrations for one of Ron's books.

A year or two later, Ron and Camilla were on the verge of getting a publishing deal with Harper Junior Books, but Camilla was no longer interested. None of us could figure out why until, a couple of years after that, we were all shocked to learn that Camilla Hall had been killed in a shootout with the LA police. It turned out she was a member of the Symbionese Liberation Army, the radical left-wing organization that kidnapped Patty Hearst. Camilla had fallen in love with Nancy Ling Perry, the girl known as "Mizmoon," who was the second in command (and reputedly the real brains) of the SLA. Police said they shot Camilla as she was charging aggressively out of the house, but, having known her, I know that was a lie. More likely, she was trying to give herself up.

* * *

I knew my Tree Music tape was flawed, but I felt that anyone with ears could hear in it the potential for me as an artist. This was before you had to have master quality demos to get a record deal, or so I thought.

I brought my new tape over to Joni Mitchell's house and played it for her. She liked it enough to play it for her manager, Ron Stone, who was El-liot Roberts' partner in Lookout Management. Ron lived just a few houses up from Joni on Lookout Mountain. He liked the tape enough to agree to shop it to record companies. I was ecstatic. Being represented by Lookout Management was a big deal; they were the hottest managers in the busi-ness at that time, plus they had a class image. They were not the old school hucksters of the bad old days of the music biz. These guys were young, hip, really understood and cared about their artists and had a bit more integrity than had been the norm.

Coming out of an elevator in Hollywood one day, I ran into Bill Szymczyk, the guy who had engineered and helped produce one of my sessions with The Lost in NYC. I congratulated him on the work he had done as producer of the first few albums by The J. Geils Band and the de-but album by The James Gang, which had just come out and was creating quite a buzz. He was now working on an album with the legendary blues artist, B.B. King. He invited me to drop in on him in the studio, and since I had my newly-finished tape, I did not hesitate to bring it along. When Bill Szymczyk heard Ted Greene play, all he wanted to know was "Who is that guitar player?" and "Where can I get ahold of him?"

"I don't think Ted is playing rock sessions anymore," I told him. "And besides, you've got Joe Walsh!"

"This guy blows Joe Walsh away," was his reply.

But Bill didn't have much to say about me, or my music, so I moved on.

In 1974 Bill Szymczyk produced his first album with The Eagles. In 1975, perhaps not coincidentally, Joe Walsh joined the band and Szymczyk produced *Hotel California*, one of the best-selling albums of all time.

Ron Stone spent a couple of weeks playing my tape for a few of the major labels, and he got passes across the board. Even my old friend and mentor, Al Coury, who was now a senior vice president at Capitol in LA, turned me down. I was finding out that the bar for excellence in the music business was rising fast, and I had to rise with it, or wash out. With the tepid reaction from the record companies, Lookout Management decided not to represent me after all. I was back to square one.

Chapter Twenty-Eight

Left Brain, Right Brain, Razzamatazz

It wasn't long before Tree Music and the small stipend they provided also fell by the wayside. They were unsuccessful at getting any covers on my songs and the LA office of Tree soon closed down. They stopped paying me, thereby nullifying my contract, so I was a free agent once again.

The problem of earning a living now took center stage. In those days, one would actually pound the pavement, stopping into retail establishments asking if they needed any help. It was on such a mission that I walked past a little dress boutique on La Cienega one day. Inside I spied a cute little red-head and decided to wander in and chat her up.

"Hi, nice shop you've got here."

"Yes, it belongs to me and my sister." She indicated another girl who was waiting on a customer across the way.

"What's your name?"

"Pam."

"How did you get your own boutique, Pam?" I asked, just trying to keep the conversation going.

"My boyfriend bought it for me."

Shit, a rich boyfriend, I thought.

"So who's your boyfriend?"

"Jim Morrison," she said.

And just then Jim Morrison walked through the door. He was much taller than I expected, more than six feet. He was overweight and had a full beard, but still a commanding presence.

"Well, nice talking to you, Pam," I said hastily. "Gotta run." And I split, rubbing shoulders with Morrison on the way out.

Jim Morrison and Pam, 1969. Photo: Edmund Teske/Getty Images

* * *

I had worked a few part-time jobs, mostly in retail, but my favorite came along when my old friend, Judy Miller, who had resurfaced in LA as 'Judith,' now a hyper-feminist, introduced me to her friend, Judy Kirkman, wife of Terry Kirkman of The Association. Terry had set up Judy's sister, Syd, in an antique business, and Syd was looking for a part-time person to man the cash register a few shifts a week. The store was called Razzamatazz, specializing in art deco and art nouveau antiques. It was located at Santa Monica Boulevard and Doheny Drive, just a few doors down from the Troubadour.

I fell instantly in love with the artifacts of the 1920s and '30s. In them I saw a time when people made things to last, a time when excellence trumped bottom line, a time when there was pride in work well done, a time before planned obsolescence and when the pressure to hurry up so you could make more had not yet gobbled up the last vestiges of integrity in American commerce.

Syd, a rotund, florid woman in her forties, was very knowledgeable, and she educated me as we went along. I learned that art nouveau flourished from the late nineteenth century through the 1920s and drew upon nature for its inspiration, while art deco ('moderne') started in the '20s and was inspired by man-made objects; straight lines and geometric shapes—the cubists. Art deco introduced the concept of 'streamlining' and coincided with the new skyscrapers that began to rise in cities everywhere.

The store was a wonderland of history. I was left alone there for many hours, so I was able to explore and examine the hundreds of fascinating objects we had for sale. And there were art prints all over the walls by popular artists and illustrators of the day like Louis Icart and Maxfield Parrish. The photo-realistic fantasy illustrations of Maxfield Parrish were my favorites, and I acquired a number of antique prints of his work in lieu of payment from the store. Unfortunately, owning these beautiful works of art, and eventually some furniture as well, did not contribute to the rent or putting food on the table.

We got quite a few celebrities at Razzamatazz. One day two pretty blond girls pulled up in a Mercedes convertible. They were barefoot, in long skirts, and looked like a couple of hippie chicks. They gaily flitted about the store, gathering quite a few items to purchase. They were very sweet and friendly. It wasn't until they paid me with checks that I realized I had been waiting on Goldie Hawn and Julie Christie. Other celebrity patrons included Elton John and Mick Jagger, although I didn't get to meet either of them. My friend John, also a musician, who usually took the evening shifts, told me he smoked a joint with Mick in the back room. I worked at Razzamatazz for about two years, until it went belly-up in 1973.

* * *

Warren (of Warren and Diana) had been diagnosed with a brain tumor, and had been successfully operated on by a brain surgeon named Joseph Bogen. Warren, who held a PhD in Sociology, theorized that all of the information that had been in the left hemisphere of his brain where the tumor was, 'evacuated' through his corpus callosum (the bridge between the two hemispheres of the brain) over to the right hemisphere, where he could still access it. Out of this theorizing came the notion that people were either 'left-brained' or 'right-brained,' and that each hemisphere had its own 'style of thought.' For instance, right-brained people were more intuitive and artistic and left-brained people were more linear and technical. I could certainly identify with being 'right-brained,' since I had been math/science-challenged all my life, yet instinctively good at anything involving art or music.

So Warren and Dr. Bogen created a proposal to do a study that involved giving a large cross section of the population a long questionnaire that would presumably determine whether they were right-brained or left-brained. And the study got funded. I was hired as one of the interviewers that would go out and find people to take the questionnaire, and administer it. This and the job at Razzamatazz kept me alive for the better part of 1971 and '72.

Although opinions vary about the validity of the 'right-brain/left-brain' theory, there is no denying that the terminology it spawned has become firmly rooted in our current lexicon.

* * *

Meanwhile, I focused on my songwriting and my singing, which was in dire need of improvement. V, whose husband was now off on yet another overseas production, allowed me back into her life and worked with me on my singing. As a consummate actress, she gave me techniques that applied to both acting and singing, like: "Become one with the material; forget that you're singing, just focus on the emotion of the song. Be the character who is telling the story. Never 'vocalize.'" Tips like this really helped and made me improve fast. V started helping me write songs as well. She became my collaborator, my muse and the inspiration for just about every song I wrote during the 1970s.

I was spending more and more time at her place. It was like heaven on earth. I loved everything about her and we fell deeper and deeper in love.

One night I showed up at her house bearing two hits of LSD. "Are you up for this, baby?" She was.

We dropped the acid and spent the next eight hours wrapped in each other, in indescribable ecstasy. As before, the lovemaking was spectacular, perfect—pretty much like it had been 'on the natch,' only about a hundred times more intense.

At some point I concluded that the Universe is one big orgasm. When the church coined "God is love," they were onto more than they realized. I mean, when people have an orgasm, what do they say: "Oh God, oh God, oh my God," right? I rest my case. There is pure ecstasy going on all around us all the time, but we filter it out. If we allowed it in, we would not be able to function in the 'normal' world.

After loving for a long, long time, we were downstairs in her bedroom, looking out at the garden that sloped down to the floor of the canyon below us. "Look," I said, "It looks like the plants are all glowing, like they're on fire!" There was an uneasy pause. We looked at each other wide-eyed, then frantically ran upstairs.

The curtains in the living room were all ablaze. They had caught on one of the candles. It looked to me like the whole house was a goner. I picked up my guitar. "Let's get out of here," I yelled, and I was out the door. Once outside, I realized V was not with me. I put down the guitar and went back in. She had pulled down the burning curtains and was smothering the flames with a blanket. I grabbed another blanket and started to help, but, in moments, it was all over. She had snuffed the blaze single-handedly.

After that, I looked at her with new eyes. This woman had more grit and cool under fire—much more than me—than I ever would have given her credit for. The house was trashed and the fire department was on its way. I had to get the hell out of there. Her husband had to fly back from wherever he was to deal with the insurance company and fixing up the house. It was two months before I could see her again.

Chapter Twenty-Nine

Movin' On Up

Almost the last thing that happened at the Kirkwood Drive house was the Sylmar Earthquake on February 9, 1971. It had a magnitude of 6.1 and lasted twelve seconds—a very long time when you're in it. It was the first earthquake I had ever experienced. The day before it happened, my old friend and fuck-buddy from college, Ginny Sue Robbins, dropped in out of nowhere to visit me, sans motorcycle, but with a baby. She and the little tyke had been hitchhiking all over America, and she had finally made it to the West Coast. That night the baby bedded down in my guitar case and Ginny Sue got into bed with me and said, "Now, just pretend you're all alone. There's nobody here…" She burrowed under the covers and gave me the second-best blow job of my life—the best being the first one she had given me at Goddard six years earlier.

Around dawn, the place started shaking like crazy. I was pretty sure the ceiling would fall in on us. Ginny Sue jumped out of bed and covered the baby with her body. He started crying. She picked him up and put him to her breast, then got back into bed. We all huddled together until the shaking stopped. It was a cold February morning in Laurel Canyon. After things calmed down, I turned to her and said, as straight-faced as possible, "The earth really moved for me last night, baby."

After that, wild stories began to circulate that, in the next big earthquake, half of California would break off, right along the San Andreas Fault, and tumble into the Pacific.

* * *

Warren and Diana got a divorce later that month and neither one of them wanted to remain in the Lookout Mountain house. They offered to rent it to us for the cost of their mortgage payment: $300 a month. This was a huge bump up from the $175 we had been paying for the place on Kirkwood, but it was such a beautiful house, we had to go for it. Ron, who was now a licensed psychotherapist, proposed to use one of the downstairs bedrooms as his office—as well as his bedroom—and start seeing private clients. He also would lead group therapy sessions once a week in the living room. I had my piddling income from my job at Razzamatazz, and we had acquired a third roommate, who we hoped would soon find some visible means of support.

David was a guy who had been a rabid fan of The Lost back in Buffalo, NY—one of our biggest strongholds—and had somehow tracked me down upon coming to LA. Ron's friend Tony had returned to Chicago some months earlier and David, a fresh-faced blond kid of about twenty, arrived virtually on the heels of Tony's departure, immediately ingratiating himself by doing all the housework and making himself our ward and houseboy. We became a sort of structured triumvirate: Ron was called 'Dr. Dog' after one of his children's books. I was 'Boy One' and David was 'Boy Three,' soon shortened to simply "Three." Why was there no number two, you ask? Well, would you want to be number two? So Three moved into the other downstairs bedroom and I took the master bedroom upstairs. Suddenly I was living like the rock star I longed to be. It was definitely a step in the right direction.

In our backyard at Lookout Mtn. L to R: Ron (holding Fang), me,
David – March 1972

* * *

My job at Razzamatazz afforded me free entrance to the Troubadour just about any time I wanted to get in. When Van Morrison came to town, I hit up my friend at the box office for a hand stamp and joined the throng outside waiting to be let in. Suddenly I found myself eyeball-to-eyeball with two of the prettiest blue eyes I had ever seen—and she was returning my stare. She was gorgeous—and smiling at me wantonly. *Holy shit*, I said to myself, *that's Jane Fonda!* Then she was swallowed up by the crowd. Once inside, I looked all over for her, but she had disappeared—probably to the backstage area. Damn, another near miss!

Then Van and the band came on, and there was my old friend, Jack Schroer, on woodwinds. Van was at his zenith, the songs were great, the band was great. I thought he was the best solo artist then extant in America. Afterward, I got to tell Van how great I thought he was and sit down with Jack and catch up. Jack and Ellen were living in San Rafael in Marin County, and they had a little girl. He gave me their address and number and invited me to come up there and visit. The idea of seeing Northern California again appealed to me.

I looked around the backstage area for Jane, but there was no sign of her. Maybe she had been a hallucination.

* * *

Our old friend Darlene introduced us to Bob Cooper, a director of low budget hardcore porno movies, which he exported to Japan. Bob was a tall guy with shoulder-length sandy hair. He always wore a headband made out of a kerchief, Apache-style. Bob was looking for shooting locations. He came over and, once he checked out our house, he offered us $300 to shoot there for just one day. Suddenly our rent was paid for the entire month. We drew straws, and I won the honor of presiding over the house on the day of the shoot. Ron and Three had to make themselves scarce.

The crew consisted of Bob, a camera guy and a sound guy. The talent consisted of Darlene, who was average height and build and had shoulder-length brown hair and very white skin with freckles, a short, blond girl with an odd-shaped body—small breasts and a wide waist, and a taller, slinkier brunette girl with kinky hair. There were two guys: a shorter, muscular blond guy and a taller, bearded guy with the biggest schlong I had ever seen. It turns out this was the fabled John Holmes, soon to become perhaps the most infamous male porn star of all time. Not just for his body of work, which included both heterosexual and gay porn, but also for his alleged involvement in the notorious Wonderland Avenue murders that took place in Laurel Canyon in July 1981, ten years later. How any of those girls were going to get that thing into any of their orifices was beyond me.

In between takes, I overheard Darlene trying to get Holmes hot. She sprayed some whipped cream on his cock and proceeded to lick it off. "Does that feel good?" she said in her most seductive voice.

"No," replied Holmes, expressionless.

He impressed me as someone completely devoid of human feeling. What a joker that God is. He attaches the all-time greatest pleasure-making tool to someone as numb as a stone.

The shoot went off without a hitch. The script, if there was one, was minimal to say the least. I think it was a home invasion scenario, with the two guys breaking in on a houseful of nubile babes. They shot a series of sex scenes with different combinations of players, in each of the three bedrooms. Bob and his crew were completely professional. They got in, they got out and he paid me in cash. I had to change all the sheets, but it was the easiest $300 I had ever made.

Chapter Thirty

A Road Trip with Van

A week later I was driving north on the I-5 on my way to visit Jack and Ellen. I got the warm and fuzzies driving over the Golden Gate Bridge, thinking of my time in Northern California and tripping with that sweet young girl in Mill Valley. That seemed like ages ago, but I had been in LA just two years.

Jack and Ellen rented a modest house on a quiet, tree-lined street in San Rafael. Ellen was as beautiful as I remembered her and she had an incredibly cute, golden-haired little girl about three. We hung out and talked about old times and then Jack suggested we go over to Fairfax and see Van and Janet.

Van and his wife Janet Planet—I guess she took that name because of her avid interest in astrology—lived in a spacious, rustic-modern home nestled among a stand of tall sycamores. The living room, which was on the upper level, was all glass and wood and was surrounded on two sides by a wide wooden deck that overlooked the front driveway and the woods beyond. Van was short and barrel-chested. He was looking the best I'd seen him, with his long red hair and a mustache and goatee. Janet was a real beauty, with hair the color of Tupelo honey and big green eyes. She seemed somewhat highly-strung and was clearly the dominant personality in this household. Van was obviously devoted to her. She invited us all to stay for dinner.

Jack told Van I was a songwriter. "Oh yeah?" he said, "I'd like to hear your music sometime."

"How 'bout now?" I asked brazenly, and whipped out my tape.

We all adjourned downstairs to the garage, which had been turned into a recording and rehearsal studio. Van seemed to actually like my music. He was not the kind to dish out phony praise. One song, called "The Raptures," was his favorite. "It's because there's a gypsy in it," Jack confided. "He likes anything with gypsies." Then Van put on a tape of his new album, which was as yet unreleased. From the first song, "Wild Night," I knew it would be a hit. My favorite, though, was the title track, "Tupelo Honey," which was transcendent, and no doubt written for Janet. I felt incredibly fortunate to be in that place at that time, and I said so.

Van asked me if I might be interested in working for him as road manager/'rehearsal manager.' In the latter role I would be his 'stand-in' at rehearsals, teaching his songs to the band and doing the lead vocals. On the road I would be in charge of making all the travel arrangements and overseeing the crew that carried and set up the equipment. He offered me a salary of $300 a week, big money in 1971. But it meant I would have to put my own musical career on hold. I told him I would have to think it over.

At dinner, Janet had an important announcement. She had done numerous consultations with the heavens and there was now no doubt in her mind that the Big Earthquake, the one that would break California off and drown it in the sea, was coming within DAYS. There was only one thing for us to do: pack up our essential belongings, get in our cars and drive east.

No one doubted her veracity.

The next day Van and Janet in their green Audi, Jack, Ellen, their daughter and I in their camper (a pickup truck with a camper shell), and a third couple, Axel and Lily, in their Opel, all hit the road eastward, headed God knows where.

What followed was a mini-Exodus, an epic pilgrimage. We meandered across California and Nevada, and then headed north for a bit into Wyoming, then back down into Utah. Like the Children of Israel, we wandered, with no direction home, through the American wilderness. At Salt Lake City we stopped at a motel.

It was mid-August and blisteringly hot. We sat around the motel swimming pool. Van, who was covered from head to toe to protect his snow-white Irish skin from the desert sun, seeing I was getting a lovely tan, lamented that he envied me my complexion. I confided to him that it was because I was part gypsy. He ate it up. But the bigger issue was that we lacked a destination. Jack suggested his parental home, Albuquerque, New Mexico. We all immediately agreed. But then Van and Janet announced that they were tired of driving. They gave me the keys to their Audi, along with some money for gas and food and we drove them to the airport.

With me helming the Audi, we made our way further east into Colorado and then south, snaking our way along precarious Rocky Mountain roads toward New Mexico. The cars overheated often, as they would back then, and we had to stop frequently to add water to the radiators. The Audi, which was touted as a luxury car, impressed me as a big green lemon.

Finally, we made it to Albuquerque. Backing out of a parking space at a 7-11, I backed into a car that was parked behind me. No damage to the other car, but the Audi needed a new taillight. I didn't have enough money, so Jack had to take care of it. Fortunately, we got it fixed before Van found out.

Jack's parents were surprised, but very hospitable. We stayed in Albuquerque a few days, with me sleeping in the camper, Van and Janet in a hotel and the others staying in the house. We waited for the Big One to hit California, but we waited in vain. Finally, we could put our lives on hold no longer. We headed home. Van and Janet caught a plane, and I was left the task of driving the thousand-or-so miles back to Marin County.

During the trip I had a lot of time to think about Van's offer. The challenge of making the high rent on Lookout Mountain combined with my dim prospects as a musician led me to decide to accept. When we got back I told Van I would take the job. I just needed to go back to LA to put my affairs in order. My plan was to retain my residence on Lookout Mountain by continuing to contribute to the rent there and also establish a residence here in Marin. V was also much on my mind. Her husband was still very much on the scene, and I didn't know if or when I would be able to see her again.

Upon arriving back in LA, I let my roommates know what had transpired. I would be making an entire month's rent every week working for Van, so they needn't worry about making the rent. I was able to speak briefly with V and break the news. She said it was probably for the best, as our love was doomed to failure anyway. When I was ready to leave, I phoned Van, almost as an afterthought, and told him I was on my way. "Who?" he asked.

"It's me, Ted," I said, "You know, the guy you hired to be your road manager."

"Oh," said Van vaguely, "nah, I hired somebody else."

Rock Star Etiquette, Lesson #2: *What is true one day, may not be true the next; always strike before the iron freezes.* And so ended another California adventure. Square one revisited.

Van Morrison and Janet Planet. Photo: Ron Landy/Getty Images

Chapter Thirty-One

Going in Circles

When I finally regained access to V's domain it was miraculously transformed. Wall-to-wall white carpeting, two round silver velvet cushions the size of tractor wheels dominated the living room, and there were two silver velvet couches along the walls. Over by the window was a white baby grand piano and in each of the four corners of the room was a huge, white Altec speaker, the size of a small refrigerator. She had installed a stereo with quadraphonic sound, a new process which created the illusion of surround sound by throwing the two discrete stereo tracks out of phase and putting the out of phase tracks through two additional speakers. It made the sound rather ringy and less present, which I did not find terribly pleasing.

But what mattered was that I was back in her heavenly presence. We collapsed onto one of the cushions, put *Abbey Road* on the turntable, lit up a joint, and just held each other for hours.

* * *

We started going to the Golden Temple to meditate with the Sikhs, followers of Yogi Bhajan. These turban-headed yogis were practitioners of Kundalini yoga, in which the "serpent force" is awakened through chanting and prana yama (breathing exercises) and channeled up the spine, through the various chakras, and ultimately out the top of the head. V and I started using these techniques in our lovemaking, since this seemed to be occurring naturally anyway. At one of these gatherings we met a woman V knew from the movie business. She called herself Jaiananda, and it turned out she lived right near us in Laurel Canyon. Jai, an attractive brunette in her early thirties, was working with the director of a film that was being shot in England called *X, Y & Zee*. It starred Elizabeth Taylor and Michael Caine, and Jai was helping to develop the script. When she found out I was a songwriter she asked me if I'd like to collaborate with her on a song for the movie. Being decidedly not busy, I agreed immediately.

In a series of meetings, Jai and I went through the script and started crafting a lyric from the main character's point of view. I came up with a minor key melody that I thought sounded like a typical movie theme. I was thinking of "Windmills of Your Mind," the theme from *The Thomas Crowne Affair*, which had been a big hit in 1969. I even co-opted the circles-themed lyric of "Windmills." We called the song "Going in Circles." From what I had observed of music in Hollywood movies of the '60s and '70s, too much originality and hipness would not serve us well. What we needed was mediocrity.

Jai financed the demo session, and I brought in Ted Greene on guitar and Jack Conrad on bass. Ted introduced me to a drummer named Eddie Tuduri, who turned out to be a great choice. We got a classically trained female pianist, which was very appropriate for this song. The instrumental bridge sounded very Bach-like and was played by a recorder ensemble. The demo turned out amazingly. I was singing the best I ever had, and the quality of the recording surpassed anything I had done previously. It was also the first time I had ever been in complete control of one of my recording sessions.

We sent the demo to the director, and he loved it. We were in! I had achieved critical mass mediocrity-wise for this first level of acceptance. But we needed to parlay this into something that would actually create some money. We needed for the song to be cut by a major recording artist for the soundtrack of the movie. Jai and I set about making a list of potential artists.

There was Johnny Rivers, who was in the twilight of his career, but whose voice would work on the song, there was Dusty Springfield, who I loved, and who had sung "Windmills of Your Mind," and thinking of Dusty somehow brought Jackie DeShannon to mind, and then there was a great singer named Mike Harrison, late of the English band, Spooky Tooth. And then we thought of Three Dog Night, the band that was neither fish nor fowl. Three Dog Night represented themselves as a band, but was in reality three blue-eyed soul singers fronting a four-piece backup band. What songwriters loved about Three Dog Night was that they didn't write most of their own material. They were famous for putting aspiring songwriters on the musical map. These included, among many others, Laura Nyro, Hoyt Axton, Paul Williams, Randy Newman and Harry Nilsson. We put a big star next to them on the list.

But before we even got started shopping the song to artists, I got a call from Lester Sill, president of Screen Gems, Columbia Pictures' music publishing arm. Lester came on strong. "Hey kid, congratulations! We need you to get down here to sign the papers right away."

"Huh?"

"You wrote the song 'Going in Circles,' right?"

"Yeah…"

"Well, I need you to sign the publishing contract."

"Really? Why's that?"

"Well, your song's in a Columbia Picture, therefore we take the publishing."

"Oh really? What're you gonna give us for it?"

Then Lester went ballistic. "Give you? We're giving you the opportunity to get your song in a major motion picture, that's what!" But I was cool.

"*We* got our song in the picture, not you. What kind of advance are you offering?"

"You little punk. You're nobody! This is a chance of a lifetime for you. Now, get over here and sign the contract!"

"I'll have to get back to you," I said sweetly and hung up. It felt great to have some leverage with one of these assholes.

I called Jai and asked her to talk to the director. "Find out if we're obligated to give the publishing to Screen Gems. And see if he can refer us to an attorney." She did as I asked, and got back to me with two phone numbers. First, we called Lalo Schifrin, noted film composer. He confirmed that a major studio generally got the publishing on a song written for a major motion picture. Next, we called Bruce Raymer, the lawyer that had been recommended to us. He agreed to represent us. It should be noted here that, a few years later, Stephen Spielberg named his mechanical shark in *Jaws* 'Bruce,' after his attorney, Bruce Raymer. Ultimately we signed the publishing away to Screen Gems, but they gave us an advance of $1,500, plus they reimbursed Jai for the cost of the demo. Now we set about trying to find an artist for our song.

We sent the demo to everyone on our list, and then some. We found out that Danny Hutton of Three Dog Night lived near the Canyon Country

Store on Little Laurel Canyon Boulevard. One morning we knocked on his door. He answered, bleary-eyed, in his bathrobe, obviously unaccustomed to being awakened at the ungodly hour of eleven in the morning. We awkwardly introduced ourselves, told him about the song being in the movie, and thrust the cassette into his hands, then fled.

Nearly a year passed, and we never heard back from any of the artists. Post production was winding down on the movie. The director had recorded a version of our song with an unknown artist he had found in England and told us that this was the version he was going to use. We hated it. Our demo wiped the floor with this version. We were heartsick. For me, it looked like another 'close, but no cigar.'

It must have been December 1972 when I got the call. It was Tom Thacker, who worked for Three Dog Night's management, Reb Foster Associates, calling to let me know they had stumbled upon my cassette in a pile of stuff in their office and they loved "Going in Circles." They were going to cut it, even though they realized it was probably too late to get it in the movie.

"No, it's not!" I yelled, my voice strangled with a mixture of panic and elation. "It's in the final stages of post-production. How quickly can you get into the studio and record it?"

But there were more shenanigans from Lester Sill. When he found out Three Dog Night was cutting the song, he first congratulated himself on getting the song to them, and then he told them it had to be the A side of their next single, or else they couldn't cut it. Was this guy *nuts*? Here we have a guaranteed million-selling record, and he's trying to sabotage it. I had Jai call the director, the director called the head of Columbia Pictures, and he called Sill and told him to just get Three Dog Night to cut the record.

A week later Jai and I were invited to Richie Podolor's American Recording Studios on Ventura Boulevard to hear the finished song. I was not that attached to the song, which as stated earlier was a calculatedly commercial effort from the start, so I was not at all upset that Three Dog Night's version was nowhere close to my original concept. I was thrilled to be in the studio with them, and they were all super nice to us.

The track was rushed over to Columbia's editing room on Gower Street where the director dubbed it onto the end titles of the picture. It turned out the song, at more than three minutes, was a lot longer than the credits, so on the original cut of the film, there is circular credit that says "'Going in

Circles' performed by Three Dog Night, written by Ted Myers & Jaiananda" and it stays on the screen for a full minute at the very end.

The timing was so tight that there was no time to get the finished film on a commercial flight to New York for the premier, which was the following night. So Three Dog Night took the film and flew it there on their private jet.

The song came out on the B side of Three Dog Night's next single, "The Family of Man" which, ironically, was a song written by my bass player, Jack Conrad, and Paul Williams. A few months earlier Jack had asked me to try to come up with a lyric for it, and I came up with "Long Gone Train," not one of my more inspired lyrics. Later, Jack took it and reworked it with Paul Williams, who had already enjoyed considerable success as the writer of Three Dog Night's "An Old Fashioned Love Song."

The single peaked at #12 on the charts and sold over a million copies. "Going in Circles" also appeared on Three Dog's next album, *Seven Separate Fools*, which sold in the millions, as well as a live version, which appeared on the next album after that, *Around the World with Three Dog Night*, which also went gold. I ended up receiving royalties on over six million records. My calculated bid for mediocrity had paid off bigger than anything else in my career. But I was not so cynical as to stop following my true creative vision and start cranking out soulless crap. I was sure that this success would be a springboard that would enable me to share my real talent with the world.

Although there had been a screening for Three Dog Night, I never got to see the film until it came out on video many years later. If I had, I would have realized that John Barry, who composed the score, used melodic themes from "Going in Circles" all through the movie. You don't really get any royalties for something like that in the US, but in Europe, where the movie was huge, I was told they pay for cues in theatrical showings of a film. Probably not enough to raise a stink about, though. Actually, I was quite flattered that Barry, a very big film composer in those days, liked the song enough to lift from it.

Chapter Thirty-Two

Young, Hip and On the Scene

We went to lots of concerts in the '70s. With her money and connections, V would get tickets to Led Zeppelin at the Forum three nights in a row, all of them in the first three rows. When we walked down the aisle to our seats, people would look at us, decked out in our platform shoes and velvet splendor, and wonder what branch of the Rock Royalty Tree we had fallen from. We got to see The Who, The Stones, Queen, just the best of the best. And always the best seats in the house.

Once, we dropped acid and went to the Santa Monica Civic to see The James Gang opening for Steve Miller. Joe Walsh was doing some amazing slide guitar work with an Echoplex and a pedal that panned the stereo guitar sound from hard left to hard right and back again. We could 'see' the notes, zooming back and forth across the wide stage, which had a solid wall of Marshall stacks on either side of the drums. By the end of The James Gang's set our minds had turned to Jell-O. Walsh had put us in a place we did not want to come down from. We decided not to stay for Steve Miller, as we were sure his lightweight pop songs would bust our balloon. We got to our car, only to realize the parking lot had filled up and cars surrounded us on all sides. Instead of doing the sensible thing—go back inside—I got behind the wheel and started inching forward, and back, turning the car slightly each time toward a narrow opening through which our car would just fit. It took us about fifteen minutes to get out of that parking space, but on acid it seemed like hours. On the drive home we felt like a pair of escaped prisoners, having just broken out of the big house.

* * *

I had been in contact with my high school girlfriend, Sophi, who was now married. She and her husband, Derek, came out to visit me. Sophi was suffering from random panic attacks, and Ron undertook to help her with psychotherapy sessions, which he did pro bono. Sophi was still a brilliant and beautiful girl. She had cut her hair short, in sort of a bob, but otherwise looked much the same as she had in college. Derek was an ectomorphic Brit with a frizzy halo of flaming red hair. They were as rabid a pair of rock fans as V and I.

We got tickets to see Deep Purple at the Long Beach Arena, and six of us—Derek and Sophi, V and I, Ron and Three—all piled into V's big gold Mercedes and drove down to Long Beach. Deep Purple were no Led Zeppelin, but they were quite stellar that night. Ian Gillan sang the shit out of "Highway Star." After the concert we exited through a side door that put us at the foot of a long ramp that led to the backstage area. "Wait here," Sophi said, and she walked up the ramp and disappeared. We waited. After about fifteen minutes, Sophi emerged with Ritchie Blackmore, the lead guitarist of Deep Purple. She was literally leading him by the hand! She introduced him to all of us. He was very quiet but pleasant, and he invited us all to a private party in West Hollywood at the Black Rabbit on Melrose. I knew the place; it was one of those trendy little restaurants that are the 'in spot' for about two months and then fold. Anyway, we were happy to attend, and so we told Ritchie we would see him there.

The Black Rabbit was packed with revelers. We told the door person we were guests of Ritchie Blackmore and were let right in. We found ourselves a table and were served all kinds of lovely free food and drinks. We scanned the room for Ritchie, but could not see him. Three hooked up with an attractive young girl and disappeared at some point. The next day he showed up and told us that he had gone home with Robert Mitchum's daughter and had sat up all night smoking joints and talking with Mitchum himself.

At last I spotted Ritchie way in a back corner, sitting at a table by himself, looking morose. "Hey, Ritchie," I said, "we've been looking for you!"

"Fuck off and leave me alone," he muttered drunkenly, as much to his beer as to me. Rock Star Etiquette, Lesson #3: *In the fast lane, mood swings are as common as speeding tickets.*

V and I also got to attend several memorable gigs by major acts at the Whiskey: Chicago, the J. Geils Band and Aerosmith (before they broke big). Elmer Valentine, the owner of the Whiskey, was a friend of V's husband and always reserved us a great table. When we went to see Chicago, we were waiting outside amidst a huge crowd of people and Elmer had someone come out and page V, then lead us through the throng, and seat us at our table before they let in the hoi polloi. It was quite a time to be young, hip and on the scene.

Ritchie Blackmore, 1972. Photo: Jorgan Angel/Getty Images

Chapter Thirty-Three

Fang

One day a rotund hippie chick named Lorie, whom I always thought of as 'Mother Earth,' walked into Razzamatazz with the cutest little puppy I had ever seen. I was not actively seeking a dog, but there was something about this one that made me really want her. She was off-white and shaggy. She looked like a powder puff with eyes. I knew Lorie was an animal nut and already had a small zoo in her apartment, which was nearby.

"Oh my god, Lorie, that's the cutest dog I have ever seen!" I said. "Where did you get it?"

"The vet across the street gave her to me. She was abandoned."

"I can't believe anyone would abandon a cute little thing like that."

"You'd be surprised," she said.

"How many animals do you have now?"

"This is the third dog, and I have five cats."

"Jeez, how big is your apartment?"

"One bedroom," she said, smiling.

"Listen, Lorie, I really love this dog. I just moved into a huge, three-bedroom home in Laurel Canyon, with a big dog door and an acre of land. She would have that all to herself. And me and my two roommates would look after her like she was our own child."

"Well…"

"C'mon, Lorie, you know how much happier she would be up in the canyon…"

"Well… okay."

So Lorie gave the unnamed little ball of fur to me.

Sophi and Derek were still staying with us when I brought the dog home. Sophi melted. She attached herself to the dog and wouldn't let go. Because of her fragile mental state, I let Sophi be the puppy's temporary mommy. We had been doing a Soupy Sales thing lately in the house. Soupy had been on TV all through the '60s with a quirky kid's show for adults. He had a character on his show called White Fang. All you would see of White Fang was a giant paw extending out from the camera toward Soupy. White Fang would sort of speak and growl at the same time. Instead of "hello," White Fang would say "reh-row," and that was our current gag around the house, everyone extending a paw and saying "reh-row." So, sitting around discussing what to call this sweet little girl puppy, we naturally came up with White Fang, which was shortened almost immediately to Fang. It was the perfect misnomer for my little white ball of fur.

Almost simultaneously, Kyle, my old band mate from The Lost and Chamæleon Church, showed up. Kyle had been knocking around Europe, working as an actor and musician and had now decided to check out the West Coast. I was, of course, happy to see him again, but, as we sat around catching up and talking about old times, I began to sense a weird dynamic developing between him and Sophi. He sensed her high-strung state of mind and seemed to take some pleasure in needling her. She responded with hostility, which merely incited him to further teasing. When Derek came in, Kyle spotted a kindred spirit. Seeing them together was like seeing Kyle and Walter together, the perfect symbiotic recipe for trouble. Derek even looked like Walter, except for the red curly hair. With Derek as the passive enabler/cheerleader and Kyle the aggressive showoff/bully, I suspected we were in for a bumpy ride. Kyle took Fang and threw her across the room, just to enrage Sophi. That was it for me. I couldn't believe my old buddy would do a thing like that. "What the hell is wrong with you?" I asked. I was beginning to think he was high on something.

"Aw, c'mon," he said, "I was just playin.'"

"That's just a little puppy. You better play nice with her from now on." I was ready to throw him out, but he didn't have any place to stay and he didn't know anyone in LA except me. Sophi pulled me aside and begged me not to let him stay, but I didn't know how to turn him away.

So Kyle crashed on our couch that night.

At about three in the morning, I was awakened by the sounds of Jimi Hendrix playing "Voodoo Child" booming through the hollows of the canyon. I got up and looked outside. All the lights at V's house were blazing. I quickly got dressed and went over there. She answered the door immediately and let me in. On the couch, nursing a bottle of brandy and three sheets to the wind were Kyle and Derek. I was furious. "What the hell are you guys doing here?"

"It's alright," V said gently, obviously trying to keep tempers calm, "I let them in."

"You shouldn't have," I said. Then to Kyle: "What made you think you could bust in on her at three o'clock in the morning?"

"She's just so sweet. We just wanted to say hello."

Something about this reminded me of *A Clockwork Orange* and the thought passed through my mind that they might have meant to actually do her harm, consciously or unconsciously. "Why does this not make me feel better?" I said. "C'mon, you guys have to get out of here—now."

"Oh, relax, Teddy. Everything's cool."

"No, nothing's cool. You gotta go."

I walked over and grabbed Kyle's arm in an effort to move him toward the door. He was much bigger and stronger than me and always loved to fight. He pushed me away hard. I stumbled back. Then he came after me and was about to haul off with a punch. From the couch, Derek was observing with glee. V was horrified. As he raised his fist, I threw both my arms around him and hugged him. I stroked his head lovingly. I whispered right in his ear, "I love you, man. Don't do this." Then I released him. "Okay?" Kyle motioned to Derek and they both left. I grabbed V and we held each other, shaking.

When I went back to the house, there was no sign of Kyle and Derek. Sophi was in the living room, sitting in the dark. "They went to a party," she said flatly.

"At this hour?"

"They were there earlier. It's an all-nighter—with groupies and drugs."

Then she broke down crying. I put my arms around her. Through her sobs she told me things had been getting very shaky with Derek lately. She didn't drink or do any drugs, and he had started drinking heavily; maybe doing some other things as well. Their marriage was crumbling. That night I let her stay in my room. Fang and Sophi both slept in bed with me. I didn't put the moves on either of them.

The next day Three came home. He had been at the same party. He said Kyle and Derek were still there. Sophi made him take her over there. She walked in on Derek in bed with two girls. She woke him up so he could see her, and then left. She came back to the house and shut herself up in the downstairs bedroom. We didn't see her for the rest of the day. The following day she got a call from Derek. He was in New York. "He just left me here," she said, heartbroken. Sophi stayed on a few days more, and then she too flew back to New York. I don't think they ever lived together again, but her panic attacks subsided.

Fang remained my best friend and closest confidant for the next fourteen years.

Me & young Fang, 1972

Chapter Thirty-Four

Opportunity Knocks and I Knock Back

One night in 1972, V and I were leaving the Mayfair Market on Santa Monica Boulevard. As we walked through the darkened parking lot the door on an old VW bus slid open and an arm appeared holding a Gibson Melody Maker electric guitar. It was proffered majestically, like the Lady of the Lake bearing Excalibur, and it had about it the same portent of destiny. A voice whispered from within the van: "Psst! Wanna buy a guitar? Fifteen dollars." The whole thing reeked of 'hot,' but I didn't hesitate. I really needed an electric guitar, and this one fit nicely into my pathetic budget. I never even saw the face of the guy I bought it from. I thrust the money into the van, grabbed the guitar and off we went.

When I got it home, I saw that the neck had been broken and reset badly. This would throw off the intonation and make the guitar impossible to tune. I took it to Valley Sound on Sunset, the most prestigious instrument repair shop in LA, and who should appear behind the counter to take my order? None other than my old friend and lead guitarist from Ultimate Spinach, Jeff "Skunk" Baxter. He looked pretty much the same as he had in Spinach: shoulder-length brown hair, but his beard was gone and his mustache was bigger and fuller. He generally wore glasses, except when he was performing, and he was wearing them now. Jeff had always been good with fixing stuff and being up on all the latest gear, so it made sense to see him working there.

"Whazzhapnin'!" he slurred in his trademark hipster voice.

"Wow, fancy meetin' you here," I said. "I didn't know you were in LA."

"Yeah, been here a few months. I've been doing some studio work with some guys over at ABC Dunhill on Beverly Boulevard."

He looked at my guitar and deemed it fixable. He showed it to the guy who specialized in guitar building, and they gave me an estimate I could afford, so I dropped off the guitar. Before leaving we exchanged numbers.

When the guitar came back from Valley Sound, it was perfect. Before I was through, I would buy two Humbucking pickups and have them installed, making it a Les Paul Jr. My guitar arsenal was once again complete.

It was maybe two or three weeks later that Baxter phoned and told me he had formed a band with these guys he had met at Dunhill Studios, Don Fagen and Walter Becker, plus a couple of other guys. They were going to call it Steely Dan after a strap-on dildo in William S. Burroughs' *Naked Lunch*.

"Fagen and Becker are writing all the songs," he said, "but Fagen is very uptight about his voice, so we need a lead singer. Would you be interested in auditioning?"

Well, frankly, I wasn't sure. I was primarily a songwriter myself and a singer second. I'd have to really, really love these guys' songs to give up my songwriting at this point, especially right after my first flush of success.

"Can I hear some of their music?" I asked.

"Yeah, we've got one song on tape. You wanna come over and hear it?"

I agreed to come over to Baxter's apartment and listen to the tape.

Chez Skunk was a nondescript modern apartment in a nondescript apartment building near Valley Sound, which was located at Gardner and Sunset in Hollywood. It was devoid of furniture, except for a mattress on the floor, a dining table and a couple of chairs. And amps, keyboards, guitars and a pedal steel guitar. Jeff put the tape on for me. It was a song called "Bye Bye Dallas," which sounded distinctly country. Jeff played pedal steel on it, which was his latest passion.

"Well," I said, trying to be tactful, "the band sounds great—all the players are excellent—but it sounds very country to me. I don't wanna waste your time. I don't think I'd be the right guy for this band."

A month later, Jeff invited me to Steely Dan's debut performance at Under the Ice House in Pasadena. Their songs knocked me out. "Bye Bye Dallas" was not in the set—and never appeared on any of their albums. Two weeks later, their debut single, "Do It Again," hit the charts and wound up going to #6. The guy they hired as lead singer, David Palmer, sounded a lot like Donald Fagen, and once Fagen got his vocal chops up to speed, Palmer was gone. There but for fortune…

Steely Dan, 1972

Chapter Thirty-Five

Once More Into the Breach

I figured the best thing I could do to capitalize on the success of "Going in Circles" was to get credible management. Terry Kirkman was kind enough to introduce me to Pat Colecchio, the manager of The Association. Pat, in turn, assigned me to his junior partner Lee Leibman. Lee agreed to manage me on a handshake to see how things worked out. If he could get things moving for me, we would sign a formal contract.

All I can remember about that experience is that Lee tried to get radio stations to flip "The Family of Man" over and play "Going in Circles." As far as I could tell, he achieved no results. He couldn't really shop me a record deal because the only studio tapes I had were the Tree Music tapes, which everyone had heard and passed on and the "Going in Circles" demo, which did not embody my sound as an artist. I needed to record a really good studio tape, and I had no budget to do it. I was not to receive my first royalty check for "Going in Circles" for another six months. A quandary.

* * *

One day I got a phone call from Kim Fowley, who was already a legendary and controversial Hollywood character three years prior to discovering and producing a band of sixteen-year-old girls called The Runaways. Kim told me he liked my Three Dog Night song and he wanted to offer me a publishing deal. I was skeptical but intrigued. I had seen Kim haunting Hollywood nightspots like the Rainbow and Rodney Bingenheimer's English Disco.

He was an impossibly tall, impossibly thin wraithlike figure with blond hair and sunken cheeks. Kinda scary, really. V said I should invite him up to her place. She even leant me her Mercedes to go pick him up at the Chateau Marmont, where he was currently residing. So I swooped down and whisked him up to V's palatial digs. If he was suitably impressed, he wasn't obvious about it, but he seemed well pleased with the setup. The plan was, I was going to play him some of my songs live on guitar, but the evening that unfolded was much more interesting than that. After smoking the obligatory joint, we all adjourned to V's velvet cushions and Kim held forth on his career as a male prostitute—in graphic detail. Seeing we were not shocked, but rather amused, he dropped that tack and decided to show us his improvisational prowess. And this was indeed impressive. Kim would say, "Play something Beatles style," and I would launch into some Beatle-like chords, and he would make up a faux-Beatles song, complete with rhyming lyrics, to my chord changes, right on the spot. Then he would say, "Okay, play blues chords," then a Bob Dylan progression, and on and on. And he kept up an unending stream of spontaneous lyrics and melodies that really held water for what must have been an hour. I never did play him any of my songs and no business was discussed, but we had a hell of a good time that night.

* * *

I learned that my old friend from the East Coast, Irwin Pincus, had started a publishing/management company in LA. Irwin and his father, George Pincus, had run Gil Music out of New York for years. They had done a publishing deal with The Remains, which is how I came to know them, and they had been the first publishers to snag American publishing rights to the earliest songs by The Beatles. Most of all, I knew Irwin as a sweet, honest and genuine guy whom I trusted. We spoke, and I went over to see Irwin and his junior partner, Stan Milander, at their office in Crossroads of the World.

Irwin, who was old school but a real gent, offered welcome relief from the Hollywood shuck and jive. He had curly dark hair and wore glasses, reminding me a little of my dad. Stan was about my age with blue eyes and bushy light brown hair that looked like a lion's mane. He and I formed an instant rapport. I played them some of my new songs live and they offered to find me a producer and finance master-quality demos in exchange for my publishing.

I called Lee Leibman and Pat Colecchio, who were technically still my managers, thanked them for their efforts, and signed with Irwin and Stan. It turned out that Irwin and Stan already had an engineer/producer in mind. Bruce Ablin was the house engineer at a sixteen-track studio in Hollywood called Golden West. I went over to the studio to meet with Bruce and was very favorably impressed. This was indeed a state-of-the-art studio and Bruce, a solidly-built guy with shoulder-length brown hair and wire rimmed glasses, clearly knew his way around it. He was soft spoken and used meticulously proper diction, always a good sign as far as I was concerned. I made it clear that I had certain production ideas and that I would insist on sharing creative control. Bruce readily agreed and we were off to the races.

I wanted to start fresh with all new musicians. Bruce introduced me to Rob Moitoza, an excellent bass player and singer. Rob and I ran down a few of my songs and I liked both his sound and the parts he came up with. Bruce also found lead guitarist Gary Rolls. He too turned out to be a good fit. I had seen a band recently called Skylark with an excellent young keyboard player named David Foster. I had gotten his number when I heard him and now I called him. He was available.

At that time in my recording career, I was obsessed with the Perfect Drum Sound. It was my Holy Grail. Drums are hard to record, and The Beatles had set the bar for the ultimate drum sound, starting with *Sgt. Pepper's*. I had tried for it every time I had been in the studio but never came close. None of the engineers I'd worked with had a clue. I discussed this with Bruce and we were on the same page. The first step was to find the perfect drummer. I heard Paul Williams at the Troubadour and, while I was not that impressed with him as an artist, I was with his drummer, Gary Mallaber. Gary was a well-known session player and quite in demand. He was expensive, but we brought him in to lay down some basic tracks with me and Rob. Because his time was so valuable, there was not a lot of time to play around with drum sounds. The results of that session were disappointing. I wasn't even crazy about the grooves this guy was playing. It can be so deceptive when you go hear someone and love what they're doing with another artist and then actually try to play with them and you realize you just don't click.

Bruce came up with a drummer named Bobby (I can't remember his last name). He played great on my stuff. What's more, he came into the studio two or three hours before anyone else, and he and Bruce noodled with mic-ing and tuning the drums. When Rob, Gary and I arrived for the session, the Perfect Drum Sound had been dialed in. This was a really valuable lesson for me. Talent and chops are important assets, but the greatest asset you can have in the recording studio is *time*.

We cut solid basic tracks on four songs. Next, David Foster (who later went on to become one of the most successful record producers of all time, recording artists such as Chicago, Kenny Rogers and Barbra Streisand) came in and laid down some beautiful acoustic piano tracks. While listening to the playback of one, a song called "It's Too Bad," he commented, "I'd cut that."

But Bruce and I felt there was still something missing. The tracks needed more going on, even after we added background vocals. We decided that what we needed was a synthesizer. The next time I came into the studio, Bruce had an Arp synthesizer set up and ready to go. Only none of us had a clue as to how to get a sound out of it. Like the Moog, the Arp had several patch bays that looked like a telephone switchboard. Rob said he knew someone who could play it. The next day James Newton Howard arrived in the studio and added synth on all four tracks and electric piano on one. His spontaneous arrangements were nothing short of brilliant and my tracks really came alive. James went on to become the arranger and music director for Elton John and then one of the most successful screen composers in Hollywood.

I had been working hard on my singing. I was not blessed with a naturally powerful voice. In fact, with the Tree tapes, the reason most given by record companies for turning me down was that my voice was neither strong nor distinctive. I was painfully aware of this and made a Herculean effort to overcome it. To make matters even more challenging, I wrote songs that were very difficult to sing. I had this penchant for really sophisticated melodies with tricky soul licks. No simple Neil Young or Bob Dylan songs for me. One thing in my favor, I discovered I could hit very high notes without going into falsetto. In fact, I barely had a falsetto. This was a cool thing in 1973, the days when singers like Robert Plant of Led Zeppelin and Ian Gillan of Deep Purple were testing the limits of the vocal stratosphere, hitting notes that would have been deemed inappropriate for a male voice in an earlier era. Not that there was anything heavy metal about my music; on the contrary. Paul McCartney was more my paradigm, and he hit some pretty stratospheric notes.

One advantage to singing in the studio, as opposed to live, is that you get to go back and fix all your little mistakes by 'punching in,' recording over a single phrase or, if the engineer was fast enough, over a single note.

Bruce was fast, so my vocals came out sounding pretty good.

The ball now shifted to Irwin and Stan's court. They had a tape suitable for shopping to record companies and they ran with it.

Who knows why things click and why they don't. Maybe Irwin no longer had the music biz creds to convince record companies I was a good bet. Stan was a neophyte, so he certainly did not have sufficient weight at the labels. Record company A&R guys were very insecure. A guy could sign five hit acts and get a pat on the back and then one flop and get fired. So they relied a lot on the credibility of whoever brought in the tape. The truth was that nobody knew what was going to be a hit and what was not. So, to get a new artist signed, a confluence of favorable opinions was required. In the '60s it was a bit more fast and loose; then it was "Okay, let's go in and cut a single." But in the '70s it was all about albums, and albums were expensive; a few bad decisions could do some serious damage to a record company.

We got a lot of compliments, but no offers.

Chapter Thirty-Six

Bread and Butter Gigs

By the end of '72 Warren had moved back into his house at 8854 Lookout and we had to move out. Three stayed on as Warren's houseboy and Ron and I found a place further down Lookout Mountain, at 8530. It was a far humbler two-bedroom affair that had a faux log cabin look. The walls were all wood paneled and the floors had linoleum with a wood grain pattern. Coincidentally, this was a house formerly occupied by Danny Hutton of Three Dog Night. A few houses down was a house with a garage door that had a mural of a long-haired hippie dude. This house had been occupied by Jimmy Greenspoon, the keyboard player of Three Dog Night. I soon met the present occupants: Michael O'Brien, a drummer, his wife Jackie and their little girl, about five. They were a handsome couple. Michael had piercing blue eyes, light brown hair, and the perfect rock 'n' roll image. Jackie, an actress and dancer, was a tall stunning brunette.

Michael had the garage set up as a rehearsal studio, complete with drum riser, sound proofing and PA system. He was half of a heavy metal power duo with guitarist Rich Bertram, and their sound was both unique and impressive, but they were not any closer to signing a record deal than I was. What Michael and I both needed was a "bread and butter" gig. So we decided to form a Top 40 cover band in his garage.

We ran an ad in *Music Connection* magazine for a lead guitarist and a bass player and soon began auditioning potential players. Dan Seymour was a natural choice. He was a talented and versatile player, could sing high harmony and he had a great rock 'n' roll look, with long black hair, blue eyes and a big hoop earring in one ear—way ahead of the fashion curve in 1973. We tried out a few bass players and finally settled on Mickey Moriarty, a blond surfer dude who actually lived at the corner of Topanga Canyon and Pacific Coast Highway—right on the beach.

We immediately began rehearsing songs that were recent hits. I picked a wide range of styles and genres, as long as it sounded good with a four-piece rock band playing it. So we played everything from "Dancing Days" by Led Zeppelin to "I'll Be Around" by The Spinners. We even worked out "Jackie Blue" by the Ozark Mountain Daredevils, just to please Michael's wife. We were sounding pretty good, so we invited an agent to come and hear us in our garage.

Joe Marzetta was a booking agent who worked for Prestige Artists, a small-time booking agency in Hollywood. "You're wasting your time," he told us.

"What d'ya mean?"

"There aren't any clubs within fifty miles of here that book four-piece rock bands. What they all want is small lounge acts; a piano player, maybe one guy with a guitar and drum machine, a duo at most. They won't pay enough for four people."

So that was the end of the garage band with no name. But Dan and I decided to try to work something up as a duo. Our voices blended well and we could cover a lot of 'lite' California rock, like The Eagles and Captain & Tennille that might go over in lounge settings.

* * *

At the same time, Ron, V and I started working together on the script for a TV game show we called *The Battle of the Sexes*. It was inspired by the Billie Jean King-Bobby Riggs tennis match, which had captured the imagination of the whole world in September 1973. The idea was simple: we came up with a series of events at which you could pit a man against a woman that highlighted some skill or ability and that did not involve physical strength. For instance, we had driving, which had the two contestants in mock-cars that had screens for windshields, like an arcade video game. We tested sense of smell, hearing, quickness of reflexes, and different kinds of intelligence—even intuition—all in entertaining, comedic ways. It was a hot idea, and it was happening right now. We even built a miniature set out of Styrofoam and used little plastic dolls for the people. We had a host and two teams of contestants, the men and the women. V showed the idea to a producer she knew, and he took it to NBC Television—and they liked it.

One day in 1975, we all got to go to Burbank with our little mockup set and demonstrate the show for a female NBC VP who at the time was in charge of all daytime programming. The presentation went well and, after what seemed like an eternity, we got a green light. Not only that, but the VP wanted it as an evening show as well as a daytime one. We were ecstatic. But when the time came to sign the contracts, our NBC contact and her whole team had been fired and there was a whole new crop of people there. The furor over the King-Riggs match was old news and NBC was no longer interested in *The Battle of the Sexes* game show. *Hollywood Etiquette, Lesson #2: You don't have a deal until the ink on your contract is dry.*

* * *

Ron and I had been working on a screenplay loosely based on my experiences with The Lost and my other East Coast bands in the '60s. It was 1969 when we started working on it, so we made it about the travails of a contemporary rock 'n' roll band, but as we wrote and rewrote and the years flew by, it gradually turned into a period piece about the '60s. This actually gave the piece an added dimension: a picture, not only of a band, but of a magical era in recent American history, the like of which we would never see again.

So, sometime around 1974 we showed it to an aspiring young movie producer named Neil Sellers, and he offered us $1,500 for a one-year option. We accepted, of course. In retrospect, the screenplay—which never did get made—was far from ready for production. Likewise with the producer. Neil, who might have been a trust fund kid, knew little-to-nothing about making movies. In fact, the thing that qualified him most for the job was his wife. She was known as Becky Sharp, and she was a bona fide porn star. I knew this because, at the time, my day—and sometimes night—job was as assistant manager at a Pussycat Theater, the most successful chain of porno movie theaters in LA, and I had seen some of Becky's movies.

One night I was invited to a party at their home, a spacious old Spanish style house in the Hollywood hills. There was a fairly small group in attendance, maybe six or eight people. We were drinking wine and smoking weed, the usual fare, and Becky became very flirtatious with me. She sat on my lap and put her arm around me. I was flattered and aroused. Neil, who was sitting right there with us, was completely blasé. As the small crowd dwindled down to just us three, Neil brought out some brown Mexican heroin. "Ever snort heroin?" he asked. I hadn't. I had never done heroin in any form. "Don't worry, you won't get hooked from snorting it," he said.

"Okay," said I, and we proceeded to snort a few lines of heroin. When we were all quite relaxed, Becky suggested we all go downstairs to the bedroom. At this point I was amenable to anything. Becky was a dark-haired beauty. She was slim and lithe and was really lovely from top to toe. She looked about nineteen. In fact, in the one film of hers I had seen, she played a little high school girl. You'd think a porno actress would be sick of sex, but not Becky. She had all her clothes off before I could even get on the bed. Neil was also naked. First she went down on him while I watched, then she went down on me while he watched. I never felt so relaxed in my life.

"Well, what do you think of my wife?" Neil said.

"Wow," I said.

I nodded out for a while, then got up, went to the bathroom and threw up. But it was not at all an unpleasant experience, as throwing up usually is. It was the nicest puke I ever had.

Chapter Thirty-Seven

A Taste of My Own Medicine

Even though I did not have unfettered access to V, you'd think that winning the love of a woman like that would have been enough to assuage my insane need to prove my desirability to women, again and again, but, no.

I was invited to a party at the home of fellow singer-songwriter, Marcia Waldorf. She was a lovely person, both physically and personally. She played great piano and sang her well-crafted songs in a lilting contralto. She had straight brown hair that fell way below her waist and compassionate brown eyes. My drummer friend, Michael O'Brien, who had recently broken up with his wife, came with me. At the party I met Marcia's new boyfriend, Ron Blair, a bass player recently arrived from Florida. He was a very pleasant fellow and we exchanged numbers. Also at the party was a Farrah Fawcett look-alike named Fiona. Both Michael and I made our plays for her, and Michael, the taller and better-looking of us, came up the winner and went home with her. I left alone, in quiet anguish.

Afterward I congratulated him on 'getting lucky.' "You're the one that got lucky," he said enigmatically. Hmmm, I wonder what he meant by that…

A few days later Fiona appeared at my door. And she looked amazing. The warm flush of victory coursed through my body once again, reinforcing my addiction to love, or anything resembling it. She asked me if I wanted to come with her to her place at the beach, so I got in my car and followed her out to Malibu.

She lived in Fisherman's Village, one of those gated apartment developments north of Leo Carrillo Beach. Her place was just one room with a kitchen alcove and a bathroom, but it was just steps from the sand. As I got to know her, I came to understand what Michael had meant. Fiona did not like sex; she put up with it. If it messed up her hair or her makeup, she got very testy.

She had a scam going where she would drive way down into Orange County to the offices of certain doctors and get them to prescribe Quaaludes to her. One day she enlisted me to go with her. We would each make appointments with these same docs and double the take. Of course, I got to share in the profits. Genuine Rorer Quaaludes fetched a hefty sum in the clubs of Hollywood, and not everyone was as enterprising as Fiona.

During that long drive south we got into this inane conversation, and that's when I realized Fiona was an idiot. We were talking about why I was a vegetarian, and she said, "How do we know that plants are lower forms of life? Maybe they're smarter than we are!" Smarter than her, anyway.

But I loved the beach, and having someone living in that particular location was sufficient motivation to keep Fiona as a friend. I never thought of her as a girlfriend because she was so cold and vapid, but she looked good enough to be seen with—and I loved the beach.

And that's where I met Elena. Elena was Fiona's neighbor, a blond German girl, about thirty, a double for Yvette Mimieux, but with augmented boobs that looked like nuclear warheads. This girl was dynamite in a bikini. Elena lived in another small single apartment in the same complex, only right on the sand. Once, Fiona had to leave for a couple of days and gave me the key to her apartment, asking me to look in once or twice. I brought Elena up there and we house sat for Fiona together. I lit a candle that hung from the ceiling over the television, as we were lying in bed watching TV.

The next day I got a hysterical phone call from Fiona, saying she was going to kill me. I had forgotten to blow out the candle and her apartment had caught fire and nearly burnt down. The Fire Department had come and the damage to her place was fairly extensive. Now the idiot was me. I pled guilty, apologized, and told her I would do my best to make it right. I hardly had any money, but I gave her a couple of hundred dollars and went out to her place and cleaned and vacuumed as best I could. Of course, that was the end of my relationship with Fiona.

But I continued to come out and visit Elena. After several fun-filled afternoons, frolicking in the sand and surf, we finally wound up naked in her shower. She washed me, I washed her, and then we were making love on her living room floor. But what she wanted was not making love, but fucking. What she wanted was harder, faster, longer. She wanted it rough, and I wasn't into rough. At last I admitted I couldn't keep up her frenetic pace. But that didn't stop Elena. There was a three-legged wooden footstool right next to us and she grabbed it and got herself off with one of the legs. When V found out about this—and somehow she always did—Elena was, from that day forward, referred to as 'the foot stool fucker.'

Yes, V would always get it out of me—what I had been up to with other women. Hearing the awful truth always made her eyes flash fire and her hot Spanish blood boil. There was more than one occasion when I had to dodge flying cutlery. I was always banished, but eventually forgiven. But such was the precarious and exciting nature of our relationship. She was dependent on, and at some level devoted to her husband; I was incapable of committing to one woman, and we were both hopelessly hooked on each other. My rationale was that she couldn't demand faithfulness from me as long as she was married to someone else; her rational was that she wasn't having sex with anyone else so neither should I. In many ways, this was the perfect arrangement for me, and it certainly made the decade of the '70s the most alive and exciting of my life.

At one point she decided two could play at my game. She developed a liaison with a guy who hung out at Help, a vegetarian restaurant on 3rd Street that we often frequented. His name was John Jai, a tall, revoltingly handsome guy who wore all white and talked a good spiritual game, constantly dropping words like tantra and dharma and chakras. One day I knew she was down at Help with him and, in a blind fury, I drove down there. I pulled up, and there they both were. I confronted her, told her she could leave with me then and there, or she could have him and never see me again. She stayed. I left, blinded by my own tears as I drove home. I could dish it out, but I couldn't take it.

Chapter Thirty-Eight

Gerry, Isis, Maggie and Ringo

My friendship with Gerry and Isis started way back in '69 or '70 when I was still living on Kirkwood. One day I spotted an attractive girl walking down Kirkwood as I was driving up the hill and I turned around and went back and picked her up. Isis was slim and lithe with lovely, delicate features, short red hair and the bluest of blue eyes. She happily hopped into my car and I drove her down to the Canyon Country Store. We talked as she did her shopping, and then I drove her back up the hill. She told me she was a singer and song-writer and also a witch. So, basically, she fit the typical professional profile for most girls living in Laurel Canyon in 1969. She was living with an older guy named Gerry on a little street that branched off Ridpath Drive called Oakden. Gerry was extremely intelligent, lively, witty and affable. He had thinning blond hair, a ruddy complexion and rheumy blue eyes. He worked as a writer for TV, a job I wouldn't have minded having. He and I hit it off immediately.

Gerry and Isis produced three hits of LSD and suggested we all drop together. Sounded like a fine idea to me, and so down the hatch it went, without a second thought.

Being the lean, mean fucking machine I was, my first impulse when on a psychedelic trip was to grab the first pretty girl in sight and seduce her—and that's what I did with Isis. It never occurred to me that they were a couple, and neither she nor Gerry said anything to dissuade me. So I took Isis into the bedroom—Gerry's bedroom—took all her clothes off and start-ed making love to her. Up to that time I was under the impression that acid would make any lovemaking experience better, but, as J.J. Cale incorrectly said about cocaine, "She don't lie, she don't lie, she don't lie." No, acid tells only the Truth. So, in the middle of fucking Isis it dawned on me I was making a big mistake. She and I were not meant to be lovers... friends yes, but not lovers. I'll never forget the image that kept coming into my head as we were doing it: a snake eating its own tail, the *Ouroboros*. I had no idea at that time that this was a symbol used by almost every ancient civilization, from the ancient Greeks to the ancient Chinese, and generally symbolized the endless cycle of death and regeneration. For me, however, it symbolized the essential similarity between me and Isis and therefore lack of compatibility. Sort of like fucking your sister, or possibly just 'go fuck yourself.' Literally.

Then I started thinking that maybe she really was a witch, and maybe not an altogether good witch. Then she started laughing, like she had read my mind, and that scared me. I knew I was not where I was supposed to be, so I got out.

The Ouroboros

We came out of the bedroom as if nothing had happened. Gerry was completely unfazed. Nothing was ever said about the incident, and we all continued to be friends for another decade.

Gerry and Isis got married not long after that, and he got a plum job as Story Editor for the successful TV drama, *Kojak*. He purchased a large Spanish house on Arlene Terrace, off Wonderland Park Avenue, that had once belonged to Paul Newman and Joanne Woodward and dated back to the '20s. It had a huge cavernous living room with a vaulted oak beam ceiling and a big fireplace, quite a few bedrooms and sitting rooms, a swimming pool with elegant old tile work and a guesthouse, formerly the nursery for the Newmans. That guesthouse would eventually be my home for a while. But I'm getting ahead of myself...

One night in 1975 I went with Gerry and Isis to the Roxy to see John Mayall, who was one of our neighbors in Laurel Canyon. Mayall, and his band, the Bluesbreakers, had been the launching pad for some of the most iconic British blues musicians of all time, including: Eric Clapton, Mick Taylor, Mick Fleetwood, John McVie and Peter Green (the latter three all breaking off to form the original Fleetwood Mac in 1967).

After the show, Gerry invited everyone back to his house for a party. Many luminaries were present, including Mayall, my old band-mate Chevy Chase (who was quite distant toward me), Mickey Dolenz of the Monkees, who lived nearby, Chip Douglas, who had produced The Monkees and played bass with The Turtles, Chip's wife, Judy, who worked at the Troubadour and Howard Kaylan of The Turtles, another canyon resident. Then, in walked Ringo Starr. Everyone shouted a greeting to him: "Hey, Ringo!" But Ringo held up a defensive hand over his face and shouted, "Don't look at me—don't talk to me!" He accepted a large bottle of brandy from Gerry and retired to a corner with his entourage: his wife, Barbara Bach, his lawyer and his lawyer's wife. They didn't interact with anyone else. It made me wonder why he went to the party in the first place. It also made me feel sorry for him. Is that what fame did to people? *Rock Star Etiquette, Lesson #4: If you think stardom will make you a happy person, think again.*

In 1977 Gerry and Isis divorced and she moved out. I stayed friendly with both of them. Gerry met a beautiful flight attendant named Maggie on one of his business trips. She was tall, perfectly proportioned and had a pretty, all-American face. She was not from LA and was not what you'd call sophisticated. But she was a looker. She moved in with him and they soon got married. They had a baby very shortly after that, and in pretty short order the marriage was on the rocks. There was talk of divorce, although I can't remember who initiated it. In 1978, Gerry was diagnosed with lymphoma. I got evicted from my apartment on Gould Avenue. Gerry's guest house was vacant, so I asked if I could move in there, and he said yes—grateful, I think, to have someone he trusted who could help out now that he was sick. In those days, lymphoma was pretty much a death sentence.

So he was in the hospital, another in a long series of stays. I was sitting with Maggie on the couch in the living room. Somehow she made all this about her. This was something that was being perpetrated on *her*. "I feel so unattractive," she said tearfully.

"You're not, you're extremely attractive," I said, not missing my cue.

The next thing I knew, we were kissing. Then we were in her bed— Gerry's bed.

It would be easy for me to put all this off on her, easy for me to call her a self-centered, ignorant slut. But I was the bigger slut, and not ignorant. I knew better. Because of this all-consuming need to feed my perpetually undernourished ego, I had betrayed a trust. I had betrayed a friend on his deathbed. I had gone about representing myself as a spiritual being, a man concerned with raising his consciousness, aspiring to Buddhahood. And in the end it had come to this. I had become a completely amoral person.

There was a secret passage that led from the main house to the bedroom in my guesthouse. The next morning, Maggie, still without a trace of remorse, came through to my bedroom. I was just getting out of the shower, wearing nothing but a towel. She sat on my bed, peeled the towel off, and gave me a wonderful blow job. I'd be lying if I said I didn't love it, that it wasn't thrilling and exciting. Somehow I managed to keep the realization of the import of my actions at bay. I told myself it wasn't hurting Gerry if he didn't know anything about it, that I wasn't depriving him of anything. The next day, as I was leaving, I saw a friend of his arriving at the house. "How's Gerry?" I asked.

"He died this morning. They were wheeling him into the operating room to try to irradiate a tumor the size of a baseball in his throat. It was blocking his airway, so he couldn't breathe. The sonofabitch was joking and wisecracking right up to the end."

Chapter Thirty-Nine

I Fought My Hair and the Hair Won

I hated my hair for as long as I could remember. When I was a preschooler it would burst forth in big, billowy curls. Kinda cute, really. That was before my parents taught me to train it by plastering it down with hair tonic, a comb and a brush. The result was flat, wrinkly hair, not straight, which was the vastly preferable look, and not curly either. Just ugly. The "natural" had not been born yet in the 1950s. In the '60s I started to straighten it with a hot comb. I'd heat this metal comb up on the stove and run it through my hair, often burning the hair and my scalp. But eventually I mastered the vagaries of the hot comb and got my hair to look relatively acceptable. By the '70s I had discovered Kix Kinks, a product primarily purchased by black folks that was a white cream that reeked of sulfur and burned your scalp if left on too long. I eventually developed a regimen that I went through every time I washed my hair: straighten with Kix Kinks, wash the hair, condition the hair, then set it in large rollers, four or five of them, right across the top of my head, then slick down the sides with another product called Dippity Do. I would put Scotch Tape along my temples to keep the sides straight and then go under the hair dryer. It was one of those old fashioned little round plastic jobs with a hose protruding from it that led to a plastic bonnet, which I would put over the rollers on my head. It was pink. The result was the perfect rock 'n' roll coif for the seventies.

The perfect rock 'n' roll coif, 1973

On July 4, 1976, the 200th anniversary of America's independence from Great Britain, I figured out that I had spent well over 2,000 hours of my life fucking around with my hair. My hair launched its own quiet revolution. "Relaxation without representation is tyranny!" it cried. My hair was mad as hell, and it wasn't going to take it anymore. I remembered what it had looked like when I was a baby, and it was right in style for the late 1970s. I laid myself down in a tub of hot water and let the steam permeate it, making it revert to its natural curly state. When I got done, all I had to do was run my fingers through it and it looked fine. Over 2,000 hours, shot to hell!

The perfect rock 'n' roll coif, 1977: Photo: Michelle Mourges Marx

Well, that's an oversimplification. There was an awkward period. I had to cut off the long ends that were still straight, and that gave me a sort of brunette Harpo Marx look, but once it all grew out curly, voila!

In late 1975 Ron and I decided to get separate places. My recollection is that it was his decision—that he wanted to live alone. Stan Milander, who had been my manager-publisher with Irwin Pincus at Uptight Denim Music, was freaking out because Uptight Denim had gone belly-up, and he was now unemployed. He used to come over to our house on Lookout Mountain, lay down on the couch and lament his fate to Ron, because he knew Ron was a shrink. As with many doctors, uninvited friends would often avail themselves of Ron's services for free.

Anyway, Stan had rented the upper apartment of a house on Gould Avenue, which snaked along the western wall of the Canyon, high above Laurel Canyon Boulevard. There was a pathway that zigzagged up from the street with 150 stone steps that led up to the house. The lower floor had a small one-bedroom apartment, and Stan urged me to move in there. When I went over and checked it out, I fell in love with it. It had a small, private backyard that overlooked the entire city. The owner was a tall, scrawny guy in his eighties named William Hawley, who had been in the canyon since the 1920s. He was one of those flinty American individualists: tough, independent and stubborn. He had built this house, probably single-handedly, as well as his own, which was a few houses up the street and also perched high up on the hillside. The rumor was that the entire house was constructed from materials filched from sets on the Universal lot. The place was funky, but perfect for me, and the rent was a pittance.

* * *

Dan and I spent a lot of 1975 and 1976 learning and rehearsing a top 40 lounge repertoire, and by '76 we were starting to get gigs. We called ourselves the Ted & Dan Two Man Band—corny, but appropriate for the kind of gigs we were going for. Our best and longest-lasting gig was at Simply Blue's, a restaurant-lounge atop a tall office building at Sunset and Vine. We played there every Friday and Saturday night for a couple of months. There were other sporadic gigs as well, but it was not what one would call earning a living.

During that period, I wrote prolifically—probably my best songs ever. Dan and I started working some of these up and recording them on my reel-to-reel, sound-on-sound Tandberg tape recorder. This was a quarter-track machine that gave you the ability to overdub by bouncing everything over to the right channel, but you had to mix and record at the same time; in other words, the track you were overdubbing had to be at the exact right volume as you recorded it, because it couldn't be adjusted later. This was also how it was done in professional studios back in the early days of multi-track recording. Anyway, we managed to make some pretty good home demos of my current material that way.

For a couple of sessions, I brought in Ron Blair, Marcia Waldorf's boyfriend—or ex at that point—on bass. He was a great player and really easy to work with. I asked him if he'd consider teaming up with me and Dan and forming a band, but he had come out from Florida with a band and they were starting to gain some traction. They were called Tom Petty & The Heartbreakers, and I had to admit they were pretty good.

* * *

Dan and I signed up to play at this booking convention in Palm Springs. It was basically a showcase for all kinds of club acts to audition for a whole room full of booking agents. It was high summer—the off-season in Palm Springs—and my Datsun station wagon, filled with equipment, overheated every few miles as we trekked deeper and deeper into the inferno that was the California desert.

The Ted & Dan Two Man Band (my Harpo Marx period).

When we got back from Palm Springs, my house had been broken into. My Gibson electric guitar, tape recorder and stereo were gone. Fortunately, we had all the rest of the equipment with us. I saw that the thief had broken in through a small window in my bedroom. This was a high window, and there was a bookcase right below it. In the dust on that bookcase I saw a footprint. I'm not one for calling cops, but on the off chance they had recovered my stuff, I called and they sent someone over. I showed the detective the footprint, but he said there was no way to preserve a shoe print in dust. But I had a way: I taped a piece of Saran Wrap over it and traced it with a magic marker. The cop identified the print as having been made by an Earth Shoe, a popular brand at the time, which had a rubber sole with many parallel ridges, like the tread of a tank.

Now, as you may recall, I don't take kindly to people stealing my guitars. I remembered the MO of the last junkie thief who ripped me off and I decided to make the rounds of every hock shop in a five-mile radius. The nearest one was on Santa Monica Boulevard, just east of Crescent Heights. I hit pay dirt on my first shot out of the box. I described my Gibson and the guy behind the counter turned and took my guitar down from the shelf. Yep, that was it. "Oh, Jimmy McAllister," he said matter-of-factly.

"Oh, Jimmy McAllister!" I exclaimed, "Of course!" The guy had given Jimmy $50 for the guitar. I paid the fifty (I knew the drill) and left with my axe.

Jimmy was a bass player from Detroit who claimed to have played with Mitch Ryder & The Detroit Wheels in the '60s. I'd met him a few years earlier and we had jammed together once or twice. We talked about putting something together, but never actually did. One reason for this is that I heard he had gotten into junk. And Jimmy had stopped by to visit me in my new digs on Gould not three weeks earlier. What an idiot—he had used his real name.

I hatched a plan to get my stuff back if he still had it. If he had been stupid enough to use his real name in the pawn shop, he just might fall for this. I called him up and acted real friendly, as if nothing had happened. I told him Dan and I were getting some high paying gigs and were considering adding a bass player. Would he be interested? And he says yes. So I invited him over to rehearse with us at my place.

A few days later, there he is: a skinny, shifty-looking guy with long, stringy blond hair, mustache and bloodshot blue eyes. He's fully-loaded, with his Fender bass and a huge amplifier. Dan and I help him up the 150 steps with his amp. I notice he is wearing Earth Shoes. Earlier, I had alerted my neighbors across the street, the Paris brothers—Adeniyi and Ekundayo, who had written the Grass Roots hit "Sooner or Later"—to keep an eye out for anyone fleeing down my steps and to stop him if necessary. So we get Jimmy and his equipment into the house and I say "Sit down, Jimmy. There's something I need to show you." And I take out my electric guitar. "Recognize this? The guy at the hock shop gave me your name!" Seeing denial was futile, he collapsed in a heap of remorse. "Well," I said, "you're a very lucky guy, Jimmy. If I wanted to, I could put you in jail right now, but all I want is the rest of my stuff back. Do you still have it?" He nods. "Good. You bring me all my stuff: my stereo amp, my FM tuner, my tape recorder and the $50 I paid to get my guitar back, and I'll return your bass and amp."

"Okay," says Jimmy.

"You have four days. I don't get my shit by then, I start selling your shit."

He nods and gets up to leave. "One second," I say. I yell down to the Paris brothers, "It's okay, guys, let him go."

I had installed double-key deadbolts on both my front and back doors, so the only way to get the booty out of there would have been out the same window Jimmy came in, and that window was almost six feet off the ground. So someone had to have helped him. He had to pass each item out the window to his accomplice. And I knew who that was: his lowlife wife, Sandy. Sandy was the daughter of a fairly successful record producer from Detroit named Harry Balk.

Four days later exactly, Sandy and her mother, all smiles, pull up in a big fat 1972 Cadillac. Both women are as capacious as their car. They open the trunk and give me my stuff and my $50.

"I know you were along on the job," I tell Sandy. "You tell Jimmy it would be a good idea for you both to leave town for a while. The cops already know it was him and they'll be looking for both of you." Her mother thanks me for not turning them in and tells me she's getting them into rehab. Dan and I bring Jimmy's gear down from my place and the massive Cadillac lumbers off, almost scraping the parked cars on my narrow street. Luck had smiled on all of us that day.

Chapter Forty

The Good News and the Bad News

Another of my neighbors on Gould Avenue was Big John Brennan, a burly New York Irish guy who sold marijuana for a living. He had a dark complexion, a mustache and big brown eyes that made him look a little like Clark Gable. Big John had a seemingly never-ending supply of high grade Columbian marijuana, and he would often sell me O.Z.s. One day he offered to front me a half-pound and let me sell it off in ounces and pay him back later. I had been paying $40 an ounce and the half-pound was costing me $150. With eight ounces in a half-pound at $40 per ounce, that came to $320, a profit of $170. Big John had solved my problem of how to earn a living in a single brilliant stroke.

I could now smoke for free and make a decent living without having to find a job. I was soon taking full pounds, which carried an even greater profit, and easily unloading them in a week or two. I bought a Triple Beam scale and soon realized I had a surprising aptitude for precision measurements. My O.Z.s were always 28 grams on the dot. When the product was good and you gave people a fair count, the word spread and business flourished. I was never greedy. I never thought of myself as a dealer, just a musician trying to earn a living, while providing a valuable service to the community.

One day while picking up a 'package' at Big John's I met a cute blond babe who was doing the same thing. Her name was Dale Consalvi. Dale was very East Coast, had a killer body and a lively wit. It turned out she hailed from Boston, my favorite city, so we hit it off and got to talking. She said she was an aerobics instructor, and she looked like a walking advertisement for her product. She wanted to see my eagle's nest of an apartment, which was right across the street, so I brought her up there. We smoked a bit of weed and talked. I would have liked to have done more with her, but she kept talking about her boyfriend, who was Frank Zappa's drummer, Terry Bozzio. "He must be a damn good drummer," I commented, knowing Zappa's very high standards for hiring musicians. "Yeah, and he's good lookin' too," she said. She never said anything about being a singer or wanting to be a singer. It wasn't until 1982, seven years later, that she and Terry—now married—gained national recognition as the new wave band Missing Persons.

Dale Bozzio, 1982

* * *

Stan, who was not only my upstairs neighbor but also my de facto manager, finally landed himself another job. He went to work for Al Bart of Bart-Levy associates, who at the time was one of the top movie music agents in the business. Bart represented many of Hollywood's leading screen composers, such as Elmer Bernstein, Henry Mancini, David Shire, Bill Conti, Lalo Schifrin and others. Stan learned quickly, and when Bart's partner, Michael Levy, branched out on his own in 1982, Stan was made Al's partner and the agency was re-named Bart-Milander. Stan tried to get me into the film composing racket, but this was before computers, and you had to be formally trained in notation and orchestration, and I was far from that. Now I suddenly regretted cheating on Billy Bauer's sight-reading lessons.

Someone introduced me to Irwin Mazur, who worked for Family Productions, and took an interest in me. Family Productions was headed by legendary record man Artie Ripp. And all the legends were not that complimentary. Artie was one of those old school record guys out of New York. He had been one of the founders of Buddha Records and Kama Sutra, the label that signed The Lovin' Spoonful. Ripp also famously signed Billy Joel in his early career and continued to take royalties from Joel's subsequent albums, long after he had signed with Columbia. There was talk of mob ties.

So now Artie was out here in LA and had a recording studio in the Valley somewhere. Irwin envisioned me as an R&B singer, backed by all black musicians. Obviously, he didn't get what I was doing at all, so I passed.

Dan and I finally did add a bass player to the Ted & Dan Two Man Band, a guy named Mark, so we had to change the name of the act. For a while we played a gig way out in Anaheim as The Beagles (because we played songs by The Eagles and The Beatles), but I was looking for a name that would work beyond the club circuit, I was still thinking record deal, so we settled on Glider.

Glider, 1976. L to R: me, Mark, Dan

Not long after this I met two record producers from New York, Marc Gilutin and Freddie McFinn, who had a deal to produce albums for an independent production company called Chalice Productions. Chalice, in turn, had an ongoing distribution deal with United Artists Records. Marc was a big guy, tall and wide, bald with a big mustache. Freddie was closer to my size, with brown curly hair and a beard. Both were about my age, thirty. I'm not sure what brought them up to my place—perhaps to score some weed—but we got to talking music. We all shared a fanatical admiration for The Beatles, so I played them the tracks I had cut with Bruce Ablin and then the new demos with Dan and Ron Blair. They loved my songs.

They set up an appointment for me, Dan and Mark to audition live for the heads of Chalice: David Chackler and Lee Lassiff. Lee had been one of the founders of White Whale Records, the label that had a string of hits with The Turtles in the '60s. He also discovered and released the first album by Lindsay Buckingham and Stevie Nicks, *Buckingham Nicks*. David was out of the Philadelphia area and also had a long history of making records. So the three of us went to their office down on Beverly Boulevard and played a bunch of my songs for them. A few days later Marc and Freddie called me up and told me they were prepared to offer me an album deal. There was only one catch: they didn't want Dan and Mark, only me. They wanted to get better musicians to play on the album. Mark was the newbie, and not the greatest bass player, but Dan and I had formed a strong bond. We worked well together. He might not have been the greatest guitar player in the world technically, but his playing and arrangement ideas were right for my music, and his singing blended well with mine. I should have fought harder for him, but I had gone seven years without a record deal, and I wanted this badly. I didn't want to start off my relationship with my producers by fighting with them, so I bit the bullet and did as I was asked. I knew letting Dan go was a bad decision then, but it became even more apparent later on.

Stan was happy to step in and help me negotiate the deal. Of course, Chalice wanted the publishing, but Stan got me a decent advance and a weekly stipend for the publishing. At last, the elusive album deal was once again within my grasp.

Chapter Forty-One

Orgy Anyone?

I met Peggy Warner at one of Jerry and Isis's parties. She was a cute redhead with cherry red lips and bright blue eyes—almost a cartoon of a girl. We started going out together and I soon found out that Peggy was a swinger. She had a membership at Sandstone, a private retreat deep in the mountains of Topanga. Sandstone was a massive estate with a Jacuzzi and an outbuilding that housed an Olympic-sized swimming pool and some saunas. It was more than a nudist colony; it was a free sex club. The first time she took me there I thought I had died and gone to heaven. Everywhere I looked there were lovely young bodies, and not a stitch of clothing to be seen.

Upstairs there was a big living room and kitchen. Dinner was generally served around seven and everyone lined up with their trays, got their dinners and settled into one of the comfortable chairs or cushions to eat. Then, after soaking in the Jacuzzi for a while, Peggy suggested we go over to the pool house. We sat in the sauna and then dove into the pool. There was a group of about a dozen people in the pool playing a game, and we joined in: everyone would stand in waist-high water in two rows, guys on one side, girls on the other, and we would take turns passing one person, floating on their back with eyes closed, down the aisle. As the floater passed, everyone touched that person however and wherever they wanted to. Nothing was forbidden, you could use your hands, your lips, whatever. There was one girl in this group who was a true stunner, just gorgeous. When it was my turn to float, I felt her hands on me, and her mouth, and it made me feel very special. Of course, she was part of a couple. I didn't know if the guy with her was her husband, but I got the feeling he was.

Then Peggy showed me the orgy room. This was a room about fifteen by twenty feet that was wall-to-wall mattresses. It was pretty much wall-to-wall bodies when we entered. Peggy and I found a spot and she immediately went down on me, getting me off pretty quickly. Just as well, as I had a long night ahead of me. Then, in walked that couple—the great beauty and her husband. She fell into my arms as naturally as if we were old friends. I held her bare and perfect body close; every inch of us was touching. My erection had recovered in record time. We kissed and I nearly swooned. I started kissing her all over; then I was kissing her between her legs. She parted her legs and let my tongue in. I was hoping she would respond in kind, but she remained passive. Out of the corner of my eye I could see Peggy going down on her husband. Beauty would not let me enter her. She would not go down on me. She let me continue going down on her, but that was all. "What's wrong?" I finally whispered.

"I just can't."

"This was all your husband's idea, huh?"

"Yes."

"You're not comfortable here."

"No."

"Sorry," I said, "I wish we had met under other circumstances. You're so beautiful."

I turned to my right. There was a girl right next to me without a partner, moaning. She was wearing nothing but a pair of knee socks and a very short T-shirt that said 'Pussy Power.' I rolled over and I was in her. After a long while, I looked around. Peggy was with some other guy and Beauty and her man were gone.

* * *

One of the most treasured objects I obtained from Razzamatazz was a Victorian era silver cigarette case, marvelously engraved by a master craftsman of that era. The thing about this little case was: it was too thin and too short for modern cigarettes. The only thing it was good for was holding joints—and it was perfect for that. I never went out to a social function without laying a neat row of meticulously rolled joints into my beautiful case. This came in especially handy at a party I attended in 1976 at the home of Richard Delvy.

Richard was a pioneer of the California surf music movement and made his lemons into lemonade by going beyond being a musician to being a producer, manager and publisher. Among the songs on which he owned the publishing was "Wipe Out," the surf classic by the Surfaris. Richard lived close by in Laurel Canyon, and he would often throw parties during that period.

I didn't know many people in attendance, so I milled around, drinking the punch and eating the hors d'oeuvres like everyone else. Then I spotted an odd trio: a man of about fifty, distinguished looking, gray—almost white—hair, goatee and mustache and two beautiful young women. The older was about thirty, the younger maybe twenty-one at the most. They were all dressed in black and all wore identical gold pendants around their necks. I couldn't resist; I walked up to them and said, "Are you guys in a cult?" I got a laugh out of at least the guy. He introduced himself as Paul. The older woman was Carol and the younger was Sue. "Have you got any marijuana?" he asked. And that's when I whipped out my art nouveau cigarette case and proffered a joint. We all adjourned to the veranda and lit up. Paul was very cordial in a friendly, yet almost formal way. I thought he might be European. The girls were extremely friendly to me; in fact, I was getting strong sex vibes from both of them. It came up that I lived close by in Laurel Canyon and that I had a lot of grass. They wanted to know if they could buy some. I invited them to come to my house, and I would be happy to oblige.

At my house I produced a lid of my primo Columbian and Paul paid me for it. I went into the other room to stash the money and, when I came back into the living room, both girls were sitting on the couch, completely nude. Paul, still fully clothed, sat across from them in my bentwood rocker. "Why don't you take your clothes off?" he suggested. *Okay, twist my arm*, I thought. I got naked and sat between the girls. Then we all started making out. Paul seemed to be getting off just watching. Sue, the younger one, was absolutely adorable: sandy blond hair, about 5'2" and a perfect, tight little body. She got down on her knees on the floor and started sucking my now fully-erect penis, while I was sucking on Carol's gorgeous breasts. Then Sue was lying on the couch, her head in Carol's lap. "Fuck me," she said, and I did. As I was doing so, I looked up, and Paul was standing before Carol, still clothed, with his cock in her mouth. We went on like that, switching partners and trying different things for the rest of the night. At one point I got Sue alone in the bathroom and wanted to get her number. As much fun as these 'ménages' were, for me, one-on-one was still the most intimate you could get—and I wanted to get real intimate with Sue. She gave me the number at Paul's. I tried to reach her there several times over the next few weeks, but I don't think they wanted me to get her alone. There was always some reason why I couldn't speak to her, and I never saw her again.

The next time I saw Paul and Carol was at their place, and they had a new crop of young girls—two to be exact. They couldn't have been more than seventeen. But that's another orgy for another book.

Chapter Forty-Two

Glider

The recording of the *Glider* album was a yearlong odyssey that took us on 'the grand tour' of many of the best recording studios in LA. No expense was spared. I can't be sure of the sequence, but the list included: Sound City, The Village Recorder, Richard Perry's Studio 55 (which had by far the best kitchen—we called it 'Richard's Restaurant'), RCA, Capitol, Wally Heider's, and Conway. We even went to a place in Glendale called Whitney because they had a built-in pipe organ.

All the musicians did a fine job. The key players were: Gene Barkin on lead guitars, Steve Halter on keyboards, Jeff Eyrich on bass and my old friend Eddie Tuduri on drums. The stellar background vocals were provided by two guys I discovered playing cover tunes in a club in Manhattan Beach, Jeff Stillman and Scott McCarl. It wasn't until years later that I learned Scott had been in The Raspberries. There were many other players on the album, including Hugh McDowell of the Electric Light Orchestra on cello and Chad Stewart of the '60s English duo, Chad & Jeremy, and there's an interesting story about that...

I knew I wanted strings and maybe even horns on "Leaving Our Troubles Behind," a Beatlesque song with a catchy, anthemic chorus. There was a guy who worked with Chalice, an experienced arranger named Joe Renzetti. He was an older guy, but all the Chalice guys swore by him. He did a string arrangement for the song, but for some reason I was not invited to the recording session for the live strings. When I heard it I went ballistic. Shades of Alan Lorber! Not even close to anything I had in mind. As far as I was concerned the guy totally missed the spirit of the song. Unlike in my younger days, I did not acquiesce. I put my foot down. I made Chalice scrap the entire string arrangement. Of course, there was no more money for another string date (I'm sure they blew thousands on the first one), but Stan stepped in with a solution. He put me together with Chad Stewart who, along with Jeremy Clyde, had scored a big hit with "Summer Song" back in 1964. Chad had become a film composer and an arranger, and was one of Stan's clients. He and I hit it off great, and we worked together on arrangement ideas at my place on Gould. We knew we would not be able to get real strings and horns, but we worked up some parts that would work well on Chamberlain and synthesizer. Chad played the parts in the studio and it came off really well. *Arrangement Lesson #1: Good parts trump good sounds.*

At the time I was very proud and pleased with the finished *Glider* album. I *owned* every note of that album. Sure, I collaborated with producers, musicians and an arranger, but every note, every sound on that album had to pass muster with me. In reality, it was not a band album at all, but a Ted Myers solo album. I made the choice to give it a band moniker because I didn't think the name "Ted Myers" had any cachet. In retrospect, I now hear it as a collection of very pretty, well-crafted songs that were part of an outgoing era. By the time it was released in 1977, the Beatle-influenced, sweet melodies of *Glider* were borderline old hat. The lush, sometimes over-the-top production values and vocal arrangements were being supplanted by a much sparser, more minimalist approach. The era of punk and new wave was already upon us and had, for all intents and purposes, eclipsed this kind of music, which, I guess, would be lumped into the category of 'arena rock' or even 'corporate rock.' In its defense, the songs on that album were not only catchy and well crafted, they projected a positive, evolved life view, for the most part celebrating the joy of being alive and aspiring to spiritual awakening. The spirit of V permeated everything I did at that time, and *Glider* was no exception.

I even controlled the artwork on the album. For the front cover I had a concept: an Icarus-like guy (me) flying on a Leonardo da Vinci hang glider over the coast of California. But the coast is devoid of any sign of civilization or human life—so it's either the distant past or the distant future. And I wanted this painted in the style of Maxfield Parrish.

I had a poster hanging in my house that was a surrealistic psychedelic depiction of some idyllic planet, where no one wore clothes, people could fly or levitate, and where there was nothing but peace and harmony with all beings and nature. Looming in the distance, dominating the landscape, was an enormous tree, soaring high above the clouds (the Tree of Life? The Tree of Knowledge?). The artist was Cliff McReynolds and, technically as well as conceptually, he was a true master. Somehow I got his phone number and called him up. I told him how much I admired his work and asked if he would consider painting the album cover I had in mind, imitating the style of Maxfield Parrish. He told me I could use one of his existing works, but he would not paint on assignment. I opted to stick with my concept.

Glider album cover. Painting: Annie Neilson

For the back cover, we wanted a really cool photo of the band—even though, in reality, there was no band. I wanted the guy who had shot the cover of Fleetwood Mac's *Rumors*, Herbie Worthington. Herbie was a true original, a 6'2" Jesus look-alike who dressed all in white. I went to see him in his huge loft somewhere in East Hollywood. I asked him if he could suggest an artist to paint the front cover and he referred me to Annie Neilson. Annie painted giant reproductions of album covers for display in the windows of Tower Records on Sunset. If you are old enough to remember seeing these, they were really quite crude, made to be viewed cursorily and from afar, and did not take pains with the fine details. Annie was a workman-like painter, but no Cliff McReynolds. I showed her some of my Parrish prints and asked if she could duplicate that style. She said she could. Next, Herbie shot a Polaroid of me in my skivvies, hanging from a two-by-four between two ladders in his loft. I did my best to raise my hind quarters up behind me to approximate the effect of flying through the air. Annie used this image to create my vision of me flying on the renaissance hang glider over a deserted California coastline. It was important to me that she used the emblematic Parrish blues for the sky and water. Everyone raved over the end result and, seeing as I was stuck with it, I effused along with the rest.

But privately I regretted my decision not to use a Cliff McReynolds original. The poster that I had—and still have hanging on my wall to this day—depicted perfectly the lyrics to "Leaving Our Troubles Behind":

> *...Let's take a holiday*
> *Maybe we'll go to stay*
> *Somewhere the sun's coming up like pink lemonade*
> *Catfeather trees in the breeze seem to whisper*
> *You can have all that you dream coming true*
> *True for me, true for you...*

And that's the image I should have gone with for the cover.

Cliff McReynolds: "A New Earth." © Cliff McReynolds, used by permission.

Next, it was time to shoot the back cover. V's bedroom seemed to me the perfect setting, and she graciously agreed. She had an enclosed porch that overlooked the canyon with a white wicker table and chairs. The carpets were also white, and we all dressed in white or light colors and gathered around the table with the big, floor-to-ceiling windows behind us. Herbie shot it overexposed, so it was even whiter and more washed out. We had a bottle of Mumm's Cordon Rouge on the table and we all had crystal glasses of champagne in our hands. I was in the foreground, reclining on the white rug, wearing an antique Japanese kimono in muted beige and brown and white yoga pants, bare-chested and looking the picture of decadence—all too appropriate.

Glider, 1977. L to R: Eddie Tuduri, Jeff Eyrich, me , Scott McCarl, Gene Barkin, Jeff Stillman, Steve Halter. Photo: Herbie Worthington.

* * *

About the time the album had been completed, but before it was released, Marc Gilutin (one of my producers) got tickets to *Don Kirshner's Rock Awards* at the Hollywood Palladium. We managed to find street parking a few blocks away and smoked a joint as we walked through the Hollywood side streets toward the theater. On the way, we caught up with two young ladies who were decked out like they were going to the same place. We offered to share our joint with them and they accepted. We walked along, passing the joint and making small talk. It turns out they were mother and daughter, although the mother looked considerably better to me than the daughter, who was a rather bland brunette. The mother, on the other hand, was, to quote Michael Caine in *Alfie*, "in beautiful condition." She was probably in her forties, but had obviously been a real knockout in her time. We all arrived at the theater entrance together. Limos were pulling up and celebrities were making their entrances with paparazzi flashing away. I jokingly suggested we all get into the far side of one of the limos, then exit on the theater side, so we could be mistaken for celebrities. Then, all at once, the cameras were turned on the attractive older woman beside me. Reporters were shouting questions at her, calling her "Sheree" and "Miss North." She was Sheree North, an actress I had long admired, not only for her hot looks, but for her skillful handling of many a major and supporting role. She was not a showboat, but a totally professional working actress. We exchanged numbers, and she invited me to dinner at her house in Malibu not long afterward. By the time I went, I had a copy of my album in hand and was able to give it to her. She was a sweet and charming woman, and I was very sad to learn of her passing in 2005, following cancer surgery.

Sheree North, c. 1971

* * *

By the time the album was ready for release, relations between Chalice Productions and UA Records had deteriorated to a state of mutual hatred. UA promised Chalice that they would bury the next album they delivered. And guess which album that was. I did my best to forge friendly relationships with as many people at UA as I could, but mainly that consisted of David Bridger, a very nice English guy who was in charge of artist relations, and his lovely assistant Gail. She was very sweet and took me around to as many photo ops as possible (Gail and I also forged a personal relationship, the details of which I shall not include). One day I was at the UA offices trying my best to schmooze my way into the good graces of the powers that be. I was with the head of promotion, and he had a guy in his office, Fred Lewis, who recognized me from Boston (oh yeah, I used to be big stuff there). Fred was shopping a Boston band that he managed, called The Cars, and he gave me a little car pin as a memento. I guess UA passed on them, but they got signed by Elektra. I didn't get to hear The Cars until June 1978, when "Just What I Needed" broke big on the radio. This was the new sound: tuneful, but not warm and fuzzy; not airy-fairy like Glider, but cool, robotic and hard-edged.

UA spent no promotion dollars on Glider. They took out no ads (in fact, Chalice took out a full-pager in Billboard touting the album as "The Best Kept Secret of 1978," a subtle barb aimed directly at the UA publicity department. It was my very first advertising headline, a profession I would one day embrace). They made no effort to get the record played on radio and, worst of all, there would be no tour support forthcoming.

And here's where firing my faithful lead guitarist Dan came back to bite me in the ass: All of the musicians who played on the *Glider* album were in-demand studio cats. None of them had any allegiance to me or my music. If I wanted any of them—or any musician on that level—to join my band and go out and play live with me, they would have to be paid. UA wasn't going to give me the money, Chalice Productions wasn't going to give me the money, so there was no live act. If I had stuck with Dan, at least he and I could have gone out and played the Glider songs live and just maybe we could have found a drummer and bass player that were willing to hitch their wagons to our star. As it was, I had no one, and the *Glider* album died the same quiet death as my previous two albums.

Chapter Forty-Three

Over The Rainbow

By the spring of '77 Stan Milander had become successful enough as a movie music agent to buy himself a nice little house. It was just across the canyon in the 'foothills' of Mt. Olympus (a high-end housing development that dominated the east wall of Laurel Canyon, right across from Gould Avenue). Stan's house was not one of the "pre-fab mansions" of Mt. Olympus, but a cool, rather rustic little number.

With the larger upstairs apartment vacant, I saw an opportunity. I made Mr. Hawley a proposal: I offered to rent the entire house—both apartments—for what Stan and I had been paying, which I think totaled about $350 a month. I told him I wanted to move my 'road manager' into the downstairs apartment and I would be responsible for his rent. The 'road manager' I had in mind was my good friend Michael O'Brien who was still separated from Jackie and looking for a place to live. I rented the downstairs apartment to Michael for $200, well below market value for the location, and I moved into the bigger place for $150, about what I had been paying for the smaller place.

The bedroom in the upstairs apartment was cantilevered over part of the backyard of the downstairs place, and there was a big window facing south. I had my bed right up against the window, so the view from my bed was spectacular, looking down through the mouth of the canyon across the entire city to Baldwin Hills in the distance. This was a view that people pay millions of dollars for today and it was mine for $150 a month. In my new place I also had a big living room with the leather sofa Stan had left behind that folded out into a double bed, a bar with art deco bar stools and a sitting room that was like an enclosed porch near the back door, which opened onto a completely private backyard, one that was not visible from anywhere, except maybe a passing helicopter. This proved very conducive to nude sunbathing, and there were many young ladies who were happy to use my place to achieve that 'strapless tan.' This was the best place I had ever lived, despite the fact that the roof leaked, there was a smelly septic tank that constantly overflowed, no insulation and you could see daylight between the boards of my bedroom walls.

There was a footpath that snaked its way from my backyard along the hillside. This looked like an ideal location for marijuana cultivation, and Big John and I availed ourselves of this fertile opportunity. He showed me how to sprout the seeds in a shallow pan with moist paper towels. Once the seeds had sprouted the beginnings of roots, we planted them into individual Styrofoam cups filled with earth. Once the baby plants achieved a certain size, we cut off the bottoms of the cups and planted them in the ground. We had a series of connected hoses that extended from my backyard to the cultivation site. As the female plants flowered, we removed the male plants, thus creating *sinsemillia* (seedless marijuana, and therefore more potent). By the end of the summer we had a nice crop of homegrown. The bad news was, the Columbian we had been getting from New York, even with its seeds, kicked our weed's ass. There was more to growing great marijuana than you could read in a manual.

The best thing about that magical apartment was how its sheer elevation seemed to draw songs out of the ether and channel them through me. I wrote the best songs of my life there, and more of them than ever before.

I'd heard or read a story that Paul Simon told about the mystique of writing songs. He said, "You know how you'll be driving somewhere and a great song idea comes into your head, but there's no way to write it down or record it? So you rush home and sit down to write it, but it's gone; you've forgotten it." Then he says, "Oh well, somebody else must've gotten that one." And that's really the way it is. I always felt songs came *through* me, not *from* me.

In the winter of 1977-1978 it rained for weeks. The hillside behind my house was beginning to slide down, leaving a deep layer of mud that threatened to push my whole house down into the canyon. I would look out of my windows and see just clouds—from above. The fog would settle into the hollows of the canyon, and I would be looking down on clouds.

"Rainy Day"

I sit and watch the rain
I wonder why I'm blue
All the world is crying
I guess I'm crying too

Rainy day
Sweet are the tears of heaven's sorrow
Rain today
Cry with me now, we'll laugh tomorrow

And the songs kept coming. I had my tape recorder, two Shure SM 57 microphones and an Altec mixing board in a permanent state of readiness. I had used the board for the PA system with the Ted & Dan Two Man Band. It had a crude spring reverb in it, but somehow the demos I made with this setup sounded great. Not suitable for presentation to record companies, not really suitable for presentation to anyone, but they conveyed the essence of the songs—for me at least. I was beginning to not give a shit what anyone thought. I knew that what I was doing was good. V knew it too, and that was enough for me.

"Hard to Please"

Hearts stronger than mine
I have seen them wither, fade and die on the vine
Pouring out their souls on bits of paper
Feeling sure that sooner or later
The men who pull the strings will surely see

But they're hard to please
You can't please all the people all of the time
You can't even please some of the people most of the time
But I don't mind
Just as long as I can please you

* * *

The Rainbow on Sunset was the undisputed hangout of choice for the rock 'n' roll set. The musicians—mostly wannabe rock stars like me—in their platform shoes and Rod Stewart haircuts and their attendant babes, the girls who would do anything to get next to a real rock star, but would settle for a fake one on a slow night, all gathered there and milled about trying to score—drugs or love—until 2 a.m. when the staff kicked everyone out into the parking lot. There the scoring frenzy continued for another hour.

I had been hanging out at the Rainbow since it first opened in 1973. It had proved a reliable source of adventures for me that ranged from wonderful to terrible and everything in between. But I wasn't one to stay home at night waiting for V to call me. Most of the time she would not answer her phone, and now it had grown into months between phone calls from her.

One night in 1976 I was milling about with the rest of the throng in the Rainbow parking lot. It was looking like I'd gotten lucky. A cute, voluptuous racially-mixed babe named Nola seemed to have taken a shine to me. I was chatting her up about my newly signed record deal (the truth for a change), and she was eating it up. Just then, a couple insinuated themselves into our conversation. The guy was a rather suave Englishman with sandy hair, typically Anglo features and natty attire. He introduced himself as Robert, and his wife, an attractive, petite brunette with a fashionable bob haircut, as Sue. They were wondering if there were any dance clubs that stayed open late. It so happened that a new club had recently opened on Beverly Boulevard called the Odyssey, which did not serve alcohol and which stayed open 'til 5 a.m. Robert let it drop that he was Island Records recording artist Robert Palmer. I had heard of him; his debut solo album, *Sneakin' Sally Through the Alley*, had been a minor hit in 1975. Nola asserted that she wanted to go dancing, so I agreed to drive us all to the Odyssey.

We piled into my beige Datsun station wagon, Robert and Sue in the back, Nola and me in the front. It was one of those foggy LA nights, and the windshield was covered with condensation. Having all these people breathing in my car made the windshield fog up worse. "Bloody fog," I said, turning on the defroster full blast.

"Bloody!" said Robert with a laugh. "Is that the way you talk, 'bloody?'"

Everyone started laughing at me. I felt my face burning with embarrassment. Being around a Brit had made me affect a British-ism. I had done it without thinking and this asshole gleefully seized upon it, just to make me look a fool, knowing full well that I was trying to impress the girl beside me, whom I barely knew.

"Fer sher, dude," said Palmer affecting an exaggerated California surfer accent. And everyone laughed even harder.

I tried to formulate some kind of face-saving comeback, but I came up empty. I should have thrown them out of my car, but I didn't. I started the car and drove us to the disco.

If only I had uttered the lines that came to me in the ten thousand times since that night that I replayed this scene over and over again in my head: "You don't like it? You can bloody well get out and walk!" Later, another, darker vision came to me. In this one I had a big knife, a switchblade. I'd turn to him, snap the blade open, and say "How would you like me to show you what we mean by 'bloody' here in America?"

We got to the club and Robert, Sue and Nola got out and walked in while I parked the car. Once inside, I looked around, mainly for Nola, as she had been a shoe-in to come home with me that night. But all three of them had vanished. That prick had ridiculed me, and then absconded with my date. Oh, the ignominy!

The wrath of a Scorpio lives long. When Palmer died in 2003 of a sudden heart attack at age fifty-four, all I could think was, *I wish I knew where his grave was so I could dance on it.*

* * *

Several of my Rainbow adventures happened in the period after 1979 when I began using and dealing cocaine. One night, a couple of young "nubiles" whisked me away in a limo with some guy who looked fat, puffy and haggard, but vaguely familiar. He was introduced simply as "Rick." We all went to his hotel suite.

Ever the magnanimous gent, I laid out a series of lines on a mirror. Our host snorted up almost all of them, so I laid out some more for the girls.

A lot of that night is still a blur for me. I guess there was some sexual activity going on with the young girls, but I can't be certain. The one thing I do remember is that, around dawn, our host pulled out a Gibson guitar catalog and said to me, "Let me show you my new signature guitar." And he showed me the Rick Derringer Signature Les Paul. "You're Rick Derringer?" I sputtered in amazement. He was younger than I was, but he looked ten years older. He was a wreck. "Wow, man, sorry I didn't recognize you!"

"That's okay," he said. "Some days I can barely recognize myself."
Rock Star Etiquette, Lesson #5: Fame is not for sissies.

* * *

By the middle of 1979 I was using cocaine to get chicks just as I had used my guitar in an earlier era. Now everyone had a guitar, and everyone was about to become a rock star. But not everyone had a nearly inexhaustible supply of pharmaceutical grade cocaine.

Upstairs at the Rainbow—or "Over the Rainbow," as it was called—was where the elite hung out. You had to get permission from Michael the manager to venture into the upper reaches. So there I was, schmoozing with the likes of Cheap Trick and Mötley Crüe, and there was this sleek, sexy redhead, wearing a horizontal-black-and-white-striped dress leaning against a post, with one foot propped on the post. "You look like Irma la Douce," I said.

"Thanks, I guess," she replied. She was a cool customer. Her name was Cassandra and I could tell at once she was not only sexy, but smart and interesting. I bought her a drink; we made each other laugh. We connected. Then she said, "I have to go."

"Really? Can I walk you to your car?"

"Okay."

We got to her car, which was parked in the 9000 Sunset building across the street, and I casually asked her if she'd like to do some coke for the road. She said yes and we got into her car. I took out my little glass vial with the tiny spoon attached by a chain to the cap and we each did a 'one-and-one.' She told me she was very impressed with the fact that I hadn't said anything about having coke until that moment. It was a sign of class. I had read her right: she had it in spades. She asked me if I'd like to follow her to her house. *Does the Pope shit in the woods?* "Sure," I said.

She lived in a nice but unremarkable apartment on Beachwood Canyon. The more I got to know her, the more I realized I was dealing with an extremely clever, resourceful person. "What do you do for a living?" I asked.

"I take photos of topless blond girls for Japanese girlie magazines. It's easy to find great-looking models because they get to keep their panties on. Japanese magazines don't show total nudity, only breasts."

We talked about a great many things. She was quite knowledgeable on a variety of subjects. We had a few more drinks and a few more lines, and then we were naked in bed. Suffice it to say the sex was as great as she was. She was, by far, the classiest, smartest woman I had ever picked up at the

Rainbow (and there had been many). At some point it came out that she did not live alone. She lived with her boyfriend and he was out of town, so this could only be a one-night stand.

I called her a few days later and told her how much I enjoyed being with her and wanted to see her again, but no dice. She was with someone, and that was that. However, if I was interested in buying a pound of primo weed, she had one for sale. I agreed to buy it, just so I could see her again. We consummated the deal in the office where she worked at 9000 Sunset. That was the last I saw of Cassandra Peterson—until a couple of years later, when she appeared on late night TV as "Elvira, Mistress of the Dark." She was unrecognizable in the black wig, over-the-top makeup and pushup bra, but the name rang a bell and, looking hard, I realized it was indeed my little redheaded 'Irma la Douce.'

Left photo: Elvira. Right photo: Cassandra.
Photos: IPE Collection.

Chapter Forty-Four

Incognito

I never signed a management agreement with Stan, and he never took one penny in commissions from me. He was busy becoming a very successful film music agent. But Stan did more for my career than any manager. After the demise of Glider, he shopped some of my new material to some publishers. He had a friend, Donna Young, who was at Interworld Music Group, a publishing company started by Mike Stewart, formerly President of United Artists Records (before I was signed there). Donna liked my stuff and offered me an exclusive publishing deal with a weekly draw against royalties of $300.

Almost immediately Donna told me she had submitted one of my songs to Seals & Crofts and they were cutting it! It was not one of the new ones, but an old guitar-voice demo of a song called "Fish Gotta Swim," which I had cut in the studio with Bruce Ablin back in '74. Although the title was obviously inspired by the lyrics of Jerome Kern's "Can't Help Lovin' That Man of Mine" from *Showboat*, it bore no resemblance to that song. It was inspired by one of the many tearful goodbye scenes I had played with V:

> *Fish gotta swim in the sea*
> *Birds gotta fly in the sky*
> *I've gotta love you forever*
> *Even if you say goodbye*

Even though Seals & Crofts' career was on the wane by 1978, I was thrilled and excited. It had been a long time since a major artist had covered one of my songs. I couldn't wait to hear their version. As it turned out, I never did. A few weeks later Donna told me they had cut the song, but that it didn't make it onto their album. Why I didn't press Interworld to get me a copy of their version, I can't say. Maybe I was just too disappointed to think about such a thing. In those days, we didn't think about taking photos or videos of key moments in our lives, we just lived from moment to moment. I never thought that someday I would wish I had a copy of that unreleased recording.

* * *

Also in 1978, I met Joey Alkes and Chris Fradkin, two songwriters from New York City. They had been collaborating with a guy named Peter Case who had recently formed a new wave band called The Plimsouls. They urged me to go hear The Plimsouls in one of their first gigs at Madame Wong's in Chinatown. I remember going all by myself. For some reason, neither Joey nor Chris could go with me. It was my first exposure to the burgeoning LA club scene. At that point, The Plimsouls were a three-piece, with Peter singing lead and playing all the guitar parts, Dave Pahoa on bass, and Louie Ramirez on drums. They were pretty raw, but exciting. I loved Peter's voice, sort of like a young John Lennon. I introduced myself after the set, telling him that Joey and Chris sent me, and how much I enjoyed his music. I was to hear many subsequent Plimsouls gigs in the coming years and watched them grow into one of the most promising new bands in Los Angeles.

Soon afterward The Plimsouls added Eddie Muñoz on lead guitar and, by 1982, they had a string of local hits, which included several that were co-written by Joey and Chris: "Hush," "Now" and "Million Miles Away." Unfortunately, "Million Miles Away," which was featured in the film *Valley Girl*, was the only one to make the national charts at #82, more than a year after its original release. I had predicted that The Plimsouls would go all the way. I would've bet money on it. Glad I didn't.

I started writing songs with Joey and Chris, and we found we had a good chemistry for coming up with catchy, poppy song ideas. Working with them also infused a more contemporary element into my songwriting style, something I sorely needed. These songs were clearly vehicles for a band, not a solo singer-songwriter, so I started looking around again for musicians with whom I could build not just a recording act, but a live, performing band. Fortunately, the times were ripe for such an enterprise. There were a lot of good musicians around, and they were hungry to play.

Lots of different guys came up to jam at my eagle's nest on Gould Avenue, among them, a tall, lanky lead guitarist named David Dellarosa. He had a mop of unruly brown curls (not unlike mine) and sleepy brown eyes. He was a cool guy in every respect. Women loved him as did everyone else. His motto: "Everybody relax." I loved the way he played and how quickly he came up with good parts for my songs. He could also sing—and he was up for being in a band; and that meant rehearsing and playing live without any guarantee of money.

My good friend Rob Moitoza asked me to co-produce some demos with him for a girl named Teda Bracci. She was a wild woman with a Janice Joplin-like persona and voice. Teda was interesting to work with in the studio: she kept pulling up her shirt and showing her boobs to everyone. Why she did this, I still can't figure out; it wasn't like she had great boobs, and she was, as far as I could tell, completely into chicks. She wore a tangled mass of chains and necklaces around her neck, and they made so much noise when she did her vocals, we had to tape them down. I had written a song called "Too Tough to Cry," which turned out to be perfect for her, and we also cut three other tracks. Rob assembled the players: him on bass, Carlos de la Paz on lead guitar and Herb Quick on drums. Herb was a standout: technically excellent, great taste, a clean, precise drum style, and easy to work with. It was through Herb and Carlos that I met a whole cadre of excellent musicians in Alta Dena.

Victor Bisetti, another first-rate drummer (heavier and more rock-oriented than Herb), John Avila, an awesome bass player (technically amazing, but more fusion than rock-oriented), and a few other guys all shared a large house with a garage in which we could rehearse. For a while, the personnel shifted constantly, with Victor on drums some days, Herb on others. John played bass for a while, then got too busy with other gigs and we found Paul Eckman, who was not the technician John was, but more of a rock player and better for what I was doing (John proved to be a good enough rock player a few years later when he became the bass player for Oingo Boingo). David Dellarosa was a constant on lead guitar.

Once, early on, we held a rehearsal in the garage of my friend Brie Howard, who had been married to James Newton Howard and was the drummer in the pioneering all-girl band, Fanny. None of the usual suspects on bass and drums were available, so David, who had one foot in the world of heavy metal, brought along bass player Rudy Sarzo and drummer Frankie Banali, both of whom were playing in a metal band called Dubrow, which eventually changed its name to Quiet Riot and caused quite a stir on the Sunset Strip a few years later. But they weren't right for my music, which rocked pretty hard, but not as hard as they wanted to.

By 1980 the final lineup, with Victor on drums and Paul on bass, was in place. We worked up a few of the best songs I had for a rock band that sounded very 'now' and commercial, including two I had written with Joey and Chris. I believed this would be my final stab at 'making it,' and I meant to employ all the music smarts I had gained from every bitter lesson of the past to avoid making any more mistakes. I decided to call the band Incognito. I had this vision of everyone wearing sunglasses.

Incognito. L to R: David Dellarosa, me, Victor Bisetti, Paul Eckman.
Photo: Richard Millstein

* * *

There was a guy at Interworld—Barry—who said he would take us into the studio and record us doing my best four new songs as soon as we were ready. This motivated me to whip the band into shape and, within a few weeks, I felt we were ready to record. I added Steve Halter, who had played keyboards on *Glider*, for the session.

Barry took us into a little studio in Hollywood in which Led Zeppelin were rumored to have done some overdubs. Right from the start I got a bad feeling. They had us set up my guitar amp and David's guitar amp right next to each other, separated only by a thin baffle. The plan was for everyone to play at once on the basic track, with none of the amps in isolation, which meant the electric guitars would be leaking into the drum tracks and into each other. When we played at sufficient volume to achieve the desired guitar sound, the engineer told us we were too loud and would have to turn down. Led Zeppelin, my ass!

I pointed out to Barry and the engineer that this was the wrong way to go about it. We should go for a good bass and drum track with no leakage by having me play and sing in an isolation booth. Then we should overdub all the other instruments, one at a time, then the vocals. Barry told me that it would take too much time and that time was money. He knew what he was doing, he said. I took issue with that. Even before we had recorded a note I knew we would get nothing usable out of this recording session. I got on the phone to Donna and told her so. I told her Barry was flushing Interworld's money down the toilet. But there was nothing she or anyone else could do, and we went ahead and did it Barry's way. Not surprisingly, the results were disastrous, and it made me look bad at the publishing company. I was furious at Barry. He disavowed any blame and put it all on me.

Chapter Forty-Five

Snowblind

In 1979, right after I had to move from my eagle's nest on Gould to Jerry's guesthouse on Arlene Terrace, a friend named Larry started fronting me eighth-ounces ('eightballs') of pharmaceutical grade cocaine, which Larry called 'The King.' According to Larry, the King was manufactured differently from street cocaine in an exclusive lab process that approximated the manufacture of actual pharmaceutical cocaine. The King came as large, glittering flakes. A gram of the King would fill a two-gram vial because the large flakes created greater volume. If you put it through a Deering blender (a strainer made for grinding up cocaine—an indispensable piece of paraphernalia), the volume reduced to normal and a gram would fill a one-gram vial. Of course, it was more attractive to offer a gram that looked like two grams—especially since it sold for twice the going rate.

By 1979 coke was the undisputed drug of choice among the Hollywood hip set. I was one of the holdouts. I wanted to stay 'organic' and 'chemical-free,' until I realized that cocaine was a natural, plant-based substance that underwent a chemical refining process and was theoretically no more harmful than pot, which, if you smoked enough, would probably give you lung cancer as quick as cigarettes. No one at the time considered coke to be a dangerous, addictive drug. It was a 'harmless recreational drug.' That's what everybody said. So I began dealing it, along with marijuana, to my growing clientele.

I had read the book *Snowblind* by Robert Sabbag a year or two earlier and, while on one level it was a cautionary tale, on another it was exciting, romantic and titillating. Because I still had some vestiges of spiritual awareness left, I saw myself as 'the righteous coke dealer,' not greedy like the others. And I was scrupulously honest with my customers, never stepping on (adulterating) the product, always offering the finest product on the market and even looking out for my clients' safety. I always offered to grind the stuff up for them, since it was harmful to the epithelial tissue inside your nose to snort big chunks of coke. Not only would it eat a hole in your nasal passage, it was wasteful. When ground up into tiny particles, the coke would dissolve more quickly in your system, and less of it would get you higher faster.

I was also generous to a fault, spreading the stuff around like it was Pez. I soon became the darling of the Hollywood club set, spending more time in club bathrooms than out on the floor listening to music. I quickly became very popular, gaining many new friends—not all of them as high-minded and well-meaning as me—and perhaps, underneath it all, I was more interested in being the belle of the ball than making a lot of money. I was content to make a living and have the time of my life.

And then there were the girls. Coke attracted beautiful girls like my guitar never did. Sure, some of them were 'coke whores,' but many of them were really cool and smart and not so different from me. It was a new decade—the '80s. We weren't getting any younger and we were all out to have as much fun as possible. I never considered myself terribly attractive, and I was still obsessed with somehow proving myself wrong. The fact that I was luring women with drugs didn't seem to invalidate my conquests—not in my mind anyway.

I soon learned that the King, while it had a certain novelty value, was not the real deal. It *was* like pharmaceutical: it was smooth, subtle and had a strong numbing effect, but it wasn't designed to get you high. It was another friend, an enterprising musician/entrepreneur like me named Nat, who turned me on to Peruvian flake. Peruvian flake came in glittering pinkish shale-like rocks. If you touched one with a razor blade it would fall apart and the layers would separate into big, opalescent flakes. The high was the essence of the cocaine high: euphoric but not speedy. I used to call it 'powdered self-confidence.' Just what I needed. Nat's in-laws were Columbian. He started fronting me ounces of the stuff. He encouraged me to take more, to move weight, ounces, not just grams and eightballs. But I wanted to keep it small, below the radar of law enforcement.

* * *

Coke became the new currency in Hollywood. After my acoustic guitar was stolen out of my car, I got a new one for an eightball. Owners of recording studios were also open to doing business this way, and by trading coke for studio time, I was able to bring Incognito into some of the best studios in LA for a rate that was advantageous to both parties; I was not paying as much for the coke as they would have had to, and they were not paying as much for the studio time as I would have had to. We went in during off hours, usually late at night, and I would also have to compensate the engineers, unless the studio owner was also the engineer. Between 1980 and 1982 we recorded and mixed nine master-quality tracks.

The drugs did not affect my ability to sing and play, in fact, my skills had reached a new zenith due to the constant rehearsal, occasional live gigs around town and the incentive my fellow band members provided by their high level of skill. On some of the songs, my lead vocals on the guide tracks were better than the ones I overdubbed later, and we wound up keeping many of the original lead vocals for the final version, essentially a live performance. Those tapes still hold up today in terms of energy and quality, albeit the music sounds distinctly '80s. Our sound was somewhere between The Cars and Tom Petty & the Heartbreakers, a little new wavier than The Heartbreakers, a little rockier than The Cars. It was catchy, memorable, high quality rock 'n' roll.

When I played the first group of finished mixes for Donna at Interworld, I told her I thought they sounded like masters. She did not agree. But there was one song, "Tracy," that I had written with Joey and Chris, that sounded like a hit to everyone. When Mike Stewart heard it, he called me into his office. I went in there expecting big kudos, but instead I got a shit storm.

Mike was a corpulent man around fifty, with thinning reddish hair and a red face, probably due to high blood pressure. He was one of those blustery old-time record guys who had more glory days in his past than his future. He told me that by collaborating with Joey and Chris I had violated the terms of my contract (what, I'm supposed to *read* these things?). It seems I needed Interworld's permission to collaborate with another writer, and they had to have that writer's publishing. He told me that, unless Joey and Chris signed the publishing over to Interworld on everything we wrote together, he was going to sue me for breach of contract. I asked if they would offer

Joey and Chris an advance in exchange for signing the publishing over and he said they would not. I was scared and I was screwed. I spoke to Joey and Chris, and of course, they wouldn't go for a deal like that; why should they? So my ass was grass.

Once again, my friend and ally Stan stepped in and saved the day. He noticed something that no one else had: we had never actually signed the contract. It was an oversight on the part of the Interworld legal department, and it saved my ass. The upshot was that Interworld wanted nothing more to do with me, my stipend ended, they kept the publishing on the songs I had given them so far, but I was able to walk away unscathed.

* * *

Incognito played a number of live gigs around LA, including an "industry showcase" at Stone Fox, a rehearsal studio complex on Cumpston Street in North Hollywood where we now had our own rehearsal room. This was in May of 1980. We didn't start recording our masters until November, so we still did not have a presentable audio tape at this point, which makes me question the wisdom of arranging the showcase so early.

By this time I had moved out of Jerry's guest house and was sharing a quite palatial ranch style house at the top of Pacific View Drive with a married couple, Artie and Veronica (jokingly referred to as 'Archie and Veronica'—look it up, kids). Artie and Veronica helped me organize the event and we even catered it with hors d'oeuvres and champagne. We sent out invitations to everyone who was anyone in the music business, but no record company people showed up, only a couple of personal managers and a gaggle of friends. I arranged to have the show video taped. The idea was to have a live video of the band I could show to local club bookers as an audition. The result was underwhelming. There was a single camera on a tripod at the back of the room, so that made it extremely static visually, there was a big post right in the middle of the stage, which made the setting quite unattractive, and our sound engineer took the wrong mix—the monitor mix—and fed it into the video, so the mix was bad and the sound all distorted.

Ultimately, we did play some club dates around town. There was no money in it, but bands all did this for the exposure; that next big record deal could be right around the corner. We played at the Troubadour, a tiny room in the Valley called the Bla Bla, Club 88, a place in Santa Monica called Blackie's and the Improv. The Improv on Melrose had been strictly a comedy club, but now they were featuring music on some nights. I liked playing that room because it was set up as a listening room, so people were actually sitting down paying attention. We did a good set that night, and when I came off stage there was a cute little brunette named Sherry, who had been a play-mate of a friend of mine, waiting for me. She invited me to her place, which was nearby, and we stayed up all night snorting coke and having wild sex.

The next night, Incognito was to play at Madame Wong's—Wong's West, I think it was—and I had to call them and cancel. My voice was shot. I told everyone it was because of the gig the previous night, but Sherry and I knew the truth. My music career was starting to interfere with my partying.

Incognito – live showcase, 1980. Photo: Richard Millstein

* * *

There were a few more feeble attempts to get a record deal for Incognito. Stan pitched us to a guy at EMI—Ira Jaffe. They called him 'The Ear.' According to Stan, our tape "knocked his socks off." There was a mad scramble to get him the 15ips tape he requested. We got it to him, then heard nothing. And so it went. I became increasingly cynical and disillusioned with the music business. Months later, I sent the same tape to the same guy. When I followed up, he told me, "Sorry, I don't hear anything in this." I guess his socks stayed on that time.

I had it in my head that the artist's role stopped after the creative process; then it was up to the businessman to take over. This was a paradigm that had, unbeknownst to me, already met its death. No one was going to lift a finger to help you until you had proven yourself as a viable product. This meant: do tons of gigs and develop a huge local following, put out your own records, get a lot of press and media coverage, or all of the above. It was the era of DIY (Do It Yourself). But I didn't.

Through my cocaine lens, I had already achieved the life I had always sought: hot-and-cold-running babes, enough money to live comfortably, and more backstage passes than you could shake a stick at. Schlepping equipment around to two-bit LA clubs seemed way too much effort for not nearly enough pay-off. In the world of cocaine, gratification needed to be instant. The memory of V and all she stood for slowly receded into the mists of the past. Coke and V were simply not compatible.

Once, in a coke-induced frenzy, I hoisted myself over her high iron gate and knocked on her door. Mercifully, the husband was not there. I had lost a lot of weight, and had been doing gymnastics, so I was very thin and muscular. She looked at me like I was from another planet. I was wearing a black tank top, black kung fu pants, and Chinese shoes—sort of a coked-out ninja. She let me in and we talked. But the cocaine was blocking the old chemistry. The connection was no longer there. Later, she told me I reminded her of a black spider. But why should I care? The coke whores still liked me.

Chapter Forty-Six

Coke Whores

I met Sharisse through Ben, the owner of one of the studios in which Incognito was recording. Ben was a male coke whore. He was a guy who seemed to have everything going his way: a beautiful wife, a cute little daughter, a beautiful house, and he was owner and chief engineer at one of the most prestigious recording studios in Los Angeles. He engineered our first sessions and he was really talented. By the last time I saw him (maybe 1985) he had lost it all—to cocaine.

One day, Ben brought this gorgeous blond to one of my recording sessions. By gorgeous, I mean she was perfect looking. Sharisse could have graced the cover of any glamour magazine; the quintessential blue-eyed American beauty. She was shoveling piles of coke up her nose, so I knew she was fair game. At some point I let it be known that I was the source of all this white stuff, and I asked her for her number. Of course she gave it to me, and in less than a week we were going out.

The first date I asked her on was to a wrap party for a movie. A guy I knew was a producer on one of the iterations of *The Hills Have Eyes*. Strictly B horror stuff. But the party was held in a big, lovely home in Holmby Hills. Sharisse caused quite a splash. One guy tried to trade me his wife for her. If his first-born had been there he probably would have thrown her in too.

After the party I took her home to my place on Pacific View Drive. I was now living the complete rock star life: an endless supply of drugs, beautiful women at my beck and call, and this big, beautiful house at the very top of the Hollywood Hills—and without the fame and its attendant burdens and stress. We had a 180 degree panoramic view of the entire San Fernando Valley from our huge deck. The house must have been more than a hundred feet long: there was a big kitchen, a large dining area, a spacious living room with multiple couches and luxurious appointments (the owners had left the furniture), then a long hallway leading to the bedrooms; first mine, the smaller bedroom that looked out on the lanai with a bathroom right next door but not adjoining, then the master suite, Artie and Veronica's room, with its own bathroom. Before the Universal Amphitheatre added a roof, we could hear the music from the concerts emanating from it.

Sharisse and I settled onto one of the big sofas that was actually three sofas arranged at right angles. We had some drinks and a few more lines. She called herself Sharisse Lamont, but her real name was Mary Ann Burgolio from Norwalk, California. She wasn't much of a conversationalist. In fact, I guess you'd have to say Sharisse was a complete moron. Her picture was in the dictionary next to the word 'bimbo.' But being stupid was no crime, and if you had looks like hers, you could get by in this world—if you just knew enough to keep your mouth shut. But that was Sharisse's fatal flaw. She was given to just blurting out anything that came into her head. There was no censorship mechanism between her brain and her mouth. As I got to know her better, this characteristic became more and more of a liability. For instance, we might be in a group of people exchanging fairly civilized conversation and some guy's name would come up whom we all knew in common, and Sharisse would blurt out, "Oh, I was just with him. Boy, does that guy ever have a small dick!" This is not an exaggeration. One time I brought her with me to the home of a singer, Cynthia Manley, who I not only respected as a singer, but also kind of had the hots for, and Sharisse says to her, "Yeah, Teddy just fucked me, but he didn't make me come." When I say, "you can't take some people anywhere," I really mean it.

But let's get back to the romantic aftermath of our first date. We were pretty high, so I asked her to take all her clothes off, and she complied. She was truly a masterpiece among God's creations. She stretched out on the couch that was at a right angle to mine. Her body was slim and perfectly proportioned. Her pubic hair was shaved. "Well, aren't you going to do anything?" she asked.

"Not for the moment. I just want to look at you."

"Why?"

"Because 'a thing of beauty is a joy forever.'"

"Wow, thanks," she said, missing the quote.

Then I moved over next to her. I unzipped my fly and told her to get down on her knees on the floor and suck it. And she did. This went on for quite a while. If she had been a little better at it I might have come, but that's not what I wanted to do. I wanted to impress her with my power and control. One of the properties of coke—at least for me—is it gives you a certain detachment in sexual situations that enables you to 'perform' in an almost superhuman way. So, after a while, I said "Okay, that's enough," and I put it away, still stiff as a dead cat. I told her to put her clothes on and I took her home. It's possible my attempt to impress her in this way was totally lost on her, but not on me. It made me feel really good and really powerful to know I had that kind of control—over myself and others.

The next time I saw Sharisse, she asked me to take her to a party at the home of a movie director named Iván Nagy. Nagy (pronounced "nāj") was a middle-aged Hungarian guy with silver hair and a manner that was slick bordering on sleazy. Apparently he had directed some movies I had never heard of and some American TV in the '70s. Sharisse had told me he wanted to buy some coke, so I brought along a few gram vials for sale, one of which he purchased. He lived in an exclusive gated condo complex in Century City.

The other guests impressed me as mostly Euro-trash and about as sleazy as Iván. In the bathroom he introduced me to two little girls. I mean, these two couldn't have been more than fifteen—perhaps runaways scooped up off Hollywood Boulevard. Nagy showed me a Polaroid he had just snapped, looking down on one of these girls who was sucking his cock in the bathtub. He tried to convince me to take these little girls home and leave Sharisse there. "Uh-uh, nothing doing," I said. "Sharisse came with me and she's leaving with me." And I got her out of there as quickly as possible. God knows what would have been her fate in the hands of that creep. I felt sorry for the two little girls, but there's only so much one man can do in this wicked world.

Years later I saw a documentary depicting Iván as the boyfriend of the notorious Heidi Fleiss, 'Hollywood Madame.'

* * *

Things were beginning to unravel on Pacific View Drive. I had been giving Artie and Veronica coke in exchange for doing all the housework. I thought of us as one big happy family—with them as the parents and me as the kid ('Child Drug Dealer Bribes Parents with Cocaine to Do Housework'—wait 'til Rupert Murdoch hears about this!). Add to this the resentment Artie must have felt seeing me ushering in and out an endless stream of nubile young babes, while he had to sleep with the same—albeit charming—wife every night and go to the same boring job as floor manager at a department store every day. But there was something more at work here. Artie was becoming unhinged. His behavior had become volatile and irrational. Maybe the coke had something to do with this, maybe not. I had volunteered to pay for cable TV when we first moved into the house. My preference was cable because of the movies, but Artie was a rabid sports fan and he lobbied for Direct TV, a satellite service that offered lots of exclusive sporting events. I acquiesced, and Artie loved hosting football parties and the like at our house. I became the 'idiot savant of the NFL,' successfully predicting the winners in the majority of games between teams I neither knew nor cared about.

Tensions between Artie and I rose and, at last, it was decided that I would look for my own place. It didn't take me long to find a nice little hideaway at the end of a cul-de-sac on Walnut Drive in my old neighborhood, Laurel Canyon. Coincidentally, this was a place my pal Big John had lived a few years earlier. The *coup de grâce* between me and Artie occurred when I gave the order to shut off the Direct TV. Artie had scheduled a big party to watch a championship boxing match that was only viewable on Direct TV. I gave the service explicit instructions to turn the service off *after* the date of the big fight. So, the day of the fight/party, I get home, and I'm locked out of the house. Artie has the door chained and, through the crack, he lets it be known that the Direct TV had been turned off before the fight, ruining his party and making him look like a fool. There is no doubt in his mind that I did this on purpose to fuck him up. I swore up and down that I had ordered the shut-off on a later date, but Artie was having none of it. So I moved out of Pacific View on a sour note with Artie, if not Veronica.

I heard from Veronica not too long afterward, and she told me Artie had lost it completely. Their marriage had fallen apart, he had lost his job at the department store, and he was homeless, living in his car. The thought that just knowing me might have contributed to his downfall troubles me to this day.

* * *

My new place on Walnut Drive was considerably less impressive than Pacific View, but it was quiet, peaceful, and all mine. It was really just one big room with an alcove for the bed, an alcove for the kitchen, a separate bathroom, and a walk-in closet that doubled as my 'office.' This was where I kept my drug stash and Triple Beam scale. I had a neighbor, a fellow musician named Frank Demme, just a couple of doors away. Frank was the bass player in a band called Small Talk, who had a regular gig every weekend at a club in Studio City called the Sash.

I went there on Saturday night and was dazzled. Not by the band—they were good, of course—but by the waitresses. The Sash waitresses all dressed in candy-striped body suits that required the wearer to wear nothing underneath. If you wore a bra or panties, the lines would be visible, so you basically had to have a perfect body to be a Sash waitress. I quickly made friends with several of them; a guy with cocaine makes friends easily. To say I was like a kid in a candy store would be overstating the obvious. We would often have soirees after the club closed.

One night a few people were over at Frank's place, and that's where I met Merri. She was not a Sash waitress, although her body was certainly good enough. To tell the truth, I'm not sure how she ended up at Frank's, but she sure did like coke. She was a rather tawdry-looking blond with big blue eyes, full lips, and a nose that came a little too close to the lips to qualify her as a full-on glamour-puss. She had a slight resemblance to Bette Midler, but much more svelte. And she dressed very suggestively. Anyway, Merri wound up coming back to my place with me that night and we showed each other a good time. She was a lot smarter than Sharisse, and she and I had good chemistry together—in and out of bed.

She shared an apartment in the Valley with two guys who worked for TFA-Electrosound, at the time the largest sound and lighting company, working with every major rock band and tour. Through this connection, Merri was able to get us in, and sometimes backstage, to some great shows. The first one she took me to was Tom Petty & The Heartbreakers at the Universal Amphitheatre. I don't remember much about the concert, but I remember Merri nearly caused a riot with the outfit she had on. The top was so low-cut that it just barely covered her nipples, her midriff was bare, and her skirt was more like a wide belt. The girls might have been looking at Tom Petty, but the guys were all looking at Merri. The next show we went to was the X-Fest in San Diego. This was a multi-artist festival put on by the hip FM rock station in San Diego, 91X. On the bill were the Stray Cats, Modern English and Bow Wow Wow. It was the summer of 1983.

For the San Diego trip, Merri had me pick her up in front of an apartment building near Crescent Heights and Sunset in Hollywood at dawn—we had a three-hour drive to get to the show. "Who lives here?" I asked, as she got into my car.

"Oh, just a guy I know," she answered, vaguely.

"Who? Come on, I won't be jealous."

"Well, he's this older guy. He likes to snort coke off girls' tits. There were three of us up there, and all he did was snort coke off our tits, I swear!"

We had an incredible time on our trip to San Diego, and after that, Merri kind of became a fixture at my place. I don't think she ever moved her stuff in, but she was just there all the time. I was working on a writing project with Ron at the time, and I remember her calling me at his place in Santa Monica, asking me—in a voice that was a bit too whiney for my liking—"When are you coming home?" That's when I started getting a bit nervous about Merri. I did not feel romantically inclined toward her. I thought of her as a playmate, a good-time girl, but it appeared she was beginning to feel differently about me.

* * *

The most epic bender of my cocaine career happened not long after this. I went to the Sash, then over to Frank's for another after-soiree. Some of Frank's band mates were there, a few Sash waitresses, some guys I didn't know, and Merri. There was a short, bald guy named Max. When it started getting light, Frank threw us all out, but Max, me, Merri and two of the most beautiful girls I had ever seen, Sash waitresses Suzanne and Arlene, came over to my place to snort some more coke. We partied on into the morning. I lost all sense of time. At some point Max invited us to his place up on Mulholland Drive. If you lived on Mulholland you were rich. Anyway, I volunteered to drive, so Merri, Suzanne and Arlene piled into my car and we followed Max up to his spacious home overlooking the Valley. We hung outside around the swimming pool.

Suzanne was a dark-haired beauty, about twenty-two. She said people told her she looked like Valerie Bertinelli, but the truth was Mrs. Van Halen couldn't hold a candle to Suzanne. Not only was her face a thing of wonder, her body was like one of those unreal women that Vargas used to paint for *Esquire* and *Playboy*. But she was very real. Her waist, like her age, was twenty-two, which made her other formidable curves even more striking. Arlene was a cool, Nordic beauty with shiny black hair and sparking blue eyes. She was reserved and mysterious—qualities I loved. The less she said, the hotter she seemed.

Max challenged me to an arm wrestling match for $100. He was even shorter than I was and kind of looked like Wallace Shawn, so I agreed.

."Don't do it!" said Suzanne, with whom I had by now developed an unspoken rapport, "He's extremely strong."

I had seen Max walking around the swimming pool holding the reclining Suzanne over his head, arms fully extended, but I was undaunted. I had been chin-up champ of my junior high school and, more recently, I had been taking gymnastics lessons and my upper body strength was considerable. The element of reach is very important in arm wrestling, but as this guy was shorter than me, he did not have this advantage. So I took a $100 bill out of my pocket and slapped it down. "Let's go," I said.

He took me down in about one minute. He was awesomely strong. "Okay, man, I'm impressed! Here's your $100." But he wouldn't take it. He had put himself through college by hustling much bigger, stronger guys than me into arm wrestling matches. And he had always won. Next to 'Can't tell a book by its cover' in the dictionary, there's a picture of Max. But I came out the big winner that weekend.

After god knows how many days of bingeing, it was at last time to go home. Merri, Suzanne and Arlene all piled into my car and we headed back to my place, where their cars were parked. But everyone wanted to come inside for a few more lines.

So we drank a little more and we snorted a little more. I had a small collection of vintage Japanese kimonos in my closet, and I offered them to the girls. They were short, and the three of them looked pretty adorable in them—with nothing underneath. "I'm taking a shower," I said. "Anybody that wants to join me is welcome."

I was already in the shower with the water running when I heard the bathroom door open and close. I expected Merri, as she kind of had a prior claim on me. I knew the girls would work it out, and that's what I wanted. But it was Suzanne. This was my dream come true. She doffed her kimono and got in the shower with me. Suddenly that body of unreal proportions was up against mine and we were kissing. We washed each other, but we didn't make it—not in the shower.

When we came out, I could tell Merri and Arlene thought we had already made it. "Okay, everybody on the bed," I said. And suddenly I was face-to-face with six of the most magnificent breasts I had ever seen. *Oh my god, now what do I do?* I said to myself. *Three? I don't know if I can handle three by myself.*

"Why don't I go get Frank," I suggested. The three of them shrugged. There were no objections, so I went next door for reinforcements. But, when I looked into Frank's window I saw him passed out on his couch with his hand down his pants, and I thought better of waking him up—even for this. I went back to face the music. The girls were already making out with each other when I got back, so I got naked and dove right in.

What followed had to be the pinnacle of any guy's sexual history. Nothing compared or would ever compare with my experience with V, but, on a strictly carnal level, this took the prize. Merri and Suzanne were having a sort of friendly competition, demonstrating their fellatio skills on my penis. Then they collaborated—setting a new high bar for my erotic experiences. Arlene was more passive, so I went down on her and kissed her all over while the other two were working me over with their tongues. Then Suzanne went down on Arlene while Merri and I got it on. Amazingly, I still had not reached orgasm. I knew just how and where I wanted to come. I rolled over and grabbed Suzanne, and I held her close, then entered her. We came together, and on that night, the beautiful Suzanne became my new girlfriend.

I had forgotten that I had arranged for Big John to come by that morning to drop off a pound of weed. He walked in and surveyed the scene—unconscious girls everywhere. He looked at them. He looked at me. He shook his head. It was not easy to get a raised eyebrow out of Big John, but I got one that time.

* * *

I needed to faze out Merri so that I could be with Suzanne, so I introduced her to Len. Len was a tall thin black man with very light skin and light brown hair and beard. He always wore one of those big Rastafarian knitted caps, so his hair was always covered, and he had a full beard and mustache. Len had a commanding presence. He had that unmistakable New York City speech pattern and a booming baritone voice. He was smart and people tended to gather around him and become his followers. If he had been a psychopath, he could have been another Charlie Manson. But Len was no psycho. He was a pimp; at least that's the way it seemed, although he never said as much. He had a gaggle of young women—and some not so young—ready to do his bidding. He had a nice apartment in the Fairfax district. It was beautifully decorated and always immaculate. There was a big round coffee table in the middle of the living room, and people would sit around it on cushions on the floor. Len started out buying weed from me and then, like the rest of our world, got into the white stuff. He presented himself as sort of a self-help guru, counseling people—especially girls—on how to make money. He would tell a story about being rousted by the cops on the street—he hadn't done anything, other than be a black man. The cop searched him and found a roll of cash—$750. "$750! Where'd you get all that money, boy?"

"Shit," said Len disdainfully, "that ain't no money."

When I brought Merri into Len's circle, there was an instant rapport between them. They each had qualities the other needed. I can't swear I did her a favor, or him either for that matter, but I felt she was in good hands with Len. He even got an apartment just for her in his building. I guess she was turning tricks for him, but wasn't that what she was doing before I met her? Only this time, at least she was getting money instead of just drugs. And I was now free to bring Suzanne into my life.

* * *

Suzanne shared an apartment in Van Nuys with Arlene, and sometimes I would go over there and party with both of them. It was starting to feel odd for me to just have one woman in my bed. I went to the club often, and Suzanne started staying at my place more and more. The crowd from the club would wind up at Frank's or my place, we would stay up and party 'til dawn, then Suzanne and I would sleep most of the day, until it was time for her to go to work again that night. Sharisse was frequently present for these soirees as well, and she would sometimes stay over with me and Suzanne. If this wasn't the rock star life, I don't know what was.

Another band that often played at the Sash was Jack Mack & The Heart Attack, an R&B cover band, fronted by Max Carl Gronethal, that had a horn section and was really tight and fun to listen and dance to. The bass player of this band was a guy named Freebo, and he had the hots for

Suzanne. Apparently they had some history together. One night, while Suzanne and I were together, she went out with him, and I didn't see her for a few days. And I was jealous as hell. I suppose that's when I realized I was actually falling for Suzanne. There was a gorgeous blond waitress at the Sash named Yvette, and I guess to get back at Suzanne, I shacked up with her and Arlene in someone's apartment where they were house sitting one weekend. I knew that all the juicy details would get back to Suzanne, because Arlene was there, and we did have words about it afterward, and that's when it came out: Suzanne had fallen for me too.

* * *

While Suzanne was still MIA, I ran into Francis Delia, a guy I used to know long ago back in Boston. He had been just a kid then, and he had a band with his two brothers called The Brothers. It was when The Lost were at their peak, so Frank always saw me as a rock star. Now he was an up-and-coming music video director. Coincidentally, he was about to direct the video of The Plimsouls' "Million Miles Away," and the shoot was to take place around the swimming pool at Joey and Chris's apartment building on Clark Street and Sunset, right across the street from the Whiskey. It was supposed to look like a party and, indeed, that's exactly what it turned out to be. I decided to take Yvette; she wasn't working that night and, besides, she looked more than good enough to make a favorable impression. Then it occurred to me that I should really take Sharisse, and I should use my influence to get her a prominent role in the video. So I decided to take both of them. I would arrive with a brace of breathtaking blonds. I called Sharisse and told her to get her wardrobe, hair and makeup perfect, because tonight I was going to make her a video star.

Yvette was totally cool about my taking Sharisse along once I made her understand it was 'business.' So I picked up Yvette, and then we went into Hollywood and picked up Sharisse at her neighbor's place. Her neighbor, a hair and makeup stylist, was quite a looker too. Before we left, she slipped me her number—in case I ever needed any hair or makeup assistance. Sharisse looked the best I had ever seen her in a tight-fitting leopard pattern dress and perfect '80s teased-out hair. When we got to the party, I had no trouble convincing Frank to cast her as the femme fatale of the party scene, and my promise to immortalize her came truer than I could have ever imagined, as the video is still viewable today on YouTube, and there Sharisse's beauty will never fade. When Yvette and I decided to leave, Frank had Sharisse floating around the pool, fully clothed, on a raft with a little dog. She didn't look very happy. We waved goodbye and split.

Back at my place, Yvette turned out to be a bit of a dud sexually. It seems she had been molested as a child by her older brother and hated to give oral sex. Even the missionary position felt like an obligation for her. At last, I got frustrated and let her crash out on my couch. I called the hair and makeup girl, and she came right up, ready to go. She didn't have the flashy beauty of Yvette or Sharisse, but she had warmth and genuine enthusiasm. While we were going at it, Sharisse called, genuinely distressed. She begged me to come get her out of there. So I called my old friend and manager, Ray Paret. He was living in LA now, just as caught up in the cocaine culture as I was, and managing The Blues Brothers, among other artists. I asked him to go down and pick up Sharisse. I told him to tell Frank he was her manager, and she had done enough work for free for one night. I told him to tell her I had sent him, and that he wouldn't be sorry. He wasn't.

Sharisse was a whole lot happier a few months later when we were all able to watch her on MTV together.

* * *

Suzanne moved out of her place in Van Nuys and in with me in my tiny, one-room cave. In another time, in another place, Suzanne and I might have been happy together. We connected at some visceral level. But cocaine permeated our lives. I started giving her little half-gram vials to take to work and sell to her fellow employees, so she would return home with maybe $100 or $150 almost every night.

Max invited us to a pool party at his house. A lot of the Sash crowd was there, as well as a nice assortment of Hollywood's 'beautiful people.' There was a lot of coke being spread around, and not all of it by me for a change. After a while a bunch of us wound up naked in the Jacuzzi. Then, some of the girls decided to dive off the diving board into the pool. Me and the other guys just watched from our perfect vantage point in the hot tub. It was like a fashion show with a diving board instead of a runway—and no clothes. When Suzanne walked out on the board and dove in, everyone's jaw dropped. Of course, as her boyfriend, my ego was practically bursting out of my skull. There was a guy in there with me, Joe Burk, and I didn't like the way he was looking at her. Well, of course, everyone was looking at her that way, but it was the fact that Joe Burk was young, handsome and athletic, with fashionably long sandy hair and a rugged all-American face—and a large penis. I found out he was a photo journalist, a photographer who would venture into war zones and, armed with nothing but his Nikon, snap award-winning pictures of African babies in burning huts—just before he whisked them to safety. Or, at least that's what was running through my imagination.

Making love to Suzanne that night at my place was never better, stimulated by the envy of all those other guys.

* * *

One night, I went to the Rainbow, just for a change. I met a cute young girl who said she was really into chicks as well as guys. *Oh,* I said to myself, *Suzanne's into chicks, I think I'll bring her home as sort of a present.* So, when Suzanne got home from work, there I was, in bed naked with this strange woman. Not exactly your bouquet of roses. Suzanne was furious. "But, baby," I said, "she's into chicks. I brought her home for *you.*" It didn't fly. Suzanne locked herself in the bathroom and started breaking things.

We decided to drive our guest back home—to Santa Barbara. It turns out she didn't have a car, and the only way we were going to get rid of her was to drive her to Santa Barbara. Now, for some reason—maybe my car wasn't running quite right—we had to take Suzanne's green Volvo. I drove, Suzanne sat in front with me, and our guest sat in the back and gave directions. It was already light when we left. To say this was an uncomfortable trip would be an understatement. Suzanne was high and drunk and excoriated me mercilessly all the way to Santa Barbara. I was becoming more and more annoyed. Through the distorted lens of cocaine, I failed to see how presumptuous I had been to bring this girl home without consulting Suzanne.

We dropped off our disconcerted guest and returned to LA. The ride back was even worse than the one going up. With no one in the car but the two of us, Suzanne took to trying to turn the wheel so we would run into other cars and putting her foot down on top of mine on the gas pedal. At some point I made her sit in the back seat, but that didn't help much. Our passenger had left a pack of cigarettes and some matches, and Suzanne started lighting cigarettes and burning holes in her arm; then she stuck one into the back of my neck and I had to pull over. I threw the cigarettes and matches away and made her promise to stop risking our lives, or I would throw her out of the car and leave her by the side of the road.

When we got home there was no let up. She started hurling my crystal wine glasses against the wall, showering the apartment with tiny shards of glass. She tried to cut herself, and me. I had to physically restrain her and, to my shame, ended up losing my cool and slapping her. I had never hit a woman before, and haven't since. In the end, I told her I was throwing her out. I literally picked her up and threw her out the door. I then locked the door, as she pounded on it, screaming and alerting all of the neighbors who had not already heard us, while I got her stuff together in her big trunk, opened the door and dumped it all outside. She picked everything up, got it into her car, and drove off.

A few nights later I got home late and there was a tearful message from her on my answering machine: she had racked up her car on a traffic island and she was begging me to come get her. By the time I got it, the message was hours old, so there was no way I could get to her. There were no cell phones back then. I would have gone to her rescue in a heartbeat. I missed her terribly.

And guess where she went: straight to Joe Burk, combat photographer.

I drove out to Van Nuys to the apartment she had with Arlene. Arlene had been seeing a Columbian guy who was heavy into the *yayo*. When she answered the door I hardly recognized her. She was kind of gray. All the spark and sparkle had gone out of her. Her hair looked like it was falling out, and her eyes were dull and glazed. Suzanne was not there. She was living with Joe on some street in the Hollywood Hills off Beachwood. She told me the name of the street and I drove up there, looking for her green Volvo. And there it was. I knocked on the door and Joe answered, but said she wasn't there. I had found a little gold necklace I knew Suzanne would like: a little gold heart framing a tiny gold key dangling in the middle. I had it in a box all gift-wrapped, and a card telling her how much I still loved her, and I was sorry. I knew he was lying about her not being there, so I gave him the present and left. Part of the reason for my visit was to show her that I could find her anywhere she went. I had a talent for that sort of thing, given my history of tracking down guitar thieves.

Later I heard that she quit the Sash and got a job at the Country Club in Reseda. I stopped hanging around there—she had told everyone that I had inflicted those cigarette burns on her arm.

In retrospect, of course, I realize that my behavior—and Suzanne's—was reprehensible. I'm appalled when I look back on that period of my life and the Cocaine morality that distorted my perceptions.

* * *

I first met Melissa through my hair stylist, Robert W (the W was for Weinstein, but he didn't think that sounded too cool for a hair stylist). Robert was extremely talented. He did great hair and was also an excellent photographer. He worked out of a salon on Melrose called Wave. I used to hang around there a lot and soon got to know all the employees as well as a lot of the regular customers. My hair was always cut on the barter system. The trouble with having your hair cut by someone on coke was that he sometimes got a little carried away and, one time, he snipped my ear. I had some joke business cards made up for him that read: "Don't worry, it'll grow back. – Robert W."

One night in 1980 I was invited by Robert and some of his cohorts on a trip down to San Diego to see The Joe Perry Project. This was during the time that Aerosmith was broken up and Joe Perry, the lead guitarist, had started his own band. We had a carload of freaks. One of the girls in the car was Melissa. Her boyfriend was Ralph, the lead singer of The Joe Perry Project, and she was the one that had gotten us all backstage passes. I, of course, was there to spread the coke around and, as always, I accommodated with a smile.

After that, I would run into Melissa from time to time. She was always with a different rock star or wannabe rock star. She was the quintessential groupie. It was 1982 by the time she got around to me. I gathered that, by this time, having a steady supply of coke had become more important to her than being seen with burgeoning superstars. She called me one day and asked if I wanted to come with her to see The Who at the Los Angeles Coliseum—and to the after-party backstage. One of her best friends, Maxine, had been a waitress at the Rainbow and had married John Entwistle, so that was our in. The opening act was The Clash, and I really wanted to see them as well, but Melissa and I spent so much time snorting coke and trying to get our shit together that we missed them completely.

I had seen The Who quite a few times, and this show was far from disappointing. But it was the first time I'd seen them without the late Keith Moon, and I did miss his energy. Then came the backstage party. I got to talk briefly with Roger Daltrey, whom I hadn't spoken to since that early gig in the U.S. in 1967. I schmoozed with Morgan Fairchild. Then Melissa told me we had to get the car and meet John and his party at the Rainbow.

The Who was—and is—one of my top three all-time favorite bands, so sitting at the center table downstairs at the Rainbow with John Entwistle, with all my rock 'n' roll wannabe acquaintances looking on in envy, was one of my proudest moments. I had given Melissa a small vial of coke to share with John and Maxine, and they made frequent trips to the 'private' bathroom behind the kitchen. I struck up a conversation with the guy sitting opposite me, a guy with blondish hair, bad skin, a puffy face, and glasses.

"So what do you do, man?" I said. "You look like maybe you're into graphics or something."

At this, John leans over to me and whispers loudly, "That's Joe Walsh! Yeah, he's 'graphic' all right!" I was totally embarrassed.

"Oh wow, sorry, man. I haven't seen you since the James Gang concert in 1972."

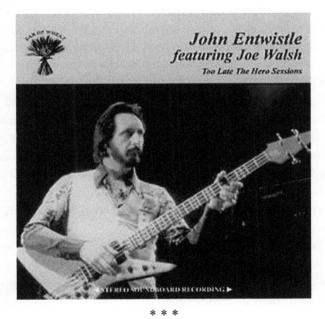

* * *

My place on Walnut was the lower apartment in a house that was divided into two apartments. The upper apartment was a modest two-bedroom place that was occupied by a young German doctor and his wife and child when

I moved in. After they moved out, the place was vacant for quite a while, which was very conducive to my lifestyle, which often involved happenings occurring very late at night. Then the house was sold and the new owner, one Bruce David, moved in upstairs. I could see him through my living room window as he moved his stuff in. He was a tall, nice-looking chap with dark hair, but there was something foreboding—even dangerous—about him. He saw me as he repeatedly passed my window, but looked at me unsmiling and said nothing.

When, a few days later, he finally decided to come by and introduce himself, I was on the tail end of a two-day floating orgy with Alissa, a girl I had known from the music scene for several years, a couple from out of town, and a stripper whose name I can't recall. We were all there in my tiny apartment, fortunately fully clothed, gathered around my big wooden table, which was about eighteen inches off the ground and surrounded by velvet cushions and a velvet-covered 'floor couch,' made from a single mattress. It was pretty clear we were doing drugs. I asked Bruce if he would like a drink, a joint or some cocaine. He accepted the invitation to snort a couple of lines. I took this as a favorable omen. He was still unsmiling and said little. The nameless stripper was asleep on my bed. He looked at her and said she had been in his magazine. It turns out Bruce David was the editor of *Hustler* and Larry Flynt's right-hand man.

A week or two later he called me up to his apartment and told me he didn't want a coke dealer living in his house. I protested my innocence, telling him I did coke as a recreational drug, but did not sell it. He pointed out the inordinate amount of traffic coming and going from my place. I told him I sold small amounts of marijuana. I got the impression—in fact, he might have told me—that someone close to him had died from cocaine. In the end, all my protestations were in vain. Bruce was a nasty sonofabitch, but he had my number. I was given thirty days notice.

My friend, Herb Quick, had introduced me to a couple living up the street: Bernie and Josephine. They had a similar setup to the one I was living in—a house with a one-bedroom apartment downstairs—and I was able to move in there. Bernie and Josephine were cool; in fact, they had been buying drugs from me, so my new situation was actually an improvement.

* * *

One day I went and picked up an ounce of the best blow Nat had ever gotten. This was the classic pink Peruvian flake. I stuck the coke under my driver's seat, along with the bag of bogus Quaaludes I needed to return to the asshole who sold them to me. I had my guitar in the back of my station wagon, as well as my Triple Beam scale. On the way back to the Canyon, I stopped at Lady Snow's, the head shop at Crescent Heights and Sunset, to buy some glass vials. Heading into the Canyon, I just made it through the light at Sunset. Just north of Hollywood Boulevard, I was pulled over by a Sheriff's car that had been tailing me since Lady Snow's.

After telling me I had gone through a yellow light at Sunset and it seemed like I was in a little too much of a hurry, the two officers made me get out of the car and stand near the sheriff's squad car. One of them stayed with me, while the other one searched my car. I knew I was sunk. In a minute, the guy searching my car held up the bag of Quaaludes and said to his partner, "Look, Ted, Quaaludes!" (The guy I was standing with was a Ted). I waited for him to produce the coke, but no. The other cop had pocketed the O.Z. of coke. I breathed a sigh of relief. Thank god for corrupt cops.

I had just lost $1,500, but all they had were some bogus Quaaludes which were made of god knows what, my Triple Beam, and a bunch of glass vials. In the cop car on the way to the sheriff's station, we were all having a pleasant, civilized conversation. I was saying stuff like, "Boy, you guys sure have a dangerous job. I really admire you." And Ted, the honest cop who obviously had no idea his partner had snatched the evidence, said to me, "Man, you sure are calm. You've got a lot of guts, kid."

I had to spend the night in the hoosecow. I had Ron call a lawyer we knew and Ron's girlfriend, Annie, put up the mortgage on her house to go my bail. They came and got me out the next morning.

The lawyer cost me another $1,500, but he got me off with 'Diversion.' The Diversion program simply meant that I had to attend a certain number of classes on the evils of drugs, and my record would be expunged because it was a first offense, and they had no real evidence I was selling. After that, I had to redouble my selling efforts and cut down on my partying for a while so I could pay back the money the bust had cost me.

* * *

But there was one party I couldn't turn down. This was the result of a plane trip Sharisse had taken back east. It seems that on the plane she had met

Ahmet Ertegun, a small, homely Turkish man who was at the helm of the world's biggest and most profitable recording empire, WEA (Warner/Elektra/Atlantic). I'm pretty sure Sharisse had never heard of him, but I certainly had. I guess she rendezvoused again with Ahmet after the flight, because she told me he was into some pretty kinky shit sexually. Bottom line was, Ahmet had invited Sharisse to a private party he was throwing at Spago, celebrating the tenth anniversary of the band Genesis, and she wanted me to escort her.

Spago, Wolfgang Puck's restaurant just off the Sunset Strip, was the newest, coolest, in-est place in Hollywood, so of course I had been there several times; I was even introduced to Wolfgang. But this party was going to be on a whole new level of coolness.

I rented a limo for the evening, ensuring that we would arrive in the proper style, and also that we wouldn't have to worry about driving home. When we arrived, the party was already in full swing. Ahmet was seated at the head of the main table with Phil Collins and the other members of Genesis. During this period (January, 1984), Phil was doing double duty, as both a successful solo artist and as lead singer for Genesis. This had been going on for several years already, so Phil was an incredibly successful guy. Sharisse introduced me to Ahmet and I gushed appropriately, making sure he knew I was aware of his early musical triumphs, discovering and producing the likes of Ray Charles and Ruth Brown in the '50s. He was a highly cultured and erudite man and—his unusual sexual proclivities notwithstanding—one of the true gentlemen of the music world.

Over by the bar we encountered a lovely, petite blond and started to chat with her. She was Terri Nunn, lead singer of the band Berlin, who were riding several singles off their first album and getting a lot of airplay in LA, their home town. I had just met Ahmet and Terri had not, so I took her over and introduced her to him. "Berlin," he said. "Ah yes, I think they are on one of my labels." (Geffen—*his* label?). Sharisse and Terri were hitting it off, so I gave them a small vial of coke to take into the bathroom. When they came out, Terri pointed. "Hey, there's Prince," she said. "Boy, I'd sure like to meet him!" Prince, looking extremely sullen, was trolling around the party, shadowed by his bodyguard, a seven-foot blond guy with long hair and a mustache who looked a lot like Hulk Hogan—only bigger and scarier.

"No problem," I said. "I'll introduce you." I popped up in front of Prince like a jack-in-the-box. "Hey, Prince!" Prince stopped. The bodyguard started to pounce. I held up my hands. "Don't worry, I'm harmless. I just wanted to introduce you to two of your loveliest fans." And I introduced Terry and Sharisse. Prince acknowledged them with a perfunctory nod, said nothing, and moved on, never breaking his perfectly sullen expression. Maybe he was like Keely Smith, I thought, who never smiled while performing because she was afraid it would give her wrinkles.

Then I spotted someone I would never have thought I would meet— here or anywhere: Dr. Timothy Leary. "Dr. Tim!" I exclaimed, pulling up a chair next to him. I introduced myself and we shook hands. I told him he had influenced my life in a very profound way, how I had literally turned on, tuned in and dropped out. He seemed to enjoy that.

Unlike his partner in crime at Harvard, Dr. Richard Alpert, who had gone to India and become Baba Ram Das, a holy man, as a result of his psychedelic experiences, Dr. Tim, it seemed, still retained every bit of his ego—and then some. Dr. Tim had gone Hollywood. A lot more like the route I had taken, I guess.

I was a little disappointed that I couldn't get Terri Nunn to come home with us, but all-in-all that evening represented a high point in my roller-coaster life, which was about start on the downward plunge.

Ahmet Ertegun (left). Photo courtesy of Ashkan Sahihi.
Genesis (right). Photo: Rob Verhorst/Getty Images

Terri Nunn (left) and Prince (right)
Prince photo: Ron Galella/Getty Images

Dr. Timothy Leary. Photo: Ron Galella/Getty Images

Chapter Forty-Seven

Death and Resurrection

It was Len who taught me how to smoke the stuff. He also showed me how to 'cook' it, a process that transformed water-soluble cocaine hydrochloride into heat-soluble freebase. What eventually evolved into a street drug called 'crack,' started out as a much more elite drug called freebase. Chemically they are basically the same, but crack is made by gangster drug dealers that only care about turning a profit, while freebase was something we made ourselves, almost ceremonially. We bought certain very specific equipment: large glass vials, glass pipes, a certain kind of coffee filter. We made torches out of cotton swabs with long sticks wrapped in more cotton and tied with thread. We ignited these torches by dipping them in 151-proof rum, which burned at exactly the right temperature to give you the optimal high when you took a hit.

And it was that first hit of the evening that it was all about. I would sit with Len and a small group of his inner circle around his big round table and pass that pipe. That first hit felt like it must feel to mainline heroin. You get this incredible rush, hear a ringing sound in your ears and fall back on the nearest cushion (or girl) in a velvet cloud of ecstasy. But it was all downhill from there. You'd spend the rest of the evening chasing that first rush and never quite achieving it. By the end of the evening—and about a quarter-ounce of coke later—you'd be filled with a terrible feeling of regret, foreboding and paranoia.

At Len's we tried to be strong and disciplined about it. We stopped when we said we would stop, and then everyone went home, shaking with withdrawals. I laid in a supply of pills: muscle-relaxers, sleepers, Valium when I could get it—or, even better, Quaaludes—to help me through that crash and into slumber.

* * *

It was about this time I met Kat. She was a sleek number, with a fabulous body, big brown eyes and dirty blond hair. I met her at the home of a guy who also used to sell coke at the Sash. She told me smoking freebase was her favorite high. I invited her over to my place to show her my incredible cooking technique. Kat would have been a perfect smoking partner—because I naturally tied the ecstatic freebase high to sex, and was eager to experience the two together—only Kat was married and had a little boy about two. Her husband was a giant blond bodybuilder named Ace. And Ace worked for Sylvester Stallone as a bodyguard. He broke people's arms for a living.

So it was a very odd arrangement, but somehow appropriate to the weirdness of the drug. Kat would come over to my place to party. Ace knew where she was and who she was with. He knew she was not fucking me, and she wasn't. I did not pressure her to go all the way, but we did get as far as her taking off her top and letting me fondle and suck her breasts while in the throes of freebase ecstasy. As with the drug, there was an intense rush of pleasure, but never a complete consummation. Once or twice, I brought in another girl to join us, one with whom I could consummate a sex act while experiencing that indescribable head rush. Once, I did it with my head buried in Kat's magnificent breasts while another woman's lips were wrapped around my penis—the height or the depths of degeneracy, call it what you will. By early 1984, I was a full-blown junkie.

One night, Kat and I were smoking at my place. She took a hit and went into convulsions. Her body shook and jerked violently and her eyes rolled back in her head. Then she very was still. I took her pulse. Nothing. I looked for breath. Nothing. Kat was dead. I had a dead girl on my couch; a dead girl with a husband who broke people like twigs. I had taken CPR many years ago in Boy Scouts, and had seen enough on TV to try it. It was my only chance. Suddenly I was extremely calm and focused. This was do or die—literally. I pressed firmly on her chest rhythmically at one-second intervals about ten times, and then breathed into her mouth, while holding her nose. I kept doing this, yelling "Breathe, Kat, breathe!" At last she woke with a start, took a deep breath and looked at me questioningly. "Kat, what's my name?" I yelled.

"Ted."

"And that rhymes with dead, and that's what you were."

"Really?"

"Yes, you were dead, and I brought you back."

There was a long moment of silence, and then she said, "Thanks for saving my life."

"Thanks for coming back," I said, "'cause I would have been dead with you very shortly."

* * *

I knew it was time to quit. I had smoked up all the coke anyway, and all the profits as well. Nat, my dealer, came and I had no money for him, so he took my two electric guitars—the Gibson Melody Maker and the Fender Strat—my vintage Fender Concert amp and my Wurlitzer electric piano. I convinced him to leave me my acoustic guitar, the only thing I had left with which to write songs. There were two other people to whom I owed money, and I had to stiff them. I had never done anything like that before. I was like a hunted animal; I couldn't afford luxuries like morality and spiritual evolution. This was survival mode.

I had to get out of LA. Dorothy, the sister of my old friend Diana, was gracious enough to offer me safe haven at her home in Escondido—which, in Spanish, means 'hidden.' I got a guy with a truck to help me move out.

I spent the summer of '84 holed up in Dorothy's garage with all my furniture. None of my old crowd knew where I was. I was in touch with only Ron and V, and Diana, who had become my guardian angel.

Fang was getting on in years. She became very ill with a kidney infection and had to have one of her kidneys removed. The operation cost $500. V sent me the money. Dorothy worked for a concert promoter, and she let me help out on one of the productions—Crosby, Stills & Nash at the local baseball stadium after a Padres game. If not for the kindness of these people I would likely not be alive today.

When I moved back to LA in the fall, Diana found me a room to rent at the home of one of her friends in Pacific Palisades and a job as a night clerk at the Marina Pacific Hotel in Venice. My car died just as I reached LA. I had it towed to a mechanic in Santa Monica, but it was a total loss. I called

V and she came and got me. We had lunch at the Bicycle Shop, a restaurant on Wilshire Boulevard. It was such a sad time for me, but seeing her again raised my spirits. When we parted, I had no idea that we would never see each other again.

I stayed on the West Side, far away from Hollywood and Laurel Canyon. It was now clear that my life as an aspiring rock star was over. Songs still came through me, but I didn't record any of them. I went about the business of trying to claw my way back to some semblance of respectability.

The woman I was staying with in Pacific Palisades had two young sons, maybe eight and ten. One day, when I was at work, they left the front door open and Fang, who was now deaf, wandered out. She was not wearing her collar. I searched for her for days, even weeks, but in vain. Then one day I saw a note posted on a bulletin board at the local supermarket: "Found: shaggy dog, beige in color…" I called the number, got the address and went there, and there she was, my dearest companion, safe and sound. When I came in she jumped up into my face and took a good hard bite out of my upper lip. My swollen lip served as a reminder for weeks that I needed to take better care of my best friend, who was now an old lady.

I got a bad cough in the Fall of '84. I walked around with it for several weeks before consulting my old friend, Dr. Kevin. He told me I probably had pneumonia, and I needed to get antibiotics. I had to go downtown to County General and wait for hours, but I finally got the drugs. I guess that's what they call 'walking pneumonia.' I couldn't work for two weeks and consequently lost my job at the hotel. I wondered if smoking the freebase had damaged my lungs.

My friend Joe, a keyboard-playing composer I had met through Stan, introduced me to his brother, Vinnie, a drummer. Vinnie and his friend, Brian, a bass player, had been playing together in bands for years. Now they needed a lead singer for their latest attempt. I didn't regard this as a serious gig. I had no plans to record masters and shop to record companies. I was done with that. But it was a fun and creative outlet and offered a nice respite from the dreary life in which I now found myself. We had a rehearsal studio and worked up a few of my newest songs. It was fun, and that was all. It was nice that Vinnie was the leader of the band and I had none of those responsibilities. I acted like just another band member and went with the flow.

Brian was a married man with a new baby. He worked in a one-hour photo lab, and he got me a job there. It was a Fox Photo in Encino. Brian showed me how to operate the Noritsu film processing machines, and before long I was printing color photos like a pro. I even got to do enlargements. I was beginning to acquire employable job skills. I was slowly entering a new world, 'he real world,' the world of working for a living, paying the rent and getting along as best you could.

I moved a couple of other times during that short period in late 1984, ending up in a guest house in Northridge, way up in the North Valley, where I had gotten another film processing job on Balboa Boulevard. I had a beat-up Opel station wagon that got me to and from work, but just barely. When the Opel died, my dad sent me his 1979 Chevy, a far more reliable car with relatively low mileage. I was still scoring coke in small amounts—snorting, not smoking. I would buy an eighth and sell most of it to a small circle of friends to get a gram for myself.

Diana introduced me to Toni and Francis, a married couple who owned La Patisserie on 4th Street in Santa Monica, a wonderful restaurant with delicious breakfast and lunch fare. Francis was French and a master baker—croissants to die for. I would hang out there on weekends and met a couple of very entertaining waitresses: Marianna had short, reddish-brown hair, blue eyes, peaches-and-cream complexion, and Lena, who had dark hair and eyes, was thin and angular, but with full breasts that were a bit incongruous, though not unpleasing. These two were among the funniest and smartest people I have ever known. They were best friends. Lena was an artist, a recent graduate of Otis Art Institute. Marianna was brilliant, but seemingly without ambition. They hung out at the King's Head, a British pub in Santa Monica, and I started going there at night as well. A lot of the clientele were Brits and dart-throwing enthusiasts, but the crowd I hung with consisted mostly of Americans. They were all heavy drinkers and would not say no to a line of coke either. I started supplying them with coke so I could get a stash for free. I was done trying to make a living at it, but still enjoyed consuming. Sometimes we would go over to someone's house after the King's Head, drink beer, snort coke and play Trivial Pursuit 'til dawn.

That's how I met Julie. She was a friend of Marianna's who showed up at the King's Head one night. She was not the flashy beauty I was usually attracted to, but I was attracted. She had brown hair and compassionate brown eyes, a sweet smile and a lively wit. Her body was abundant and curvy, but not fat. She had a well-paying job as a paralegal, and had a rent-controlled apartment in Santa Monica. She had a phobia of driving; she thought her lack of 20/20 vision would impair her. Later, this turned out not to be so. I drove her home the first night we met. We talked until late, I think we kissed, and then I went home. We really got along well, and we went out a few more times before the relationship became romantic and sexual. She was trying to decide between me and another guy who was pursuing her—which, of course, added to her allure—and finally I won the contest.

Chapter Forty-Eight

The Kinda Straight and Kinda Narrow

Julie was a departure from the women to whom I was usually attracted in more ways than one: she really had her life together, and she was not crazy. She spoke Spanish well and volunteered at St. Joseph's center for homeless and battered women and children. She had taken a few trips to Spain, and was about to go again. By then I had moved two more times, both times sharing apartments with girls I had met through the King's Head crowd; first in Silver Lake, then in one of the few lousy neighborhoods of Santa Monica.

Then I moved in with Julie. She had a small-but-great rent-controlled apartment in a nice part of Santa Monica. It was good to be back on the West Side, near most of my friends, and back from the self-imposed exile of the North Valley. Her rent was so low that the financial pressure on me to have a full-time job was now gone. I got a part-time job in another photo lab in West Hollywood for a while, and then went to work for a friend, Sam Baldoni, who had started a motion picture product placement business. Baldoni Entertainment found opportunities for brands to be featured in major Hollywood movies. This new trend in advertising was most famously successful for Reese's Pieces in *ET* when the spot was turned down by M & M's. I started out trying to pitch opportunities to various brands, but ultimately eschewed the sales end of it to take a background role, writing up synopses of the scripts and highlighting the product placement opportunities.

One script that crossed my desk was *Overboard*, starring Goldie Hawn and Kurt Russell. I had written a song called "Overboard" in the '70s, and it still stood up pretty well. I had access to the film's producer, Anthea Sylbert;

I just needed to record a more contemporary version of the song to pitch to her. On a loan from Julie's mother, I went into the studio with members of Vinnie's band and a keyboard player with excellent synth skills named Trantham Whitley and recorded the new version of "Overboard," along with two other songs I had written recently. I pitched the song to Anthea Sylbert, but she told me they had contracted with Randy Newman to do all the music for the film, and they were not able to consider songs by anyone else.

In 1985, I turned forty. Vinnie got very sick, and the band had to stop rehearsing. The last time I saw him his face was broken out in strange spots. The next thing I heard, he was in the hospital with pneumonia. And then he was dead. Brian sat with him right up to the end. "He fought like a dog," Brian told me. "'Let go, Vinnie,' I told him. 'It's okay. Let go.'" I had no idea what was going on. I talked to Dr. Kevin, and he told me it had to have been AIDS. Young people did not die of pneumonia in this country unless their immune system had broken down. Joe, Vinnie's brother, never mentioned AIDS. It was anathema in the straight world, something only gay men got. Vinnie was not gay; he had gotten it through intravenous drug use.

Vinnie's funeral was an odd affair. It was in a Catholic church in Glendale, and it was open casket. Everyone lined up to pay their last respects. I had never seen a dead person, let alone someone I had known so well in life. In a weird, quasi-Egyptian ritual, I surreptitiously slipped a vial of cocaine into the casket for him to take with him to the 'other side.' It was both a gift for him and a sacrifice for me. His brother Joe, plus the whole band, were his pall bearers. Instead of carrying the coffin, we wheeled it on a gurney down a grassy slope to the gravesite. On the way down the hill, it began to build up momentum and get away from us. We ended up running alongside the casket, laughing our heads off, and yelling things like, "Last fast ride, Vinnie… Wheee!" I think Vinnie was laughing along with us in this last act of defiance, making what was supposed to be a solemn occasion festive.

* * *

It was good to be with Julie, safe and secure. I had made my peace with not becoming a rock star. I was okay with not having a hot and passionate love affair and AIDS had become a looming specter in the world of casual sex, and an excellent incentive for monogamy. I was still writing the occasional song, and that year I wrote one called "Summer Boy," a song about aging and having to say goodbye to my hedonistic past:

> *...I remember yesterday*
> *Life was so dangerous and free*
> *Now it's cold outside*
> *And fun is out of style*
> *Please bring my summer back to me*
>
> *Now it's fall and I'm bound to lose it all*
> *Unless I run and hide*
> *Safe and warm, I can weather any storm*
> *Except the one inside*
> *Summer is over*

In 1986, Fang's last remaining kidney failed and she died. I was heartbroken, of course, but she had lived a long and full life. Losing someone so close—even an animal—brings into clear focus one's own mortality.

* * *

I began to look around for other jobs that might lead to an actual career. My first thought was the movie business. I still harbored a lot of resentment and cynicism toward the music industry. I had an idea I might be able to pitch some of my script ideas if I got in at one of these companies. I got a series of short-lived jobs as a runner or production assistant (PA) for various film production companies. By 1988, I was working full-time at Robert Cooper Entertainment, which became Citadel Entertainment when Robert Cooper left to become head of HBO's original movie division. So Citadel was a company that produced mostly original films for HBO. It soon became apparent that there was a very strict pecking order in the film industry; a PA did not just go up to one of the bosses and pitch a script. It was just not done. There was a caste system and a PA was basically an untouchable. I was furniture, and the less visible I made myself, the better my chances of keeping my job.

At one of the places I had worked previously—Intralink Film & Design— the owner's wife ran a home for homeless cats—right there in the office. The place was wall-to-wall cats. Julie was making noises about getting

married and having babies, so I got her a kitten. That, however, turned out to
be only a temporary stopgap and, in 1988, Julie and I got married.

We went to England on our honeymoon, a place I had always wanted
to visit. When I got back to work at Citadel I was sent on a run to the Valley
at four o'clock in the afternoon the day before Thanksgiving. It was raining,
and in LA that in itself is enough to paralyze the entire city. There were no
cell phones at the time, at least they didn't give me one, and I was stuck in
stand-still traffic on the way back to the office, which was on the West Side.
I couldn't get to a phone booth to call in; I just had to sit there—for about
an hour. When I finally got back to the office everyone had gone home. The
following Monday I was called into the boss's office and summarily fired.
"You're over-qualified anyway," he said.

I had met a music editor while working for Citadel named Scott Stam-
bler. I asked him if I could apprentice for him to learn that trade, and he
agreed. He was about to start on a new picture directed by Rob Reiner,
which was ultimately titled *When Harry Met Sally*. I was present at a meeting about source music that included: Rob Reiner, the film's composer,
Marc Shaiman, Harry Connick, Jr., whose voice and piano were featured
in the film, Billy Crystal, Scott and me. They were trying to come up with
ideas for records that could be playing in the background on the jukebox in
the famous diner scene in which Meg Ryan loudly fakes an orgasm and an
older lady (played by Rob Reiner's mother, Estelle) says, "I'll have what
she's having." The year was supposed to be 1976, a year I remembered
well, so I contributed some ideas for songs that were playing that year. One
of them was ultimately used. I had often been mistaken for Billy Crystal,
and Billy, Rob and I were all of the same generation and shared similar New
York Jewish backgrounds, so we kind of hit it off. But I had overstepped my
role as 'furniture.' After that meeting, Scott was furious at me for speaking
to the director and the star as if I were an equal, and my brief career as a
music editor abruptly ended.

Julie was incredibly supportive. She encouraged me not to jump at
the first job to come along, to wait until the perfect opportunity presented
itself. Dr. Kevin hired me as a part-time receptionist in his medical office,
but I combed the want ads every day. At last I saw something interesting:
Rhino Records had recently started a record label that specialized in novelty
records and reissuing old music for the first time on the new medium of CD.
They were looking for a legal assistant, and their offices were right nearby

in Santa Monica. I had one advantage over most other job applicants at that time: Julie and I had acquired a personal computer, and I had been typing my scripts on it. I applied, and got a call back from Sharon Foster, the Director of HR. They had me in for an interview.

There were two people in the legal/business affairs department: Michelle Eagle, who sent out the licensing requests, and Bob Emmer, Sr. VP, Legal & Business Affairs, the only attorney in the house. I liked the vibe at Rhino. I had sworn off the music business, but this company was somehow different. They were not in the business of "stoking the star maker machinery." They were fans. They were record collectors who revered the greats of the past and were dedicated to preserving and propagating that greatness. And they didn't take themselves too seriously. Michelle interviewed me first, then Bob. I was honest; I told him I liked the vibe, and I liked what Rhino stood for: preserving the legacy of rock 'n' roll, and all with a great sense of fun. And, after all, I myself was a rock relic. I wanted this job.

I went home and waited for the call. It didn't come. I called Michelle, and she told me there were a few other candidates they wanted to interview. After a week or two, I called again. She was still on the fence. This time I decided to bluff. I told her I had an offer from another company, and I needed an answer from them within the week. The security that Julie provided gave me the courage to do this. I had the incredible luxury of not being desperate. It paid off. In less than a week, I got the call. I was offered the job and I accepted.

Chapter Forty-Nine

Record Nerds

The corporate culture at Rhino was wonderful and unique. From the president, Richard Foos and the general manager, co-founder Harold Bronson, on down, everyone was a self-proclaimed 'record nerd,' someone (almost always male) with limited social skills who had spent most of his adolescence in his room listening to, categorizing and alphabetizing his record collection. It was this collector mentality that pervaded the whole company. Although I had never been a serious collector of records, I found being surrounded by these nerds somehow very comforting and non-threatening.

My boss, Bob Emmer, was not a record nerd; he was a lawyer. Compared to him, my knowledge of pop music history was encyclopedic, and this came in handy. My job entailed a huge amount of typing: correspondence, letter agreements and contracts. Bob would dictate the letters into a dictation recorder that used mini-cassettes that I could start and stop with a foot pedal. I became quite a fast typist, but what was more valuable than that was my ability to correct some of Bob's factual errors where names of artists and other music minutiae were concerned. I never called attention to my corrections, but I later realized they had been duly noted and appreciated.

Working for Bob, I not only learned about contracts and licensing, I learned the meaning of hard work. I had always done what came easy to me. I had relied on my natural talent to get me by—in school, in music. If it wasn't fun, I wouldn't do it. Now, I had no choice but to dig deep and bend myself out of my natural lazy shape.

Bob was a workaholic. The first few weeks were a trial by fire. He was getting ready to depart for the big music conference, called MIDEM, which takes place in Cannes every year. Many arrangements had to be made: hotel reservations, airline tickets and voluminous correspondence with business contacts with whom he wanted to meet. A detailed schedule had to be created on something called a spreadsheet—a brand new animal to me. Bob would tell me to show up for work at seven in the morning, and we would work straight through until seven that night. I was lucky if I got lunch. I would come home each night to Julie, exhausted but proud that I had cut the mustard one more day.

Of course, the company was loaded with people whose knowledge of pop music and culture dwarfed mine, especially the guys in A&R. The term A&R dates back to the time when the record company guy would not only sign the artist, but also choose the material and produce the record. In Rhino's case, A&R were the guys who came up with the compilation concepts, researched the master ownership, hired the reigning expert to write the liner notes, and put together the label copy once the compilation was fully licensed. Now, just to be clear, I'm saying "guys" here, not because I am a sexist pig, but because there were virtually no women involved in this aspect of the business at this time.

After I had been in the legal department for a year, a job opened up in A&R as assistant to the VP, Gary Stewart. I asked Bob to have lunch with me one day and told him I'd like to try for that position. If I got it, I told him I would stay and train a successor, and he gave me his blessing. My logic was that, since I would never be a lawyer, my future in the legal department was limited, but in A&R there was the potential to carve out a career.

Julie's biological clock was ticking so loud it was keeping me up at night. The kitten had grown into a cat and had outlived its usefulness as a surrogate child. I decided that, if I was ever going to have kids, this was the woman to have them with. I knew she would make a reliable mother. I also believed that, at forty-five, I had at last become mature enough to put my own selfish desires aside and to put someone else first. That's what being a parent is.

In 1990 I was hired as A&R Assistant and Julie gave birth to our daughter that December.

* * *

My boss in A&R, Gary Stewart, was not only the ultimate record nerd, he was extremely affable and egalitarian. He also had a brain like no one I had ever met. He had the phone numbers of everyone he knew memorized and could access an encyclopedic array of factoids and figures as needed. The first thing he asked me was "Are you the Ted Myers who wrote the song 'Going in Circles' for Three Dog Night?" And when I said I was, he asked me if I had been in The Lost and Ultimate Spinach. He was, and is, an amazing human being. Unlike the film business—and most of the music business—the corporate culture at Rhino did not involve subjugating or castigating employees. If you had a good idea, you were encouraged to speak up, and go for it.

After perusing the Rhino catalog, I noticed that they had covered virtually every genre of pop music—except folk music, and when I suggested a various-artists folk compilation, Gary said, "Go for it."

My concept was a three-CD series, encompassing the urban folk music revival that took place mainly in Greenwich Village, but also in Cambridge, Massachusetts, Old Town, Chicago, San Francisco and other cities, between 1950 and 1970. The thing that set me apart from most other compilation producers was that I had lived through this movement and had in fact been a part of it. I called my series *Troubadours of the Folk Era.*

I learn best by doing, and that's how I learned how to compile a collection of music. I sought out the reigning experts in the folk genre locally and got permission to comb through their vast record collections, as well as getting their input as to what tracks by which artists should be included. I visited Roz and Howard Larman, who hosted the long-running radio show *Folkscene*, Michael Ochs, who owned the famed Michael Ochs Archives, and who is the brother of the late folk singer Phil Ochs and author and musicologist Cary Ginell. They were all enormously helpful with my research.

I had read a great article on Richie Havens by a guy named Bruce Pollock, and I enlisted him to write the liner notes. Geoff Gans, who headed the Rhino art department, was a big folk aficionado, and was especially knowledgeable about all things Bob Dylan. He went the extra mile to obtain rare photos and make the packages look authentic. It all came together in a way that made me realize there was life after rock 'n' roll. Leading a team effort, I had created something I could be proud of. I had carved out a niche of expertise for myself; I was now 'the folk guy' at Rhino. The first three volumes of *Troubadours* sold well, and gave rise to subsequent volumes: *Troubadours of British Folk, Vols. 1-3* and then *Troubadours of Folk, Vol. 4: Singer-Songwriters of the '70s* and Vol. 5: *Singer-Songwriters of the '80s.*

Rhino, which began as a small record shop on Westwood Boulevard in Los Angeles and started releasing novelty records as a lark, was now evolving, in the heyday of the CD era, into a major player in the music industry. We became universally recognized as the official archivists of pop music. By licensing masters from the major and minor labels, putting them together in creative ways, and releasing them on CD for the first time, we showed the music industry the value of their own back catalogs. We began to acquire our own music catalogs, first purchasing the Roulette Records catalog and later, by signing a distribution deal with Atlantic, we assumed control of the incredible Atlantic Records back catalog, and eventually that of the entire Warner Music Group. When I arrived in 1989, Rhino had forty employees; when I left in 2000, they had almost two hundred in the LA office and sales reps across the country.

My boss Gary was also a social activist and a believer in giving back to the community. As Rhino became more prosperous, he formed SERT, the Social and Environmental Responsibility Team, an ad hoc group of employees that designated funding for local charities and organized group activities to aid various charitable organizations. I became an active member and was put in charge of finding volunteer opportunities for fellow employees. Rhino instituted a policy of giving all employees the week between Christmas and New Year off, if they put in forty hours of community service over the course of the year. Almost everyone participated. We devoted special attention to the Al Wooten Center in South Central Los Angeles, an area riddled with gang violence. The Al Wooten Center, founded by the mother of Al Wooten, a teenager who had been killed in gang crossfire, provided a safe after-school environment for neighborhood teens. SERT organized several field trips to the center, where we threw barbeques and other events for the kids. We also did cleanup, landscaping and painting at various homeless shelters and along the now-dilapidated and legendary Central Avenue, formerly the jazz center of LA. All this made me feel like a "solid citizen" for the first time in my life, a term I had previously disdained. Somehow, being a part of this team of like-minded record nerds concerned with the greater good gave me hope for humanity, made me feel a part of something bigger and stronger than me. We focused on changing our own community, not trying to save starving orphans in Africa. If you want to change the world, start by trying to change your neighborhood.

Chapter Fifty

Folked Up

In 1992 I got a call from veteran concert promoter Jim Rissmiller. I knew the name from the '70s, when Wolf & Rissmiller were the kings of concert promotion in Los Angeles, booking every major rock act into huge arenas like the LA Forum. He had seen the *Troubadours* series and wanted to know if Rhino would be interested in collaborating with him on a folk festival—the Troubadours of Folk Festival. I ran the idea by my boss, Gary, and he took it upstairs to ownership. Everyone liked it, and Richard Foos called his friends Ben Cohen and Jerry Greenfield, founding owners of Ben & Jerry's Ice Cream. Ben & Jerry's came onboard as co-sponsors and Jim Rissmiller was invited in for a meeting.

Rissmiller was a tall, slim guy of fifty. Even in jeans and a madras plaid shirt he looked distinguished, with his close-cropped silver hair and wire-rimmed specs. He arrived with his wife, Randy, a pleasant-looking blond woman, about ten years his junior, who was his second in command. At the meeting he impressed everyone with his extremely positive, can-do attitude and confident delivery. Richard Foos, Harold Bronson and Gary Stewart gave the project their blessing and pledged to contribute $25,000 toward promotion and publicity and held out the possibility of a like amount coming from Ben & Jerry's. The details of booking the artists and choosing a venue were left to Jim—and me.

I submitted a list of artists I felt would be good candidates for the festival. Jim booked all of them and increased their number twofold, with artists who I did not necessarily agree would fit the profile of the folk revival of the

'50s and '60s. There were a few people I had never heard of, artists whose managers were good friends with Jim. As the number of acts increased, I became alarmed. How can we fit all these people in over the course of two days? I told Jim I thought he was booking too many acts. "Don't worry, I know what I'm doing," was always the response. And, of course, he must know what he was doing; he was one of the most experienced concert promoters in the world.

As the event began to take shape, the way Jim was handling things caused me increasing anxiety. He insisted that the concert take place in Westwood, on the campus of UCLA, his alma mater. The venue he picked was Drake Stadium, a 15,000-seat sports arena designed for track and field events. There was no stage, no sound and no lights. All of that would have to be brought in—at great expense. It seemed to me 15,000 was a rather optimistic figure for a folk concert. "What about the Greek Theatre?" I suggested. "It seats about 5,000 and has a stage, sound and lights." But Jim was dead set on UCLA. Was there some kind of sweetheart deal going on between him and his alma mater? As the stage was being constructed and the sound system set up, I asked, "What about the lights? You're going to need lights."

"No, we won't," Jim told me. "In June it gets dark around seven. It'll all be over by then." And so it went.

The festival was scheduled for the first weekend in June: Saturday, June 5 and Sunday, June 6, 1993. I wanted to make sure we would not be in conflict with any other events, like the annual Cajun and Zydeco Festival in Long Beach, but Jim assured me that was scheduled for the last weekend in May. In early April I found out that was untrue, that the Cajun & Zydeco Festival was, in fact, the same weekend as ours, and, of course, it was too late to change our dates. I blamed myself for taking his word for it and not getting in touch with the promoters of the Cajun & Zydeco Festival to confirm their dates.

Rissmiller had booked a total of thirty-three acts, seventeen on Saturday and sixteen on Sunday. Then there were the winners of a talent contest we had run, with the winning artists opening each day of the festival, so actually there were thirty-five acts. The headliner on Saturday was my old friend Joni Mitchell and on Sunday it was Peter, Paul & Mary. Most of the luminaries of the '60s folk revival who were still alive would be there: Judy Collins, Arlo Guthrie, The Kingston Trio, Roger McGuinn (with surprise guest Tom Petty), John Prine (with surprise guest Bonnie Raitt), Taj Mahal, Ramblin' Jack Elliott, John Hammond, Jr., Richie Havens, and the incomparable Odetta. The lineup also included some contemporary folk artists like Richard Thompson and Mary-Chapin Carpenter. The Folksmen, which was Spinal Tap's send-up of The Kingston Trio, would also be there to provide some riotous satire.

I ran into Joni at a party for the artists, held the day before the first show at a restaurant in Westwood Village. I hadn't seen her for twenty-three years, and she was chain-smoking cigarettes. "Hey Joni," I say, "What's up with the smoking? You're the person who inspired me to quit in 1969!" She looked at me blankly. She had no recollection of me whatsoever. Of course, I used to straighten my hair, so I mentioned that. I had aged well, so I didn't really look that different. I recalled the night I walked in on her when she was writing "Woodstock," but nothing registered. "Sorry," she said, "I've known so many people, and I was smoking a lot of dope back then." In 2015, Joni suffered a brain aneurysm, which affected her abilities to speak and function for years afterward. Could her lack of memory have been a foreshadowing of this event?

* * *

It never rains in June in Southern California. Never, that is, except on the opening day of my festival. I showed up on the muddy field early Saturday morning amidst a significant downpour. The people started to trickle in at 10:30 a.m. Advance sales had been disappointing, to say the least. Rissmiller had blown almost the entire advertising budget on a half-page ad in the Calendar section of the Sunday LA Times. It ran on April 16th, too early in my opinion. But what did I know? He was the expert. The rain tapered off in the early afternoon of the first day, but the crowds were thin at best. In the Greek Theater that crowd would have filled the place, but Drake Stadium looked empty.

Rhino had made a deal with PBS to use a video of the festival as a fund-raising show. PBS would give away videos of the show, released by Rhino Home Video, as premiums. We hired Stephanie Bennett's Delilah Pictures to shoot it. I roamed the backstage area with a camera and soundman both days, doing backstage interviews of the key artists.

Of course, the show ran hours late on both days. At 10:30 Saturday night, Joni was still onstage. Thanks to Mr. Rissmiller, there were no stage lights. If not for the video crew, who brought their own lights, there would have been no light on the stage at all.

In spite of some memorable performances by some great artists, the Troubadours of Folk Festival was a resounding financial failure. It was a planning debacle, riddled with incompetence on the part of Rissmiller. To make matters worse, we learned after the fact that Rissmiller had promised to pay a large number of the artists $25,000 each. Many of the artists were not paid, and Rhino made up the shortfall for several of them. Many of the crew, including the live sound engineers, also got stiffed, but there was little anyone could do.

We got some excellent video footage, and I now turned my attention to editing that with Delilah's video editor, Janis Ingles. We created a sixty-minute show that really looked quite good. Joni Mitchell had forgotten the words to some of her songs (another clue?) and, at one point, stopped in the middle of the song while her audience shouted out the words to remind her. I was in the video trailer while this was happening, screaming at the monitors, "Joni, you're fucking it up, you're fucking it up!" But Janis managed to edit out the fuckups so well it looked and sounded like she had performed the song flawlessly.

At the Troubadours of Folk Festival. L to R: Richie Havens, me, Tom Petty, Roger McGuinn. Photo: Peter B. Sherman

But it was all for naught. Many of the major artists, Joni included, refused to participate in the video. I thought the Rhino legal team would have required the artists to sign off on participating in the video as a pre-requisite for playing the festival, but apparently they too had 'folked up.' PBS made things even worse by rejecting what I thought were some great performances by excellent artists. What we were left with on the final video that got distributed was a severely truncated version of the festival. None of my backstage footage ever made it into the show. The PBS special was not even broadcast on KCET, our local LA station.

And so, even into the '90s, my life-lesson of "Just How Many Ways Things Can Go Wrong" continued.

At the Troubadours of Folk Festival. I interview Joni Mitchell. Photo: Peter B. Sherman

Chapter Fifty-One

Appointments and Disappointments

Nobody blamed me for the failure of the Troubadours of Folk Festival, but nobody praised me either. Nothing that went wrong was my fault; in fact, I foresaw and tried to head off much of what did go wrong. But the net result was clear: what could have elevated me to hero status at Rhino ended up casting me with an aura of vague disappointment. We all got over it, and I went on to produce and supervise hundreds more compilation CDs for Rhino over the next seven years, but, as with my career as an artist, I never became a star.

By 1992 I had become restless and dissatisfied in my marriage. There was no sexual chemistry, no passion or excitement. Now that my life was back on track, I craved all of that. Julie and I made love once that year, and it resulted in the birth of our second child, a boy—a powerful reason not to leave. We now had two little kids, twenty-two months apart in age, both in diapers and car seats. I owed my very existence to Julie; she had practically hauled me up out of the gutter. I felt like a heel, a cad, but by the spring of 1994 I had to leave. I remained very hands-on with my kids, and got a harsh taste of what being a single parent was all about. They stayed with me in my small apartment when they were both babies three or four nights a week. It was hard. I had no support network (Julie had both parents living near her), and sometimes the little buggers drove me crazy. But it was a good lesson in selflessness—not one of my strong traits.

Julie's broken heart mended, and a few years later she remarried, bought a house and had another child. Every relationship I've had since then has resulted in me getting unceremoniously dumped. In my youth, I was usually the dumper, now I was the dumpee. Karmic payback? Who knows?

* * *

In late 1998, I got a call from Barry Tashian, the leader of Boston's hometown heroes, The Remains. He asked me if I would be interested in re-assembling The Lost to play a double bill reunion gig at the Paradise club in Boston. Don Law owned The Paradise. I had met Don as a college student in early 1965 and he was now the most successful concert promoter in New England. I was definitely up for this. I phoned the other members of The Lost and all of them were into it. The gig was scheduled for March, 1999. Don paid for my plane ticket to and from Boston and offered the band a fee of $1,500. But none of us were doing this for the money. I contributed my share to rent the equipment we would need to rehearse. Our good friend, Erik Lindgren, founder and president of Arf! Arf! Records, a boutique label that specialized in reissues of obscure '60s garage rock, offered his rural recording studio, which was an outbuilding on his horse farm, as a rehearsal space, where we all could also sleep. It was an ideal setup.

Erik had released a couple of CDs of non-Capitol Lost recordings— some live rehearsal tapes and "Space Kids," the soundtrack for the breakfast cereal premium we had recorded at the end of our career. Since I first met Erik in 1989, we had been trying to get Capitol to license us The Lost's Capitol masters, of which there were fifteen recordings, all but six of them previously unreleased. The problem was that Capitol had a "10,000-unit minimum" rule on which they would not budge. This meant that anyone licensing masters from them would have to pay them an advance on the sale of 10,000-unit minimum We figured we'd be lucky to sell 1,000 Lost CDs. And so we were stymied—until 1999, that is. That's when I had a talk with Bob O'Neill, who had recently become chief counsel at Rhino and who had previously been chief counsel for Capitol. I got Bob to intercede on our behalf, and Capitol at last agreed to license us the Lost masters for an advance on 1,000 units. So my trip to Erik's farm had a two-fold purpose. We spent the first couple of days mixing and mastering the Lost compilation from digital transfers of three- and four-track masters, and the next few days rehearsing with the band for our first live gig in thirty years.

Willie, Walter and Kyle arrived separately. Walter and I drove to the railroad station to pick up Kyle, who was arriving from New York by train.

What a blast it was to see these guys again! I realized I was among friends who were uniquely bound together by an experience that was surely a high point in all of our lives. Our drummer, Lee, had to drop out at the last minute because he needed gallbladder surgery, so Willie enlisted his drummer, Jim Daugherty, who was much younger than all of us and played great.

I had sent out cassettes of the original recordings of the songs which I thought would make a good set, so each band member had this to rehearse with individually. I had been rehearsing by myself in my living room every day for the previous two weeks. When we actually started playing together, it didn't sound too bad, and by the end of three days, we were sounding really good. The actual gig went pretty well, in spite of the fact that I got nervous and made a couple of embarrassing flubs. We opened with our traditional opener, "When I Call," but I was so nervous I started singing in the wrong key. My other fuck-up happened on the tricky intro to "Money in the Pocket," where I was required to play a single note line in unison with the bass, but I messed it up.

The Rising Storm, a local New England band whose one album was a major collector's item among 'psych' fanatics, opened the show. The fact that they had been added actually increased the turnout significantly, as all these record collectors had heard of them and their album, which was selling for hundreds of dollars. There were even a couple of guys from Rhino who flew in for the gig. Peter Wolf was the MC, and he introduced us next. He said something about me trying to steal his girl, we all laughed, and Edie flashed through my mind. I think maybe that was what unnerved me. The Remains came on last and were, as always, extremely tight. A review that appeared in a Boston paper afterward said we sounded "rusty," and I guess that's true, but it was a stellar experience for me being back in Boston, one of my favorite places on Earth. And I was so knocked out by the fans. I saw people I hadn't seen in thirty years. Boston fans never forget.

* * *

Later that year, my boss Gary got a call from Jac Holzman, the founder of Elektra Records, suggesting we reissue *Bleecker and MacDougal*, a four-LP vinyl box set of Elektra's folk artists, originally released in the early '70s. Because Rhino now had full control of the Warner Music Group catalog, we controlled all the master rights to this box set. Gary called me in and asked my opinion of the idea. I looked at the Elektra box and told him what I thought: "The Elektra box is a randomly sequenced collection of all-Elektra folk artists. Some artists have three tracks, some two, some one. There is no apparent rhyme or reason for this. I say, if we're going to do a folk box set, let's make it the definitive box of the genre. Hopefully we can keep Jack Holzman onboard as a consultant, and maybe he can contribute to the liner notes, but let's cross license every major folk artist of the '50s and '60s from all labels." And I set about compiling *Washington Square Memoirs: The Great Urban Folk Boom, 1950-1970*. I consulted with Jac on the repertoire and called in my old friend, Cary Ginell, who also contributed ideas. I hired Barry Alfonso to write liner notes and an interview by Cary of Jac appeared as well. I wrote an intro about my own experiences in Greenwich Village in the '60s.

The box turned out to be my final project for Rhino, and I guess you could call it my crowning achievement. I left Rhino at the end of 2000 and it was released in June, 2001.

Early in 2002, I got a call from Bob Fisher, who had been the mastering engineer, telling me we had been nominated for a Grammy®. It was the beginning of a new year and I was getting some part-time work but was struggling to find a new job. A Grammy nomination boded well for the future, and a win would really perk up my résumé. I couldn't keep my head from swimming with expectations.

It was fun to attend the Grammys and meet some of my co-nominees, like T-Bone Burnett, Larry Carlton and Steve Lukather but, alas, we didn't win. Everyone kept telling me what an honor it was to have been nominated, but to me it was just another near miss.

With my Grammy medal, 2002. (All nominees get one of these.)
Photo: Rob Verhorst/Getty Images

* * *

An old friend of mine, Harry Sandler (who had been the drummer for the Boston band Orpheus), worked as an agent for a booking agency that represented public speakers—everyone from Gorbachev to Jeff "Skunk" Baxter. He encouraged me to create a talk that he could book into colleges. The money was promising, so I developed a talk called "Ripped Off by the Man: The Whitewashing of Rock 'n' Roll." The premise was to show how many hit songs by white artists, especially in the '50s and '60s, were covers of little-known records by black artists. The list of songs included: "Piece of My Heart," by Janis Joplin, "You're No Good," by Linda Ronstadt, "Shake, Rattle and Roll" by Bill Haley & The Comets, "Go Now" by The Moody Blues, and many more. I created a PowerPoint slide show with both music and pictures of the artists and the original 45s. As it turns out, my subject was not exactly in big demand by colleges. I only got to deliver my presentation once, at Rensselaer Polytechnic Institute in Troy, New York—just feet away from the Troy Armory, where The Lost had opened for Sonny & Cher more than three decades earlier. The turnout for my talk was, um, thin, to say the least. It was a big lecture hall with steep, stair-step aisles and tiered, stadium-style seating that went up and up, and it was mostly empty.

After that, Harry urged me to work up something about the new technology of Napster and illegal digital file sharing. I protested that I really didn't know much about new technology, or any technology, but he made me an offer I couldn't refuse: he wanted me to debate Chuck D of Public Enemy on the pros and cons of this new phenomenon at St. Louis University. Chuck was to be the proponent and I the opponent. My fee would be $5000. I accepted, and proceeded to give myself a crash course on the genesis of the peer-to-peer file sharing technology invented by teenager Shawn Fanning, and the arguments for and against.

Chuck was a jovial and affable guy. We shared New York roots, and we got on famously. We handled our adversarial roles more like actors, or a game. Chuck's argument was mainly that the record companies were evil. They didn't pay their artists the royalties they had coming anyway, so why should people not just steal the music (well, he didn't put it that way exactly). Rather than being a record company apologist—which I definitely was not—I took the position that intellectual property was somebody's property. That artists, musicians, recording studios, engineers and producers all put in a lot of time and spent a lot of money creating their recordings. They did this to earn their living—and it was simply wrong to take it without paying. I argued that the existence of a new technology did not make it okay to use it. Computer technology exists that can take all the money out of somebody's bank account, but if you get caught doing this you go to jail. How is stealing someone's music any different? I further argued that, once something is invented, you cannot un-invent it. The best you can do is harness and monetize it. If the record companies had recognized this simple fact back in 2000, and embraced the Napster technology instead of shutting it down, they might not have plunged into the steep decline and massive layoffs we saw in the first decade of the twenty-first century.

* * *

Over the next five years I freelanced, mostly for music industry-related companies. I produced two more various-artists compilations: *Sleepless in Seattle: The Birth of Grunge* for Livewire Recordings in Atlanta and *Four Decades of Folk Rock*, a four-CD box set for Time Life Music, co-produced with my friend, Bruce Pollack, who had written the liner notes for my first folk compilation at Rhino. Although *Four Decades* was done with every bit as much precision, care and attention to detail as *Washington Square Memoirs*, Time Life did not have the industry cachet and historical authority of Rhino, and therefore no Grammy nomination was forthcoming. Still, I was proud of the work I did on that project, which involved more writing of liner notes and more supervision of every detail than I had done on *Washington Square Memoirs*. More than a historical document, the folk rock box had a playability factor—an aesthetically pleasing flow from song-to-song—that the folk box did not have.

* * *

In 2006, I was offered a job with Concord Music Group, a large independent record company that had started as a jazz label, but was now expanding into other areas. I was hired as A&R Editorial Manager; this meant I was responsible for gathering, organizing, proofreading and fact-checking all of the copy that went into all the CD booklets. I had done much of the same kind of thing at Rhino, but this did not have the creative facet or the project ownership that my job at Rhino had. Still, I was grateful to be working again for a progressive company with good people running it and to be getting a steady paycheck. Another plus was that I got to work with actual, flesh-and-blood artists, some of whom were among my all-time idols. Concord pursued a strategy of filling niches, which the major labels had not, making us grow to become the largest independent record label, and one of the few that had not been gobbled up by a major. One strategy we followed was to sign what were known as "legacy artists," artists who still had name recognition and a large loyal fan base, but whose careers had now waned to the point where the majors were no longer interested in them. Among these were: John Fogerty, James Taylor, Ricky Lee Jones, Elvis Costello, Joni Mitchell and none other than Sir Paul McCartney himself. Although I didn't get to interact with him personally, I found working on Macca's releases especially thrilling, since he had been one of my biggest all-time influences as an artist and songwriter.

Chapter Fifty-Two

Life After Life

Sometime around 2005, I started thinking about recording another album. I had written very few songs since I started my career at Rhino, and had played and sung very rarely. Once I started working at that full-time job and raising my kids, the music didn't seem to visit me anymore. Maybe I just didn't have any energy to spare. A list began to form in my mind of songs I had written and made demos of, but had never recorded as masters or released to the public. And they all had to be songs that held up when I listened to them in the present day. None of them sounded especially dated, or especially current either. They were never trendy, and so had retained a timeless quality. Since most of these songs were slow, melodic ballads, they were probably passed over because I was always recording as a member of a rock band, and these didn't really fit on a rock album. Two of them were written in the late '60s, one in the '80s, one in the '90s, and one was written in 2009 when the rest of the album was mostly recorded. The other seven songs were written in the '70s, my most prolific period, and during the time I was under the spell of V.

I had reconnected with Sophi, my high school girlfriend, and also with Ginny Sue ('the Sex Goddess of Goddard'), and they both encouraged me to take my guitar out of mothballs. We mostly communicated via e-mail and phone, but Ginny Sue came out to Northern California with a friend and I drove up and joined them in a house her friend had inherited, and we hung out for a few days around 2003. I subsequently visited her in her lovely home in the bucolic countryside outside of Chapel Hill, North Carolina.

Ever the resourceful entrepreneur, she had bought this house with money she had earned selling marijuana, sometimes by the kilo. Being a large woman in her late sixties was an excellent cover for being a dope dealer. Looking at her, no one would ever suspect.

Her living room was set up as a fully-equipped jam space, replete with electric and acoustic guitars, electric keyboards, two acoustic pianos, a set of drums and even a PA system. We would sit around and jam a lot, and I realized just how rusty I was. My guest quarters consisted of a beautiful little apartment ('the Sweet Suite'), perched under the eves at one side of the house, with its own deck and entrance. I would take her acoustic guitar up there, and that's where I started to relearn the old songs I wanted to record for my album.

In 2006, I was at a reunion of some old friends from the Boston music scene of the '60s. We were at the home of my former housemate in the Eastman Circle house in Wellesley, Richard Griggs—now Richard Zvonar. He was in the final stages of cancer and had gathered some old friends, basically to say "goodbye," although that was never actually stated as the reason for the gathering. That's where I ran into Peter Malick, who had played lead guitar with Walter Powers of The Lost in a band called Listening. Peter invited me out to see his recording studio, Chessvolt, up in the North Valley. I told him I was contemplating another album, and he said I could use his studio—gratis.

And so began the long, slow labor of love that was to be my 'vanity project,' *LifeAfterlife*. My old friend and sometime drummer, Herb Quick, had returned from Germany, where he had lived for twenty years. He had worked there as a producer/engineer, and had been quite successful. He had Pro Tools on his Mac, and he offered to engineer, play drums and co-produce the album with me. The entire journey, from inception to release, was to take more than six years.

I made a list of the eleven songs I had so far and mapped out proposed instrumentation for each. It turned out there were only three on which I would need live drums, and so these three songs were the first basic tracks we would lay down at Chessvolt.

I called Paul Eckman, who had played bass in my '80s band, Incognito, and he came onboard as the bass player. After those first three basics were laid down, Peter called me and told me he didn't think the bass parts were tight enough with the drums and the click track. In scrutinizing the bass track, I didn't hear the rhythmic inconsonance so much as some melodic choices I felt could be better. So we had Paul redo the bass tracks. Herb was teaching Pro Tools at Calabasas High School at the time, and he had a nice recording room set up in one of the classrooms, so we had Paul overdub the new bass parts there. It worked better with me sitting with Paul and suggesting actual note choices throughout each track, rather than us playing and recording by the seats of our pants without the benefit of rehearsals. I had been living with these songs for decades. I had made multi-track demos of all of them. I'm a songwriter who hears full arrangements in my head. Okay, I'm a control freak.

I played acoustic guitar on all but one of the songs on the album. My acoustic part was the original building block on eleven of the twelve tracks. My friend Jim West had played lead guitar on all the demos I'd made since the beginning of the '90s—which were relatively few. Jim had been the lead guitarist for 'Weird Al' Yankovic's band since the early '80s. I had recorded demos of four of my songs at his home studio in 1990. Jim was one of the most gifted and versatile guitarists I had ever met. His work with 'Weird Al' called for him to mimic the guitar work on a wide range of hit records, so, in a sense, he was the ultimate 'Top 40 band' guitarist. But his skills went much deeper than that. He showed great taste and a terrific melodic sense in coming up with parts for my original songs. He was also a very good engineer and producer, and by 2006, when I started recording my album, he had a state-of-the-art home studio with Digital Performer software. His passion for Hawaiian slack key guitar had propelled him to become one of the foremost players of this style on the US mainland. He had made more than a few solo slack key albums as Jim "Kimo" West, and with each album, the recorded sound of his Taylor acoustic guitar got better and better, so it was natural for me to decide to record all my acoustic guitar tracks at Jim's studio. My Gibson J-50 is one of the best sounding acoustic guitars I've ever heard, and Jim captured it beautifully on my tracks. Jim also played all the lead guitar parts on the album, both electric and acoustic. We also recorded some other tracks at Jim's studio: upright bass, played by Paul Eckman on one track and John B. Williams on another, and a doumbek (Arabic drum), played by Victoria Carter.

Peter Malick introduced me to Marco Godoy, a keyboard player from Argentina, who could play any keyboard in any style, from jazz to Latin to R&B to rock. Marco also had a Pro Tools home studio with his keyboards all dialed in and ready to go. Unlike the old days of analog tape, I didn't have to schlep reels of cumbersome twenty-four-track tape around in order to record at different studios. I had everything on a hard drive that was smaller than a shoebox. Herb had everything backed up on a couple of his hard drives as well. So it was easy for me to take my hard drive over to Marco's and have him lay down all the electric and acoustic piano and organ parts.

There were a couple more sessions at Chessvolt: We overdubbed a live drum track on "Overboard"—something I realized was needed after we tried it with synthesized drums—and my good friend, Latin jazz percussionist Bobby Matos, played congas on "Rainy Day." Then, a second session where we did background vocals on a couple of tracks with my old friend and longtime collaborator, JC Scott, and jazz singer Rachel Lauren on vocals, and we added horns on two tracks, with Dave "Woody" Woodford on tenor sax and Lee Thornburg (late of Tower of Power) on trumpet and trombone. That was the last time we needed to use a big studio; Herb and I did everything else on his Mac, either in one of his high school classrooms, at his house, or at my place. We did all my vocals with his pretty-good vocal mic and programmed all the strings and synth parts on his tiny keyboard using a software called Reason.

Everything, that is, until I wrote "Ordinary Girl" in 2009. We had most of the album in the can by then, but this song really cried out for live strings. We tried hard to lay down the arrangements with Jim's excellent string libraries, but somehow the sound was not as convincing with the small ensemble sound as it was with the other string tracks on the album, most of which sounded pretty real. I pursued various avenues to get professional string players for very little money, but in LA, this was not going to happen. At last I approached my friend Erik Lindgren, with whom I had done the Lost compilation, and who hosted The Lost for our 1999 reunion.

Erik is an accomplished modern classical composer and often performs and records with string players. He told me that he would be able to gather the five string players I would need for an affordable price and record them at his Sounds Interesting Studio on his farm in Middleboro, Massachusetts. Even adding in the cost of my plane fare to and from Boston, this was the most cost-effective way for me to go. I was far from flush financially; my job at Concord had come to an abrupt end in 2010, when my position (along with that of nine other employees) was unexpectedly eliminated. But my lifelong dream to record my music with a live string section, along with my mania to never do anything half-assed, drove me to commit to this. Herb and I had mapped out parts for two violins, viola, cello and bass violin, and Jim, who had scored numerous movies and TV shows, used a program he had to generate sheet music for each part. I sent these to Erik, who tweaked them a little, and I booked my flight to Boston.

The string session took place in July of 2011. It was a hundred degrees outside in Middleboro, but nice and cool in the air-conditioned studio. The five young players were excellent, and a pleasure to work with. Erik was the perfect host, and wouldn't take any money for himself—I just paid the two engineers and, of course, the musicians. Most importantly, the track came out sounding great. It was a real thrill to hear my arrangement come to life in the hands of real players with real instruments.

And, to make the journey even more pleasurable (in spite of the withering heat and humidity), I got to see Kyle and Walter of The Lost, and a couple of other old Boston friends who came over to Erik's for a barbeque.

String session at Erik Lindgren's Sounds Interesting Studios,
Middleboro, MA, July, 2011. Photo: Erik Lindgren

I was not thrilled with my vocals. I had never been a naturally strong singer, and I had let it lie fallow for too long. Unlike some of my contemporaries—Paul McCartney and James Taylor come to mind—I did not have the benefit of ceaseless touring to keep my voice in shape. I managed to piece together my vocals for the album, sometimes redoing a single line over and over until it sounded okay. But 'okay' was the best it ever got.

The process of making *LifeAfterlife* involved asking a lot of favors of a lot of old friends—and they really came through for me. None so much as Herb, who hung in there with the project for six years, all the while struggling to make his own ends meet, and never taking a dime from me. The reason it took those six years was because a lot of that time was spent waiting for Herb or someone else's availability. Since they were all doing me favors on some level, I had to be patient and bide my time. I kept telling myself, *Nobody is pacing up and down, saying, "Where's the album?" These songs will not go out of style—because they were never in style.*

L to R: Me, Herb Quick, Jim West at Jim's Westernmost Studios, 2011.
Photo: Herb Quick's camera

We mastered the CD in the spring of 2012 and it was released in August. I got some nice comments from some of my friends, and especially the guys in The Lost, and some other fellow musicians. But I was also somewhat surprised by the lack of response from a lot of people to whom I had handed

CDs personally. When somebody does that to me, I generally send them a nice note, at least out of politeness. But from a lot of people I heard nothing. Clearly, it was not everybody's cup of tea, and it was never intended to be. *LifeAfterlife* was a final musical statement I wanted to make, and perhaps a legacy I could leave for my kids. I was proud of it; I truly had no expectations of public acclaim. And my expectations were met.

LifeAfterlife album art, 2012

* * *

Making music, like all art, is a crap shoot. If you don't 'make it,' it's not necessarily your fault. As I've said many times, many ways in this book, there are so many ways things can go south. It's so much easier to miss than to hit. All you can do is the best you can do, and then hope for the best; but be prepared for the worst. After completing what I'm pretty sure will be my final album, I can look back and take some satisfaction in the fact that I learned my craft. As far as the songs themselves are concerned, I think that, in the hands of a more powerful singer, some of them might have gotten out there to many more people. I know how to craft a good song, and it's not dependent upon current trends. A really good song will move people—now and always. V always tried to cheer me up by reminding me that Mozart died penniless. Van Gogh only sold one painting. Sometimes that's the price of immortality.

* * *

As soon as I had finished copies of the CD in my hands I set about searching the Internet for V. I knew she was no longer living in Laurel Canyon. I had heard from Ron, who was still in touch with her, that she had moved years ago. I came up with an address high in the hills of 90210 that looked like a possibility. I put a package together for her and drove up there one week-day afternoon. I drove up, and up, and up some more. It was on a 'private road'—there was a sign telling me so, but no one around to enforce it—that ran along a ridge that I guessed might be the highest point for miles in any direction. You couldn't tell much about what the house looked like from the street, but I could see the upper floor, which sat atop a three-car garage. It appeared to be an enormous L-shaped room with gables and pitched roofs, one facing south and one facing east, under which I imagined cathedral ceilings rose past the rafters forty feet or more. The two facades that I could see were almost entirely picture windows that looked south over Beverly Hills and the entire city and eastward toward the hills. Inside the mailbox was mail addressed to V and her husband. I deposited the package in the mailbox and drove off. I had enclosed my contact information and a little note, but I really didn't expect to ever hear from her. I had also dedicated the album to her in the CD booklet, since she had inspired half the songs.

Two months later the call came. At first I didn't recognize the voice—I was completely unprepared. Her voice was just the same; maybe my ears had changed. I stuttered and stammered. I asked her if she liked the album and she said she loved it. Hearing that was all the praise I would ever need. She couldn't believe I had dedicated it to her. "Of course," I said. "Haven't you always been my muse?" I asked her if the situation with her husband was still the same. It was. It had been twenty-eight years since we last spoke, and more like thirty since we last made love. She told me there hadn't been anyone but me in all these years. I had been the only one "inside of her." I started to respond and involuntarily, unexpectedly, a tsunami of emotion swept over me—I choked up and started to cry. I tried to conceal it, think-ing what a wimp I must seem. At last I managed to choke out some words: "You've always been the love of my life. It was always you, only you." I thought about all the marriages, all the affairs. They had been something else, not love, but some kind of narcotic, just another addictive crutch for my crippled ego.

"I love you," she murmured.

Suddenly it was as if no time had passed, as if we had never been apart. I was right back in "that place," the place where only she and I could go. My body filled with a familiar warmth, a stirring deep inside. I felt I was thawing from a long cryogenic freeze. Those words coming from her, it seemed to me, were all I would need to sustain me for what remained of my life.

But then came another voice, the Buddha voice, the big lesson I still had to learn: "You can't depend on someone else for your happiness. That's just another drug. It has to come from within. Get back to work!"

Acknowledgements

THANKS for helping me remember: Willie Alexander, Ron DeZure, Elisabetta diCagno, Kyle Garrahan, Marc Gilutin, Jim Kweskin, Russ Levine, Ray Paret, Walter Powers, Lyn Roberts, Mark Scheuren, Barry Tashian, Fred Taylor.

THANKS for making me a better writer: Erika Schickel and all my classmates at UCLA Extension.

THANKS for the read-through and feedback: Ron DeZure, The Land of Deborah.

THANKS for the PHOTOS and IMAGES: Janet Caliri, Henry Diltz, Ed Freeman, Don Guy, Erik Lindgren, Michelle Mourges Marx, Cliff McReynolds, Richard Millstein, Annie Neilson, the family of Ed Pfizenmaier, Herb Quick, Ashkan Sahihi, Romio Shrestha, Herbie Worthington.

PHOTO EDITOR: Helen Ashford (www.cacheagency.com)
PHOTO ASSISTANCE: Aram Heller, Stephen K. Peeples, Herb Quick.

All images courtesy of Ted Myers Archive unless otherwise credited.

The publisher and author apologize for any errors or omissions in the photo credits. If contacted they will be pleased to rectify these at the earliest opportunity.

Lightning Source UK Ltd.
Milton Keynes UK
UKHW010628160123
415428UK00001B/24